Designer's Guide to Girls' & Junior Apparel

Designer's Guide to Girls' & Junior Apparel

Randi Beer
Woodbury University

Fairchild Books
New York

Executive Editor: Olga T. Kontzias
Senior Associate Acquisitions Editor: Jaclyn Bergeron
Assistant Acquisitions Editor: Amanda Breccia
Editorial Development Director: Jennifer Crane
Development Editor: Michelle Levy
Associate Art Director: Erin Fitzsimmons
Production Director: Ginger Hillman
Production Editor: Jessica Rozler
Photo Research: Sarah Silberg and Suzette Lam
Cover Design: Erin Fitzsimmons
Cover Art: Angela Coppola/Veer
Text Design: Susan Day
Page Composition: Barbara Barg

Library of Congress Catalog Card Number: 2008940823

ISBN: 978-1-56367-692-5

GST R 133004424

Printed in China

TP15

Contents

■ ■ ■ *Extended Contents*
■ ■ ■

In memory of my son Kevin Conrad,
who would have thought this book was cool

Preface

Having been a successful designer who manufactured various lines of apparel that sold profitably for many years in both the girls' and the junior markets, I wrote this book with two purposes in mind.

First and foremost it is to instruct students on the process of designing apparel for the girls' and junior markets for manufacturing. Each of 12 chapters builds upon the previous chapter's information, from the designer's first inspiration to the sketches to the selection of fabric and then to the first pattern making, cutting, and pricing, until the newly designed garments are shown, hypothetically sold, and put into the production phase.

Second, the book is written to promote the serious understanding of designing clothing as a thoughtful endeavor that is carefully calculated for the purpose of making money in a competitive and often grueling marketplace. Design students often design projects for classes that have no relationship to what is currently in style, going to be coming into style, or in any way relevant to current events. I wanted this book to help readers understand that designing apparel is a process that requires careful consideration of what styles sold last season, what movie stars are wearing, why the cost of gas means cutbacks on T-shirt sales, and all the other factors that affect profits in the clothing design industry.

It is not enough in today's garment industry to be able to draw pretty pictures or know how to sew a seam. Apparel is a sophisticated global industry, which demands that designers be aware of the world around us. Students need to learn how events inspire what is worn, and ultimately, how as designers they will forecast through their designs what will be purchased by girls, tweens, and teens.

I have included several methods to stretch the student's design talent. **Designer's Diary** is written in the voice of a new designer. The designer starts out as an assistant, and by the end of the book, the designer's first line has been created and sent to market. The diary is a first-person account of on-the-job training in a position secured after graduation, which young, aspiring student designers can relate to. It is a window into what it takes to succeed as a designer, including the long hours and physicality, and the passion for creativity.

Designer's Dictionary familiarizes the student with vocabulary they will use long into their professional careers. The key words all designers need to know are **boldfaced** in the text and are then defined in the **Designer's Dictionary**. A series of **Activities** directly relate to the chapter text. A **Weekly Planner** lists tasks that follow the pace of the text and are intended to be completed each week. The objective is for each student to design groups for a mini-line, draft patterns, cut and sew three prototypes, and follow the chapters in the text as their own line is sketched and developed into completed garments that have been priced, merchandised, and shown in a class presentation by the end of the term. **Articles** from the *Los Angeles Times* bring all of the lessons into vivid focus and present diverse voices and opinions from the girls' and junior apparel markets.

At the end of the book, you will find the **Designer's Library**, where sources, as well as recommended reading, are listed. My suggestion for all students of fashion is to keep a copy of The *Fairchild Dictionary of Fashion* (3rd ed.) at hand, collect as many resources as possible with apparel pictures like old catalogues, books, and periodicals, keep current with the news and pop culture, and sketch long into the night while watching classic movies. It is the designer's job to show up at work fresh and on top of all of the latest trends.

"Art is insurance against insanity."
—Louise Borgeois

Acknowledgments

Writing this book was a huge endeavor and certainly not one that was done alone. I'm especially appreciative of my husband, Michael, who is a perfect partner both in business and in life. Additional thanks go to Barbara Dickinson. She read more about apparel than I'm sure she ever wanted to. Also, much gratitude goes to my mother, Hope, who passed me her artistic flair. She took me to Orbach's on the Miracle Mile for fashion shows and sparked my interest in design. There is nothing luckier for a kid than finding her passion at an early age.

I wish Michelle Levy could organize me as well in life as she did as my editor, and I want her to know I appreciate her help. She was fantastic. Erin Fitzsimmons took my artwork to a higher level. I would also like to say that the entire staff at Fairchild Books was remarkable. From Bria Duane, who talked me into doing a book to Jaclyn Bergeron, who guided me further. They were all incredible. Many thanks.

Photo thanks:
Susan Flame
Rich Little, One World
John Graham
Ryan Herz
Linsey Baker Upshur
David St. John, Jerry Leigh of California

Business thanks:
Jerry Leigh of California
Popular, Calabasas, CA
Smooch, A Children's Boutique, Calabasas, CA
One World Inc.
Caroline Fabrics

Designer's Guide to Girls' & Junior Apparel

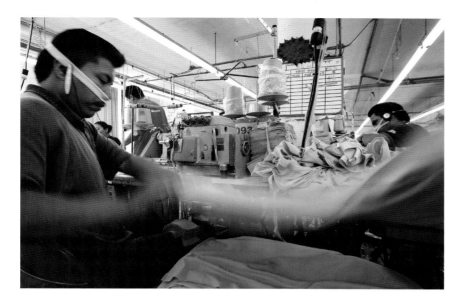

FIG. 1.4. AMERICAN APPAREL IS PROVING THAT QUALITY CLOTHING CAN STILL BE "MADE IN THE USA."

researching historical periods, girls' and junior clothing designers can find wonderful treatments, and then give them a fresh twist for current lines. Second, an understanding of the cultural influences of a particular period on clothing helps a designer draw parallels to the present and learn to forecast future trends. History replays itself. Being aware of ebb and flow of business trends gives designers a chance to plan into those business cycles.

Clothing for Girls Prior to World War I

If we check into past trends in apparel prior to World War I and look at old photos of girls, we are immediately struck by three impressions. The first is that the girls are dressed as miniature adults. The second is that they don't appear to be happy in the pictures, and finally, they never look comfortable in their clothing. There is one observation we might miss. The photos are usually of children from upper-class families. When the rare photo of poor children appears, it is alarming how unprotected from the elements they were and how pitiful they look. The visual history of clothing in the United States is similar to a family album of the upper class, while showing those members only the special occasions. (See Figure 1.5.)

The primary purpose of clothing is to protect the body from the elements. A secondary purpose is covering for the sake of modesty. The fashion eras prior to WWI emphasized full body coverage for the sake of modesty according to the rigid customs of their time, but ignored the health or happiness of the women and children who wore the apparel. It was not until John Locke put forth the idea that children were not responsible for their actions until they reached a mature age, and Rousseau suggested that children needed healthy exercise in fresh air, that the plight of youngsters was given much consideration (Sills 2005).

Social standing has a direct impact on apparel. Since society didn't value women as much as men, girls were given less thought than boys were, and they were considered miniature women and dressed accordingly. Boys were favored over little girls because a rural society needed males to labor on farms, and upper-class families needed boys to carry on the family business and name. Even in cities, society viewed children differently. Working class and poor children often worked from the time they were seven years old. There were children under 12 working in mills by the early 1800s. By the turn of the century, it has been estimated, there were one to two million children working in the United States and no labor laws to protect them. The unfortunate reality is that children were cheap to employ and disposable.

Children were not valued as individuals, and they were taught to be seen and not heard with the hopes that they could avoid childhood diseases like scarlet fever, tuberculosis, polio, and

FIG. 1.5. POSTCARDS FROM PAST DECADES OFFER A GLIMPSE INTO THE APPAREL WORN BY GIRLS LONG AGO.

influenza. Infant mortality rates were very high. Keeping children healthy was of greater concern than their comfort. Their entertainment was chiefly ignored and their education was un-regulated. The books written to amuse children didn't become popular until the mid-nineteenth century, and only a third of the children fin-ished elementary school in the early twentieth century. That percentage shrank to ten percent for the students who completed high school (Farrell-Beck 2007).

Girls' Apparel as a Dressmaker Market Prior to the 1920s

Dressmakers were employed to make all the female clothing in a wealthy home. The styles for girls copied what the woman of the house wore and incorporated leftover fabric ends into their costumes when possible. Although women rarely worked outside the home, dressmaking was an opportunity for unmarried and widowed women to make money. Dressmaking was an honorable trade for women of the working class.

Building a wardrobe for young women was not an easy affair, and the fittings were time consuming. By the time they were 11 years old, girls dressed exactly as though they were adults. Fabric was ordered, usually by mail, often imported from Europe, and dressmakers took weeks to complete garments. Girls' garments were made expandable so that they could be adjusted for growth. Less fortunate members of society had to improvise and sew their own clothing. Butterick and McCall's were the first companies to market printed, prepackaged, and sized patterns for clothing for home use in the late 1870s (Sills 2005). Mail-order patterns could also be found in some periodicals of the day, like *Arthur's Home Magazine.* Hand sewing was the method of construction and even though some of this handiwork was beautifully done, it was tedious work. Young women were judged by their needlework abilities. Little girls learned needlework skills by the hour, rather than play-ing games with other children.

Comfort Issues in Girls' Clothing

Creating comfort in girls' clothing was a slow process. The French philosopher Rousseau had written in the 1800s that outdoor play was healthy for children and that their breathing should not be restricted in the same style gar-ments that women wore. Rousseau's observa-tion ushered in the empire waistline, which draped below the bust freely, letting young girls move with less restriction when they were getting air in the garden (Batterberry & Batterberry 1977). This new silhouette was less binding than clothing had been in the past. It is doubtful that the Enlightenment associated with Rousseau was solely responsible, because the comfort benefit both to girls and to women was soon set aside. By the beginning of the twentieth century, stays and corsets became fashionable, and girls were, once again, laced up too tight.

Clothing was not comfortable for women or girls. It was hot in the summer, too flimsy for winter, heavy, voluminous, and restrictive to movement. It is hard to imagine wearing bustles and stays or corsets as an adult; for young girls it must have been tortuous. Perhaps bustles were just marginally easier to get in and out of than the hoop skirts and weighty crinolines worn by Victorian girls. When little girls were cloistered in the childhood nurseries of the wealthy, they were given some relief by wearing little dressing gowns. In public however, prior to modern times, until girls "came of age," which was prior to teenage or our junior category, they were expected to dress like adults and have an adult demeanor. The "juniors" of yesterday were often married with children. They were considered matrons, regardless of age, and they were expected to dress according to their stations in society.

In the mid-twentieth century, Amelia Bloomer exposed her exterior bloomers and is credited for the first serious suggestion that full pants, or bloomers, should be worn instead of skirts. The idea was not well received, but bloomers did stick around as athletic costumes for many years (Contini 1965). World War I forced some women into the workplace, and this necessitated the creation of less-restrictive clothing.

Women in the United States were given the right to vote in 1920. The world was starting to see women, and girls, in a new light. It wasn't until the 1920s that it was understood that children needed sunlight to prevent rickets, so **rompers** were worn outdoors while children were getting fresh air. When the "flapper" rage hit, bringing short, loose dresses that enabled the athletic moves of the Charleston dance craze, comfort was achieved, albeit briefly, but viewed by many traditionalists as racy. In 1935, *Vogue* showed jeans for women calling them *western chic,* but the look did not filter down to girls clothing yet.

Once the middle class became a larger part of society, the lives of many children changed dramatically, enabling them to grow, play, and attend public school in apparel that was comfortable and age appropriate. By 1940, play clothes for girls were commonplace. The development of nylon and other synthetics, like Dacron polyester in 1951, changed the makeup of girls' wear, improved comfort and styling, and ushered in the popular knitted apparel with stretch and convenient care. By the 1950s, magazines like *Seventeen* were advertising apparel made especially for teenage girls (Farrell-Beck 2007).

The Value of Historical Research

It is useful for a designer to have costuming books, old magazines like *McCall's* or *Vogue,* collectible Sears catalogs, and other sources on hand to rummage through periodically. The Internet has some great clothing source sites. The design inspiration that can be drawn from history is unlimited. For example, the draping of Greek and Roman tunics still influences the red carpet gowns of the rich and famous, and those garments are then copied for junior prom dresses. Victorian lace blouses have incredible pleating and decoration, which can be used in little girl dressy dresses. The **leg of mutton sleeves**, fabulous **flounces**, and draped **shawl collars**, which were popular at the beginning of the twentieth century, can still be incorporated into modern apparel for girls. In abbreviated copies, those sleeves are still used in dressy girls' clothing for Christmas dresses and flower girl gowns. By 1910, bathing attire was the rage, reaching the knees with billowing legs and overskirts. Some of these features were copied when rompers for girls were popular in sizes 4–6x. The very sophisticated tunics influenced

FIG. 1.6a, b, c. (a) Above. NOTICE THE GRECIAN DRAPE TO THIS MODERN PROM DRESS. (b) Above right. THIS GIRL HAS AN ASIAN-INFLUENCED PRINTED DRESS. (c) Right. QUAKER OR PILGRIM COLLARS ARE COMMON IN LITTLE GIRLS' DRESSY DRESSES.

by Japanese kimonos for eveningwear worn in this era can be seen whenever an Asian influence recycles in the junior market. The shirring treatments used in Victorian times are often emulated on jackets today (Figure 1.6).

Style Influences of Modern Decades

From 1920 to 2000, each decade had individual fashion statements that overlapped and merged with each other (Figure 1.7). The styles that were worn in the decades following WWI are the ones that we most often cite and copy in modern apparel lines. The Roaring Twenties are known as the flapper era, and shorter, bouncy dresses were the *cat's meow*. Each decade has its own fashion trends and its own want-to-be-

chic lingo. "Cat's meow" was the 1920s version of "cool," "rad," "fab," "bad," or "right on" in succeeding decades. The short, straight-cut, loose-fitting dresses were decorated with fringe, beads, and bangles, and the flashier the better. Waistlines on girls' dresses emulate flapper dresses every few years, and when minidresses are popular in juniors, the little flip skirts are reminiscent of those worn in the Roaring Twenties.

FIG. 1.7. ORIGINAL AND
REPUBLISHED PAPER DOLL
OR COLORING BOOKS ARE
ANOTHER EXCELLENT STYLE
SOURCE.

The long, linear dresses cut on the bias, or the diagonal direction of the fabric, that were worn during the Depression years are still copied by designers working on junior lines. The camisoles that keep appearing as trends are also reminiscent of the Depression era. The 1940s brought WWII and Bobby Soxers—teenage fans of Frank Sinatra who wore pleated skirts and rolled their socks down to their ankles. Women went into the workforce, and pants for women became commonplace. Teens were recognized as a part of society with the power to purchase their distinctive items of clothing and music. Denim jeans became appropriate for very casual activities like bicycling or horseback riding. In the 1940s, teenage girls were called *sub-debs,* and it marks the first time this segment of

society was designated as a separate group that had its own clothing preferences and styles. The young women belonging to upper-class society were introduced to the social world at 18 years of age as debutantes. When these women became debutantes, they were essentially debuting as women and leaving childhood behind. The sub-deb title was the first inkling of a junior classification of young women, a group that was neither matrons nor little girls. Teenagers were breaking through their "seen and not heard" classification and making their opinions known.

By the 1950s, teenagers had their own assorted fads, which have been copied so frequently that they are now iconic: poodle skirts, saddle shoes, small neck scarfs tied to the side, 50-yard petticoats, and tight fitting sweater sets. Little girls' clothing was slow to copy teens' clothing, and it remained conservative. Cotton dresses in little prints and plaids for school still had a hold on the 4–6x and 7–14 markets. On the strength of skirts and blouses selling in the women's market, the girls' market soon began to offer **separates** for school clothes to give a viable option in all the ranges, from 4–6x to teen apparel.

The 1960s came in conservatively, but by the end of the decade, girls wore pants and jeans anywhere and anytime, even although many school dress codes did not permit females to wear pants on school grounds. Midriffs were exposed; belly buttons were shown, bodies were painted, and love beads were sported first by hippies, and later by a huge teen demographic. *Love child* became a common expression. Youth took to the streets and rebelled against parental restraints and the Vietnam War. Peace symbols and happy faces appeared on screened T-shirts and embroidered on bell-bottom jeans. Women demanded equal rights, and fashions brought a new unisex appeal. Miniskirts and little op art dresses were worn. This was the decade where youth influenced adults visually and socially. The apparel business followed the young trends, and the important junior market was born. This new size range was for girls just entering puberty from ages 12 through 17. Today's junior clothing is designed specifically for ages 11 to 18 years, but customer purchases may extend to young women in their early 20s. The baby boomer teens had the enormous numbers to demand their own style, and apparel businesses were happy to accommodate them.

The 1970s were socially turbulent, and the fashions reflected that uncertainty. Fashion fads ranged from hot pants with knee-high lace-up boots, long skirts and wedge heels, to punk. War demonstrations, followed by a recession, influenced the previous free-spirited hippie styles and ushered in a nostalgic feeling for the femininity of the 1930s and 1940s, particularly in junior and contemporary apparel. Coatdresses competed in stores with *Annie Hall* looks, which brought in a masculine influence of vests and

neckties, and midi skirts, which hit mid-calf and caused a stir after the freedom of very short skirts. The contrasting themes of retro, punk, and *Annie Hall* clothing certainly presented a chaotic fashion viewpoint.

Girls' clothing mimicked the styles worn by teenagers. Girls' clothing manufacturers began to copy clothing styled for juniors and marketing this trendier apparel at the same time for the girls in the 7–14 size range. *Annie Hall* blouses with attached front vests and removable neckties sold well in 4–6x and 7–14 size ranges and became reorder items in junior markets.

The 1980s presented a range of fashion styles that borrowed from prior eras, yet designers managed to apply a modern twist that often seemed comical at best. The basic fashion silhouette ranged from huge, oversized shoulders with excessive padding, to slim, body-revealing, slinky dresses. Multiple gold chains around the neck and rings on every finger were hardly noticed with the demand for status logos and designer jeans commanding all the attention. It was a decade of excessive fashion swings. The girls' wear industry sustained itself on dance-trend clothing that came directly from the movie *Flashdance* in 1983. The items that sold well in junior sizes included sweatshirts with open necks and spandex pull-on leggings. Big cotton shirts in bold prints with shoulder pads worn with stirrup pants were also popular. Movies such as *Sixteen Candles* and *The Breakfast Club,* and the emergence of stars like Madonna, inspired the fashion tastes of a new generation of teens.

Olivia Newton-John became an icon in her exercise poses, wearing tights and a headband. Flashy colored exercise suits sold in neon colors made of shiny nylon, and polyester became acceptable as casual wear for juniors. Bright colors mixed with neutrals expanded the creativity in the girls' market. Bicycle shorts and *skeggings* (one-piece jump suits with bicycle shorts attached) became an important item in the 4–6x size-range and the 7–14 size-range markets.

The 1990s ushered in a tremendous array of choices in fashion. The casual American lifestyle celebrated by the general public manifested in the clothing they wore. Cargo pants crossed all size ranges and both genders. The *grunge* look came out of Seattle and crossed over into girls' attire from the teen boys' market. There was a retro feel in fashion for the 1940, '50s, '60s, and '70s. Fashion in the 1990s reflected the scattered feel of culture, and the recession created pricing considerations even for the affluent. Hip-hop and rap were strong influences on culture, but these trends affected the boys' market more than it did girls' styles.

Deconstruction may be the biggest trend story from recent years. This deconstructed trend filtered down through juniors to girls' wear with unfinished seams and hems. **Overlock** stitching was used as an inside-out finish in contrasting thread color that suited girls' sportswear.

Layering of many thin knits appealed to the junior and girls' wear markets in the new millennium. (See Figure 1.8.) Miniskirts, reflecting the styles of the 1960s and '70s made a comeback and sold well in stores.

By the fall season of 2008, retail sales in girls' and junior markets declined. Another economic cycle had begun with a bear stock market, too many foreclosures in the housing market, and continued worries across the country about the expensive war in Iraq. Department stores had a difficult time competing with discounters like Target. Junior designers sought inspiration once again in tie-dyed tops or imported Indian gauze tops reminiscent of the 1970s hippie apparel. Girls of all ages wore baby doll tops. Short dresses sold well in the junior market often worn over tank T-shirts. The knit market realized profits by offering jersey knits that had a soft, sumptuous hand that draped easily in body-hugging styles.

GIRLS' AND JUNIOR APPAREL DESIGNER PROSPECTS

The future of the apparel industry is exciting. Daily innovations in computer programs, com-

FIG. 1.8. THE JEAN MINISKIRT WITH SUSPENDERS OVER A PAIR OF TIGHTS AND A SCREEN T-SHIRT, TOPPED WITH A SWEATSHIRT, IS A TYPICAL LOOK.

puterized machinery, and fabulous fabrication strides will make garments of the future that are unfathomable to us now. Fabrics will have wireless phone and computer support capabilities. All fabrics might be treated to protect our skin from harmful sunrays and pollution, not just the few higher priced specialty garments now offered. Fabrics could mutate in order to be cooler or warmer and adjust to body temperatures. Individual measurements will be inputted to adjust clothing to fit prior to construction on a wider scale.

In the girls' market, it is not unreasonable to believe that garments will have built-in computer games because they are so popular, from Japan to the United States. It is not even hard to imagine that garments will be able to change fiber colors to match moods or other articles of clothing. Safety features like air-bag technology and monitoring of vital statistics could be put into exercise clothing to prevent injury. Security features that include tracking devices could be standard features for all children. The innovations are going to be spectacular. Designers are going to have amazing materials to work with and vast stores of styling details to draw from.

An understanding of the history of clothes and how the past can influence the future is helpful. Exposure to the business of manufacturing girls' and junior clothing is vital to the aspiring designer's understanding of the design process. Researching trends of the past and combining that with the knowledge of present business practices is necessary for the development of new and exciting apparel.

THE BUSINESS
OF MANUFACTURING CLOTHING

Clothing manufacturers are in the business of designing and marketing clothing for a profit. The company's employees design the garments, then merchandise the first samples into a line, then take that line to store buyers for purchase orders. The clothing is produced in factories and shipped to stores for consumers to purchase. Girls' and junior clothing is a specialty sector of this ready-to-wear trade.

"Made in the USA" is not usually printed on the neck labels of girls' and junior clothing. The actual production of apparel is rarely completed on U.S. soil. U.S. manufacturing companies use cheap labor in all corners of the globe and continue to chase the least expensive labor markets in order to be competitively priced. Because the junior market is so trendy, and because the girls' market is directly influenced by those trends, competitive pricing is essential to success.

The business operation can be simply put: a manufacturer must have enough cash flow to finance newly designed lines season after season that can be sold in sufficient quantity to make a profit. The garments must be produced at a high enough standard of quality for the retailers, considering the price paid, and those garments must be shipped on time plus be purchased by the consumers. There is nothing simple about

succeeding in the fashion business. Mistakes can be costly or crippling to a company's bottom line. Garment manufacturing can be very profitable, but it is a competitive and risky business. Designing great styles is just the first step in the process.

The companies that made their garments offshore years ago were called *importers,* and they dealt with a rigid import quota that protected American-made goods and kept pricing competitive through tariffs or taxes levied against goods made in foreign countries. Free trade agreements, including the North American Free Trade Agreement (NAFTA), have all but done away with most of these quotas. Thus, with the new global economy and relaxation of trade protections, it is much more economical to have garments sewn offshore.

Manufacturing in the United States is adjusting to this global marketplace by computerizing different stages of the design process. In design rooms Photoshop and Illustrator skills are mandatory. Some companies choose to upgrade to computerized processes earlier in the manufacturing process and have computers make sample patterns, production patterns, and markers. Cutting rooms can be equipped with computerized equipment that is cross-referenced with the marker-making machines. Desktop computers contain all the previous styles and the pattern numbers for immediate access, and patternmakers can make adjustments and print out the new patterns easily. This trend toward modernization is creating a new technological involvement in what was traditionally a manual and labor-intensive industry. Large corporations are usually the first to integrate these expensive innovations, but all manufacturers will have to invest in computerized equipment in order to be competitive. All large merchandisers are linked with suppliers through computer programs that send purchase orders, invoices, garment tracking, and selling information by style for quick response time. After losing thousands of jobs in the apparel industry to other countries that offer lower labor costs, these efficient methods will bring pre-production jobs back to the United States.

Physical Set Up of Facility

This portion of Chapter 1 is a guide through the physical layout of a typical clothing manufacturer and an introduction to the employees who work together to create a saleable and profitable product.

Efficiency is the driving force for the set up of the manufacturer's facility. A company that sells clothing under its own name and label is called a manufacturer, but very few garment companies in the United States actually manufacture their own products. Each company's layout is organized around the processes of production that are completed *in house.* Some companies cut their piece goods, which means they roll out the fabric and mass-cut the garments on site, and stock all their piece goods (fabric) in their own facility. (See Figure 1.9.) A company that is contracting out the garment production, starting with the cutting of the goods, does not actually produce the garments on site. This means the company pays an outside business to cut its fabric into bundled garment sections. The sewing is done in a contractor's factory. In some cases, the only garments cut and sewn on the company's premises are the sample and duplicate lines.

There is a circular arrangement to the manufacturer's organization from the beginning of the process to where the finished product leaves from the shipping dock. The logic is clear. The garment is created, then priced, then sold, and finally shipped. It is all the work that comes between the first sketch and the shipping dock that tells the story of a designer's workplace.

Five Divisions of Labor

There are five divisions of labor in garment manufacturing. These divisions, or departments break down into (1) the business department that controls the money, (2) the sales division that promotes the line, (3) the design section that creates the sample line, (4) the production department that oversees all facets of the construction of the garments, and (5) the shipping department that gets the product to the consumer. Each division is vital to the process of

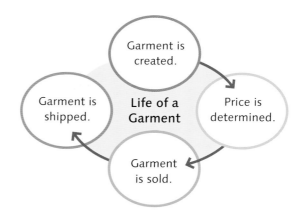

FIG. 1.9. AS THE DESIGNER SEES THE FUTURE OF FASHION IN THE CRYSTAL BALL, THE SELLER FRANTICALLY TRIES TO GET ORDERS. MEANWHILE THE PRODUCTION MANAGER IS JUGGLING THE MANUFACTURING OF LOTS OF DIFFERENT STYLES. THE OWNER HAS THE WEIGHT OF THE WORLD ON HIS SHOULDERS WORRYING ABOUT MAKING A PROFIT AND KEEPING HIS EMPLOYEES WORKING.

manufacturing clothing, and each department is dependent on all of the others.

Business Department Function

The reception area is the first space a visitor enters. A receptionist will greet clientele, answer the phones, and do light clerical jobs. In New York City this entrance may be in a high-rise building in the fashion district. In Los Angeles it could be in one of the rambling one-story, free-standing buildings scattered all over the city. In order to meet with the company's personnel, visitors must go through the receptionist (Figure 1.10). The private workings of the business are behind closed doors. Many sales representatives, buyers, or other visitors may enter, and the new designs that are being created beyond this area must be protected from people who might pass information to competitors.

The business offices are adjacent to the reception space. There is typically a bookkeeper, an order input clerk who is a computer specialist, a billing clerk, and a controller. Garment companies often finance the business with a factor, which is like a bank that funds the business, collects the receivables, and performs credit checks on the customers for a sizeable fee. Controllers are the business accountants who control the monetary flow for the com-

FIG. 1.10. WHEN A MANUFACTURING COMPANY IS SUCCESSFUL THE FRONT OFFICE STAYS BUSY CONSTANTLY.

pany process as directed by management. Large corporations will also have a human resources department and a payroll clerk.

The executive offices are located near the accounting offices. Executive personnel in manufacturing manage the business aspects of the company and participate in public relations responsibilities. They manage company finances, expansion plans, and the every day decision making that keeps the company profitable. Executives work with the sales force to forecast business trends and plan the cash flow. This is where the annual budget is determined and strategies are planned to keep the **overhead** in line with the projected sales. The controller works closely with the chief financial officer to ensure that the company is always on secure financial footing. In some businesses, the execu-

tives are the original owners of the company and may be part of a partnership wherein one of the executives is in charge of the business end while a partner may be a seller, designer, or even the production manager. It takes a diverse range of skills to create a successful apparel manufacturing operation.

Interaction between Business and Design Departments

The executives of any company are the bosses and sometimes the company owners, so it always serves an employee to heed the employer's opinion and instruction. Strong executives can mentor inexperienced designers. Since fashion trends are cyclical, which makes old styles new again; some executives have seen trends reappear more than once. Designers might find it helpful to tap into the knowledge of these experts when studying cyclical trends.

Working well with the accounting department is imperative for the design staff. In addition to payroll and expense reimbursement issues, this department is aware of all monetary concerns the company has. The design staff has to check in sample cuts and turn in signed receipts in order for the payables clerk to reconcile accounts and pay for materials and supplies. When the design department fails to keep accurate records, it is an annoying but necessary chore to go back and try to reconstruct those receipts. Designers make specific fabric selections for the line and keeping careful records is essential in order to set prices for the line and order new fabrics. Careful record keeping is often the function of an assistant designer.

Finally, a receptionist can be a great help to the designer when trade representatives stop in to show their new fabrics and trimmings. Sometimes it is difficult to keep the appointments running on schedule. A good receptionist can regulate the showing times and speed the presentations along. It is also common to see want ads in either *Apparel News* or *Women's Wear Daily* for junior-sized receptionists/fit models. It can be helpful to have the receptionist act as an in-house fit model so that the design and sales staff can see how new garments move on a real body, rather than on mannequins.

Sales and Show Room Function

The showroom is the space where sales personnel meet with buyers to show the line so the buyers can select which styles they want to purchase. Showrooms need to be attractive enough to feel comfortable to the buyer yet bland enough to not compete with the clothing. Many companies have off-site show rooms in buildings called *marts*. There are marts in large cities including New York, Los Angeles, Dallas, Chicago, Atlanta, and San Francisco.

Garments are shown in showrooms by the sales staff in order to preview the line with buyers and in order for the staff to review the line as it is being developed. Blank walls with grid screens attached make perfect backdrops for these purposes. Fancy racks usually hold entire lines of clothing for the current season, along with reorder garments from the previous line. A table may be located in the middle of the room so that a buyer may clearly view all the surrounding walls that will be covered in new styles. The table may have promotional material with company logos, but the essential items are the order book forms and pens. Fabric swatches with the entire array of colors for the season are usually arranged within binders filled with additional fabrics that are available to fill immediate orders.

The company showroom may be adjacent to the sales offices or cubicles. These areas have phone and computer stations. During market weeks, or at a buyer's request, the sales staff may travel out of town for meetings and for showing the line in buying offices, marts, or at the buyers' home offices. The sales office can be a hub of activity buzzing with the excitement of new orders. On the other hand, it can be empty and dark when the line travels with the sales staff. (See Figure 1.11.)

Sales and Designer Interaction

Designers have to "sell" their line to the salespeople before it is ever shown to store buyers. The designer's excitement about the new looks can excite the sales staff and motivate them to pass that enthusiasm on to their buyers.

Designers are often called upon to sit in on meetings with important buyers. Some buy-

FIG. 1.11. SHOWING A HOT GIRLS' LINE CAN BE EXCITING TO BOTH SELLER AND BUYER.

FIG. 1.12a, b. (a) THE DESIGNER IS VERY HANDS ON WHEN WORKING TO PUT TOGETHER THE NEW SEASON'S LINE. NOTICE THE FORM, CUTTING TABLE, AND SAMPLES PLUS PATTERN PAPER AND EVEN A STEAMER. (b) THIS LARGE SAMPLE ROOM SHOWS THE SCOPE OF SEWING EQUIPMENT AND HOW MANY WORKERS IT CAN TAKE TO PUT A LINE TOGETHER FOR A LARGE COMPANY. NOTICE THE BINS OF THREAD AND OTHER SUPPLIES.

ers want to know the designer's inspiration for an existing group, or they'll ask about the designer's "crystal ball" forecast of upcoming fashion trends. Designers of girls' clothing must be prepared to speak about overall trends in the marketplace, not just those specific to girls' wear. The sales staff will use the designer's flair to enhance its presentation. This presentation may include designer-created boards to show the color groups that are featured in the line and graphics that show where trends were first noticed.

In order to understand the interaction of the designer with the sales staff, the relationship between the buyer and salesperson has to be examined. Buyers can give important information to the sales staff on numerous issues. For example, buyers can relate news about market competition, which garments are selling well in stores, what interesting garments they've seen elsewhere, whose line is hot, or which *price points* are too high to retail successfully in stores. This information can help the designer make his or her line even stronger. If a trend is missing, the designer can incorporate it into his or her line in time for future sales. If a fabric is saturating the market place, a replacement fabric can be substituted to make a group fresher. Filling in the missing information from buyer data to the sales staff can help a designer take a line from average to profitable. Constructive criticism from buyers is always helpful.

A designer can give a sales staff a fabulous line that is easy to sell, making the designer a star and enabling the sales staff to meet and exceed its goals. Sometimes, however, the designer will create a nice line that is too similar to those of the competition. When it appears along with the other lines in the market, it loses its appeal. This is when the communication between the designer and sales staff is crucial. The information from the sales team can help to spark up the line and inspire new and fresh ideas that can be turned into stronger sales.

Design Room Layout
The layout of the design room may differ slightly in different companies, but the necessities

remain constant. The designer must have a desk with a computer and some private space in which to sketch. The design room has long pattern-cutting tables for patternmaking and sample cutting. Sewing machines line the perimeters of the room and are manned by expert sample makers. There is a single needle machine for each sample maker and steam iron equipment for the use of the entire department. There are also specialty machines to hem, make buttonholes, overlock, or **marrow edge** the samples. Somewhere, perhaps along a back wall, shelving will hold layers and layers of sample fabrics. More shelves and drawers house buttons, trims, zippers, and thread spools. Everything that is needed to produce the sample garments for the line will be close at hand. Sample-size mannequins are scattered around the room, with the new styles hanging that are awaiting trims or finishing. (See Figure 1.12.)

Also conveniently located will be the first patterns, those patterns used for the initial prototypes, and production pattern **blocks**. If the company is fully computerized, a computer system for generating patterns will also be available. Whether the company is fully computerized or still doing the original patterns manually, the patternmaker will have records of all previous patterns carefully numbered so they can be easily accessed (Figure 1.13).

Designer and Design Staff Relationship

The staff working in a design room must work in concert, like a sports team with the designer leading as the *captain*. The designer is completely dependent upon this staff of individuals who must work together to create the designer's vision. The first patternmaker has to interpret the sketch while giving the garment proper proportion and flair. The sample cutter must cut the fabric correctly according to grain lines or striping, yet conserve enough of the fabric to get as many first samples as the designer has planned. The sample makers must sew the garment according to the construction appropriate to the price point as instructed by the designer.

FIG. 1.13a, b. (a) THE PATTERNMAKER SITS IN AN OFFICE USING THE GERBER PROGRAM ON THE COMPUTER. MANUAL PATTERNMAKING IS A MORE PHYSICAL JOB. (b) THIS FIRST PATTERNMAKER DOES THE PATTERNS MANUALLY.

FIG. 1.14. THE PRODUCTION MANAGER HAS SO MANY DIFFERENT GARMENTS AT DIFFERENT STAGES OF PRODUCTION THAT HER AREA IS ALWAYS BUSY.

Assistant designers who are anxious to do their own designing must set aside their creative interpretations and execute the head designer's concepts. The assistant designer is an extra hand for the designer, doing varied tasks like completing cost sheets, checking in piece goods, filing invoices, calling sources to follow up on piece good deliveries, and anything else that helps the design room run smoothly. When a design room is in rhythm, with all members contributing their best work, the line comes together more efficiently. Time is always a designer issue because the deadlines for showing the line are determined by the clothing buyers, not by the sellers. Conversely, when there is a breakdown in the process and even one area is weak or falls behind, like a sample cutter who forgets to cut the notches, it throws the entire room into chaos, and work can slow to a crawl.

Production Department

The production department takes over in the process of product development as soon as the sales department has sold a style cut minimum, which is a sufficient quantity of a style to produce it at a profit. Each company has its own cut minimum because of differing costs from one firm to another. Examples that would contribute to the difference would be like one firm being located in a high-rent district while the competitor works out of a warehouse. The production manager orchestrates the coordination of making the production pattern, purchasing the fabrics and trims, then testing, cutting, and finally getting the garment sewn for the amount that was budgeted on the cost sheet. All this has to be completed to meet a delivery date that can be inflexible. The production manager is the juggler in the division of labor. The production manager must oversee both the quality and the timing of every shipment of clothing (See Figure 1.14.)

The crew in the production department is comprised of a production manager and assistants, who order stock fabric, purchase trims, oversee offshore and domestic factories, and control the quality of incoming goods. The production patternmaker reports to the production manager. The schedule for production patterns, for grading, and for making the markers all falls to the production staff to coordinate. If there is any part of the garment manufacturing business that is always frantic, it is this one. Even with careful handling and attention to detail, production problems arise. The ultimate responsibility to deliver a top-quality garment to be shipped before the cancellation date falls on the production manager. The stress level in this department is usually palpable!

Because of the many different combinations of outside contracting processes, it is difficult to describe a manufacturer's production layout. If the manufacturer has an active cutting room, then long cutting tables can take up a large portion of a warehouse. Fabric rolls may be stored in large shelving bins and under the cutting tables. There might be manual cutting blades or a computerized cutting system. Some companies store their own piece goods, and others have the fabric sent to an outside cutting service. All stages of the production process can be contracted out, or any single process can be done in house. The production manager oversees these stages as directed by the executives or owners of the company. Some manufacturers adapt to their growth when the company starts out by doing the production in house and then, as the company sales increase, they produce larger quantities with help from contractors. (See Figure 1.15.)

The Relationship between Production and Design

The designer's responsibility is to put together a line of garments that will sell well to the retail buyers but ultimately will sell quickly to the consumers. It is the job of the production manager to price the new design by figuring out the cost of the garment's labor and materials. If the production manager believes that the garment cannot be manufactured at a price acceptable to the sales staff, changes for that garment will be suggested to the designer. A smart designer will figure out a way to compromise and retain the look or essence of the garment and fit it within the targeted price range. The two departments could be at odds unless the designer is savvy enough to learn when to stay firm and when to make subtle changes in the design elements. Each new season brings design innovations that production managers balk at initially, but then they miraculously find ways to expand production capabilities and meet the demands of those styles. By the time the reorders start coming in, the production department usually has an understanding of exactly how to correct any problems.

The stage is set. The supporting cast has been introduced. We know the job description of designer, assistant designer, first patternmaker, merchandiser, and various production staff. The next thing on the agenda is to meet the purchasers of clothing designed for girls and juniors. It is time to meet the consumers.

FIG. 1.15. IN THIS VAST EXPANSE EMPLOYEES HAVE ROOM TO MOVE FREIGHT, PACK GARMENTS, AND STORE SUPPLIES.

Designer's Diary

Dear Diary,

I can't believe I'm finally going to do my own designs for the girls' line. Tomorrow is the big day! I'll start looking at fabrics, and they'll be my picks this time instead of me just writing down another designer's taste. Note to self: find the invoice for the butterfly print for the front office. I forgot to do that last week, and I don't want to alienate them before I sketch my first outfit! Oh, and I saw the cutest skirts on the backup singers at the U2 concert. They were like little pleated kilts with buckles, with silver and gold threads running through the fabric. Even the audience was dressed killer. Lots of fringe and dyed-to-match lace patches. Well, wish me luck. I'm ready to work my tail off to show the staff that they promoted the right assistant designer! At least the junior line designer is becoming a good friend.

Designer's Dictionary

blocks basic pattern used to create patterns with style lines, same as sloper

fashionista fashion expert

flapper name for the young women who danced the Charleston in the 1920s

flounces Piece of material either circular and bias-cut or straight-cut and gathered. Used on sleeves, front bodice, or skirt of dress, usually at the hem, singly or in series (Calasibetta, Tortora, Abling 2002, *Fairchild Dictionary of Fashion,* p. 162).

leg of mutton sleeve with full top gathered or pleated into armhole and tapered to wrist (Calasibetta, Tortora, Abling 2002, *Fairchild Dictionary of Fashion,* p. 416).

marrow edge special finish done on a marrow edge machine that makes the edge of fabric be covered in tight small stitches. If applied to a knit edge with tension it gives the edge a ruffled appearance.

overhead the specific costs that must be paid to be in business like rent and utilities

overlock a machine finish that sews the seam and finishes the edge in one application with the threads casting over one another to lock the stitch (serge)

rompers casual garments that are connected at the waist with a short pant bottom

separates apparel top and bottom pieces sometimes styled to coordinate and merchandised to mix and match.

shawl collars collar that follows the front opening of the garment. Cut in one piece, or with seam in center back, it does not have separate lapels (Calasibetta, Tortora, Abling 2002, p. 344).

synthetic fabric manufactured fibers. Textile fibers that are not found in nature but are produced through various chemical processes (Calasibetta, Tortora, Abling 2002, p. 322 under *manufactured fibers*).

Chapter 2

The Merchant and the Customer

Designing apparel successfully for the girls' and junior markets demands a thorough understanding of the target markets. Designers must consider the girls who will wear the clothes and the retailers who will sell the clothing to the girls. Manufacturers consider the retailers to be their buyers because the retailers actually select the garments that will be available for sale in their stores.

The professional purchasing agents for retail stores are called buyers. The consumers, those girls who purchase the clothing, are the retailers' customers and have the power to accept or reject styles by deciding where, when, and if to spend their money. Designers of girls' apparel need to be in touch with what the girls want to wear and what they can afford to pay for it.

A girls' clothing designer must know exactly who her customers are. Current fashion trends often overlap but there are distinct differences between little girls who wear the size 4 to 6x range, older girls who wear the 7 to 14 size range, and teenagers who wear the junior size range.

JUNIOR SIZING

This junior size range of clothing is generally sized 5 to 13 with size 9 being the sample size. This size range fits a teenager with a defined bust line, waist, and hips. In recent years, sizes 1 and 3 have been added to some lines to accommodate smaller customers. Plus-size junior lines are also marketed. For those special size adjustments, junior clothing is graded up to fit larger teens, but the proportions are meant to have the same youthful appeal. Some manufacturers have found shipping separates easier to fit the range of customers they have, and they use extra small, small, medium, large, and extra large instead of numeric sizing.

The target market for junior apparel is teenagers, and that is where the design team has to be focused. The sizing of teen clothing has little to do with age. Teenagers develop at different rates, and sometimes different parts of their bodies develop at different rates. They might stay one size for a time, go through a growth spurt, and then require a completely

Box 2.1 Assistant Designer Girls' Line Position

Post Date: August 21, 2009
Company: Just Ducky Inc.
Location: U.S.—Los Angeles, California
Job Level: Junior Staff
Field: Fashion/Apparel
Job Functions: Product Development

Description

- Support scheduling and budgeting of materials as assigned, including checking in piece goods and trimmings.
- Provide innovative solutions and best practices to garment designs. Partner with team to execute creative vision of designer.
- Partner with program management, creative, and technical production studio to execute projects on time and within budget.
- Ensure timely delivery of newly designed garments to sales staff.
- Approve color and attend quality and fit checks. Collaborate with others in production to ensure quality.
- Attend and actively participate in all weekly and project-based status meetings.
- Keep manager/designer updated on projects, initiatives, and key issues.
- Oversee staff of design room to insure productivity.
- Assist head designer in all tasks relating to production of garments for line inclusion.
- Perform any and all tasks as determined by designer which may include cost sheets, garment cutting, and patternmaking.

Specific Skills

- Must possess sketch and design skills, both manually and on computer.
- Must have excellent people, negotiation, and vendor management skills.
- Must be solution-oriented, provide options, and have a creative approach.
- Must have strong proficiency with numbers for the purpose of costing.
- Must have bachelor's degree in design or equivalent work experience at a production facility required.

BOX 2.1. A JOB POSITION AD FOR AN ASSISTANT DESIGNER MIGHT REQUIRE THE ABILITIES LISTED ABOVE.

different size and style. The sizing of junior apparel is further complicated by the fact that petite women with youthful attitudes purchase junior clothing all the way into their 30s. Our youth-obsessed culture also tempts older women to purchase junior clothing. Bloomingdale's sells Juicy Couture terry jogging suits to a predominately *over 30* customer in its California stores. Designing and sizing junior clothing is complicated even further by the fact that pre-teen girls who cannot find styles to their liking often shop in the junior department. Parental guidance has to insure that girls purchase age-appropriate clothing.

Characteristics of a Junior Consumer

There are no visual stereotypes of the junior customer. They come in all sizes, shapes, and descriptions. Surveys are constantly being taken to estimate correctly the average height and weight of American consumers. The research has shown that teens were getting taller and thinner with narrower hips than previous generations, but that trend has slowed down. The statistical charts now show teens are getting larger and heavier, but the current emphasis on healthy eating may reverse this. Fast food has also affected the bodies of all Americans, causing a thickening of the waists and raising the average size and weight. The fattening of America is counterbalanced in the junior market by the near compulsion of many teens to be skinny and petite like their favorite celebrity entertainers. The designer of junior clothing must take into consideration the customer and try to ascertain the lifestyle, including the diet, of their target

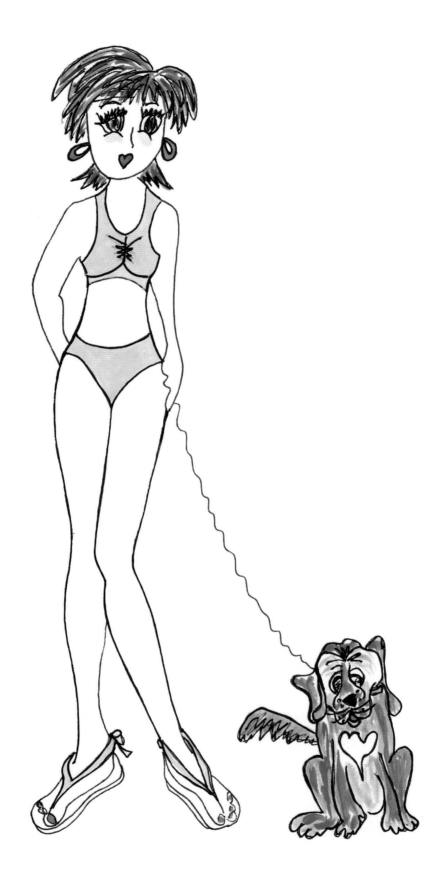

FIG. 2.1a. THIS JUNIOR HAS FILLED OUT FROM HER 7–14 SIZE RANGE DAYS. HER LIMBS ARE ELONGATED, SHE HAS DEVELOPED A BUST AND HIPS SO THAT A WAISTLINE SHOWS. NOTICE THE ATTITUDE IN THE STANCE. TEENAGERS HAVE THEIR OWN POINT OF VIEW.

YOUNG JUNIORS/TEEN GIRLS, 60″ to 63″

Young juniors/teen girls have very small busts, thick waists, and fairly small hips.

	X-Small	Small		Medium		Large
Pattern Sizes	5–6	7–8	9–10	11–12	13–14	15–16
Bust	28	29	30½	32	33½	35
Waist	22	23	24	25	26	27
Hips	31	32	33½	35	36½	38
Back waist	13½	14	14½	15	15½	16

FIG. 2.1b. THIS MEASUREMENT CHART SHOWS THE MEASUREMENTS FOR THE JUNIOR SIZE RANGE.

FIG. 2.2. Below. THIS PHOTO EXEMPLIFIES THE GENERATION GAP CAUSED BY COMPLETELY DIFFERENT TASTES IN APPAREL. TEENS WANT THEIR OWN IDENTITY AND STRIVE TO HAVE THEIR OWN LOOK.

consumer. The retailers will provide the exact measurement requirements for each style for production, but the designer needs insight into the tastes of the consumer prior to designing the line (Figures 2.1a and 2.1b).

The Junior Market Volatility

The junior-sized consumer shops in a marketplace driven by unpredictable forces that are fed by teenage angst. Teenagers' tastes in fashion are both confusing to adults and unpredictable and bewildering to the teens themselves. Normal teens come under pressure to do well in school, participate in sports, help around the house, work part time, and fit in socially. Teens are under pressure to conform to their peer group, strike out and rebel against adult taste and supervision, show individuality while walking a tricky path to avoid the pitfalls of drugs, alcohol, and premarital sex. Each teen determines how to cope with individual pressures. Each teen also determines to what extent she wants to be similar to (or different from) her friends and to what degree she will rebel against her parents' dress code. (See Figure 2.2.) On top of all the varying style input from the adult cultural cycle, this market is further impacted by the speed in which new trends hit then disappear.

If you consider only one extreme influence in the junior market you come to understand the complexity of this design segment. When *goth* was in style among a segment of teenagers, the adherents wore black clothes, dyed their hair shades of purple and black, acquired multiple body piercings, and wore crosses and thick chains. They were striking out in their own rebellious ways. However, if you really looked closely at the members of the group, they were alike. This was an extreme fashion group, but it tells the message of teen exhibition. Teens like to be different, and they enjoy being anti-establishment, but they do these things within the realm of the peer group in which they belong. This example is consistent over the many teen social groups. Whether preppie, hippie, goth, nerd, or techno types, teens today still rebel, conform, and emulate their current icons

FIG. 2.3. TEENAGERS THAT WEAR JUNIOR CLOTHING COME IN ALL SHAPES, SIZES, AND TASTE LEVELS. WHAT THEY WEAR THIS MONTH THEY MIGHT NOT BE CAUGHT DEAD IN NEXT MONTH.

en masse and simultaneously create a clothing market that is always in flux (Figure 2.3).

To add to the designer's confusion, some teens like to be first with a trend while others will only follow. Their fashion ideas come from music groups, movie and television stars, sports heroes, and street culture mixed in with regular fashion trends from conventional sources like *Lucky* magazine, *Elle,* or *Seventeen.* Because of widespread Internet access, including MySpace and YouTube, and multiple channels on satellite television where all the "in" styles are widely seen, teens want to wear the new styles immediately. (See Figure 2.4.) There is no waiting for the next season with this market. Fashion change is always in the wind and teenagers expect to find the latest styles in the stores. If they do not find what they are looking for, teens will improvise and alter basic clothing to their most recent fad by cutting, shredding, and decorating their clothing with add-ons. **Brand** labels and stores also go in and out of style. When a store is out of style with juniors, it will have a great

deal of trouble getting back into the teenagers' good graces.

Pacific Sunwear named a new female chief executive in July 2007. Sally Frame Kasaks was a prior board of director for many years. A *Los Angeles Times* (July 7, 2007) business section article by Leslie Earnest quoted Kasaks as saying, "The top priority is to reconnect with our customer." Pacific Sunwear of California Inc. is one of the largest and most successful chains of surf and skate apparel for junior customers. It had a run of very profitable years and is now struggling. Kasaks admitted the first question she asked was, "What do teenagers want? How do they communicate? What influences them?" She was still asking that question a year and a half later, as PacSun began shutting down their 154 demo stores that catered to the hip-hop urban consumer (*Los Angeles Times,* January 5, 2008).

The usual evolution of seeing high style on the couture runways, then finding it in **upstairs retailers**, and finally finding those styles copied

FIG. 2.4. JUNIORS GO IN AND OUT OF TRENDS SO FAST THAT MUCH OF THEIR WARDROBE BECOMES OBSOLETE AND THEY REFUSE TO WEAR IT. MOST TEENS WOULD TELL THEIR FRIENDS "I HAVE NOTHING TO WEAR."

at affordable prices is not the normal occurrence in the junior market. Trends can start on the street or in a surf shop and expand from there. **Retro** fads can hit, and used clothing resale emporiums can drain dollars away from apparel chains with no advanced notice. The abnormal is normal in the teen market. This is part of the appeal for designers, who love to forecast and anticipate fads and recognize which fads will become trends.

Trends in Social Behavior that Affect Apparel
American society bends and sways over time. Our girls and teenagers are in a particular period where they have the freedom to wear what they like, not what is the best choice for their appear-

ance. Part of this effort to build self-esteem was to get girls to compete with boys in mathematics and science. A side effect of improved self-esteem is that it has broadened teens' personal apparel choices by allowing them to let go of prior generational attention to making style choices best suited to individual physical assets. Clothing is not necessarily used as camouflage to cover potbellies, large hips, or even skinny legs as it was in previous decades. Anything goes; teenagers think they look good, and wearing current styles is more important to this generation than enhancing their best physical traits. There is even an accepted term *muffin top* to describe girls who wear low-rise pants with their flesh ballooning up over the top. This information serves the designer by freeing them to design for the average body, or the representative sample size proportions, knowing that if the style is right, it will appeal across all body types.

It is important to mention that within the junior market there will still be sporty and feminine tastes. Color appeal and personal aversions to prints, or stripes, or textures are factors to consider. All the normal preferences apply here that would apply in the women's wear market. The teen will just choose the current fad while considering his or her favorite colors, fabrics, and patterns.

Companies that design hot junior lines are often prompted by their retailers to add girls' sizes to their production. Conversely, girls' wear companies invest a lot of time and money studying and copying the junior market. These companies will add junior sizes in order to capitalize on the substantial profits that can be made in the junior market.

Girls 7–14 or Bubble Gum Junior
The terms *Big Girl,* **Tween**, or *Bubble Gum Junior* are used for this middle size category. Stores are inconsistent in naming this category of sizes and styles, and there are no standards for sizing. Both of these factors make this category difficult to define. Preteen clothing fills the void between junior sizing and 7 to 14 sizing. Most stores have chosen not to use preteen sizing

FIG. 2.5a. THIS SIZE-10 GIRL IS TYPICAL OF THE 7—14 SIZE RANGE BODY TYPE. NOTICE THE LACK OF CURVATURE TO THE BODY.

OLDER CHILDREN—GIRLS, 50″ to 61″

Girls are shorter than teen girls, with underdeveloped figures. This size is for girls at the beginning of a growth period that usually represents awkward proportions, and styles are more trendy.

Pattern Sizes	7	8	10	12	14
Height	50	52	56	58½	61
Chest	26	27	28½	30	32
Waist	22½	23½	24½	25½	26½
Hips	27	28	30	32	36

FIG. 2.5b. THIS IS A COMPLETE MEASUREMENT CHART WITH ALL SIZES 7–14.

but the few that do add further confusion to the mix. The 7 to 14 garment sizes fit girls from ages six to twelve years as a general rule. (See Figure 2.5a.) Retailers make the sizing even more unclear by using a 7–14 size range in some stores, while other retailers may break down this category into a 7–10 range for younger girls and 10–14 for more junior styling. Mature 12 year olds, usually those girls whose figures are already slimming down and developing, will choose to wear small junior clothing sizes. Size 10 is the sample size in the 7–14 range. (See Figure 2.5b.)

Girls in the tween size range do not have busts. Their necks, legs, and arms have elongated. They are in the process of losing baby fat and developing muscle tone. This is not a curvy category of girls. There is little difference in hips, bust, and waist. Some of these girls do gymnastics and others play soccer or other sports, and their physical activities can be strenuous. They are still modest and do not like low-cut, chest-revealing styles. As soon as these girls start to develop, they prefer to search for junior apparel. In the upper sizes of this range, the girls can be gawky and even clumsy. These are girls in transition to adolescence.

Age-Appropriate Styling

Rather than waiting until consumer tastes and characteristics stabilize, the problem of designing appropriate clothing for this size range needs to be addressed immediately. This is a

size range for girls of varying maturity both emotionally and physically. The girls—and remember these are young girls, not young women—start out playing with dolls, and they are expected to dress within this range until they are in middle school, wearing a touch of lip gloss and swooning over teen idols. These are the girls who giggle and scream in a piercing shrill pitch when they are in groups. These are girls who want to be sophisticated, but they still watch cartoons. This dichotomy creates a huge design challenge. The girls want to dress like their teen sisters or like the young movie starlets and musicians they adore. The designer must find a balance between junior styling and age-appropriate modesty. (See Figure 2.6.)

It is difficult for designers of 7-to-14-range apparel to strike the balance between the taste of their target customers, who want to dress like the popular teen idols, and the parents who want their children to be dressed appropriately. There are design methods to avoid these problems. When skirts in the junior market are very short, designers in the 7-to-14 range can offer "skorts", which are skirts attached to shorts. When crop tops are marketed to this age group, they can be sewn as twin sets with a tank or T-shirt sewn beneath the cropped bodice, which provides a measure of modesty but still offers the in-style look. There are ways to modify the trendy item to suit different tastes. If the trend is simply too mature for this age range, the designer needs to bear that in mind and get creative with fit modifications and style adjustments or pass over the trend entirely.

Taste Preferences for Feminine Girls' Styling

It is almost easier to know what tweens don't want than what they do want. Tweens do not want little girl styling. They do not want to look like boys, but they do not want to look overtly sexy either. They are body shy but emotionally daring. They are testing the waters of growing into their own skin and leaving their parents behind. They are over teddy bear T-shirts and sweet, feminine dresses that grandmothers love

FIG. 2.6. THESE TWEENS ARE WEARING JUNIOR-INSPIRED CLOTHING THAT MANY PARENTS WOULD FIND TOO SUGGESTIVE AND INAPPROPRIATE FOR THEIR AGES.

to purchase. They do not want their mothers to purchase their clothing. They don't want T-shirts that say "Daddy's Girl," unless that stencil is popular with teens at the moment. They want their own stamps on their wardrobes. They have definite color preferences. They start out with definitive feminine or unisex clothing preferences that may change overnight. They do not want to look younger because growing older is what they are focusing on. They want junior trendy clothing that fits them yet allows them to do whatever their activities demand. This size range girl still plays, even if not supervised, as she was when parents controlled activities minute by minute. Tweens do not want clothing that restrains them or binds them. They want comfortable, colorful, and practical apparel but they want to imitate the casual dress of teenagers. (See Figures 2.7a, 2.7b, 2.7c, and 2.7d.)

Little Girls' Sizing

The last size range is *little girl* or *little sister,* and it is sized 4–6x. These girls range in age from three-year-olds to small eight-year-olds. Size 5 is considered the sample size. (See Figure 2.8a.)

The size 6x is a thick size 6. It is for the girl who is still holding on to her baby fat and whose body has not yet had the growth spurt that stretches her limbs. A size 7 in the 7–14 range is thinner and longer than a 6x. A little girl does not have an elongated neck. Her head seems to sit directly upon her shoulders. The circumference of the head of a young child is very close in size to an adult head so the proportions of the neckline must be adjusted accordingly. Young girls do not like low necklines, either, so extra care must be taken to design around this preference. (See Figure 2.8b.)

Practical Design Considerations

It is important to recognize the physical abilities of girls in the 4–6x size range. It is possible that the younger children in this range cannot dress themselves entirely. They may need help determining back from front, and they may need assistance with zippers and laces. They are able to do buttoning in front, but not in back, and they struggle with sleeve buttons. None of this would matter to the designer except the fact that these girls want to dress themselves. They want to be big girls, so their favorite clothing is that which they can easily get into and out of without needing assistance. For this reason, it is prudent for the designer to take easy access into consideration.

Another factor that makes girls in this age range interesting is that they will not tolerate being uncomfortable in their clothing. If apparel

FIG. 2.7a, b, c, d. THESE GIRLS HAVE DIFFERENT INTERESTS. ONE DANCES AND THE OTHER LIKES GYMNASTICS. (a) Top left. SHOWS THEIR SIMILAR TASTE IN TRENDY KNIT DRESSES. ONE WEARS LEGGINGS THE OTHER PREFERS A SHORT DRESS. IN PHOTO (b) Top right. THEY PICK THE SAME T-SHIRT AND WORK THEIR DIFFERENT LOOKS WITH THE REST OF THE CLOTHING. (c) Bottom left. SHOWS SAMANTHA IN A FRILLY CHIFFON WITH BIG BOLD DOTS FOR HER DRESSY OCCASION ACCENTED WITH SILVER ACCESSORIES. (d) Bottom right. JORDAN STANDS OUT IN A LONG CHIFFON DRESS THAT HAS A BELT BUT NO JEWELRY.

FIG. 2.8a. NOTICE THE BODY HAS VERY LITTLE SHAPE, A SHORT NECK AND LIMBS. USE THIS GIRL AS A TEMPLATE FOR SKETCHING HER CLOTHES.

LITTLE GIRLS, 39″ to 47″

Age ranges from preschool through first grade. The styles are similar to those for boys; color and details are the primary differences.

Pattern Sizes	4	5	6	6x
Height	39	42	45	47
Chest	23	24	25	25½
Waist	21	21½	22	22½
Hips	23	24	25	26

FIG. 2.8b. THIS IS THE MEASUREMENT CHART FOR THE 4–6X SIZE RANGE IN LITTLE GIRLS.

FIG. 2.9. LITTLE GIRLS LIKE COMFORT FIRST AND THEN WILL USE THEIR OWN WHIMS TO FIGURE OUT WHICH GARMENT THEY WANT TO CHOOSE.

binds, hinders, or scratches them, they will not wear it a second time. They would just as soon take it off as wear something that hurts or constricts their movement. They do not like tight head openings that have to be forcibly pulled over the head. There should be stretch room so that they don't feel like their ears are being pulled off when wearing sweaters and crew neck knits. They do not like smothering necks probably because their necks are so abbreviated that a funnel neck or turtleneck seems like it is up to their chins. They have favorite articles of clothing that they would wear daily if allowed. These are the most loyal and sensible consumers. A girl this age will wear a worn-out favorite piece of clothing until it disappears mysteriously from her closet!

Little girls like to please. They are feeling their way to independence and enjoying the freedom that school gives them from their parents. They are now torn between pleasing their parents, impressing their teachers, and fitting in with their new classmates. These new emotional pulls can be reflected in their wardrobes. Little tomboys may suddenly want to wear a skirt to school because "only the boys" wear pants. Formerly prissy girls may demand jeans because they are hassled when they have recess and their panties show if they hang on the monkey bars. Girls in this age range have definite opinions and taste choices, and they are very verbal in expressing them. Most, however, are not at an age to enjoy shopping because of a short attention span, so the parent does the purchasing. See the girl in Figure 2.9.

Girls' Wear Fantasy

The single most wonderful thing about designing apparel for girls is the fact that they love fantasy and will dress according to their creative instincts, combining any assortment of colors and garments. Girls have very few biases about their bodies and they will try any style that appeals to their fun natures. By the time they are in kindergarten, girls will start to conform to the dress codes of their peers. They will wear jeans to school if most of the girls do, for example. Individuality is important to girls in this age range. They love color. They love dressing up, and down, and they like wearing role-playing costumes. They love screen prints of their favorite cartoon characters and feminine icons like hearts, rainbows, mermaids, butterflies, and unicorns. Think about the old saying about sugar and spice and everything nice, and this category becomes easy to target. (See Figure 2.10.)

FIG. 2.10a, b. (a) Left. THIS LITTLE GIRL JUST NEEDS TINSEL HAIR TO MAKE BELIEVE SHE IS EITHER A TEENAGER OR A CLOWN. (b) Above. GIRLS IN THE 4–6X SIZE RANGE CAN HAVE ACTIVE IMAGINATIONS THAT INCLUDES BEING A PRINCESS OR A FAIRY.

Grandmother Purchasing

It seems silly to make an issue of apparel purchasing by grandmothers but it needs addressing. Grandparents purchase a large chunk of children's apparel. As grandparents age they become more conservative in their tastes. They remember popular styles from years ago, and those styles still appeal to their nostalgic memories. Smart designers address this issue by having a group or a few pieces in their lines that fill this niche. Sometimes the dresses are just a little frillier than current fashion dictates. Sometimes the addition of bows, lace, and almost decorating the basic style like a Christmas tree fit this category, too. Grandparents rarely purchase the latest trend, and they certainly don't choose the styles that seem too grown up. Seasoned professional sales representatives in the little girl market call the styles that sell year after year *bread and butter* styles. These are the basics that only need slight modification like changing prints, updating fabrics, or lengthening or shortening sleeves seasonally and then

they just continue to sell well. Part of this bread and butter money is grandparent gifting. (See Figure 2.11.)

RETAIL MARKET CHOICES

In addition to knowing the consumer's preferences well, the designer must know the retailer's customer base. In order to get the garments into the store to reach the consumer, the manufacturer must first show the buyer a line that fits the stores price point and image. There are three basic retail groups: the upstairs market, the moderate market, and mass markets.

Upstairs Market

The upstairs market includes large, exclusive, high-end stores like Neiman Marcus, Saks Fifth Avenue, and Barneys New York. It also includes small specialty boutiques located in upscale neighborhoods all over the United States. These stores expect perfect quality garments with exclusivity and the latest fabrics, trimmings, and design features. Designing clothing for these

FIG. 2.11. JORDAN MODELS THE GARMENT HER GRANDMOTHER LIKES BUT SHE POINTS TO THE SPAGHETTI STRAP DRESS SHE PREFERS.

stores requires special attention to detail both in construction and in presentation. The high price tags often also represent known designer labels and well-established brands. Nordstrom and Bloomingdale's also fall into this category although some of their merchandise might be priced a little more competitively with moderate department stores.

The competition from U.S. manufacturers in this category would include: imports from upscale companies based in Milan, London, Tokyo, Switzerland, boutique U.S. manufacturers, and popular French couture houses.

The Moderate Market

The moderate market is an ever-shrinking assortment of department stores and smaller children's wear stores that are also called *middle-tier* merchants. Macy's is the big player in this field. The Gap fits into this range, too. The Children's Place and Gymboree would also be considered moderate retailers. The merchandise in these stores is rarely as exclusive as the high-end stores but the goods do have perceived quality over price-driven chains. There is some standard of service.

The department stores in the United States have been merging and restructuring at a fast rate. A department store traditionally is a store with many varied departments offering goods ranging from furniture to cosmetics. Each department is supposed to be staffed with experts in that area. Service and reliability have always been the promise at these retailers in addition to the convenience of shopping in one store for a variety of items. Department stores are perceived by many customers as dependable places to shop. This is because the stores have a reputation for handling product returns with customer satisfaction as their primary purpose. A department store customer knows that the purchase will cost a little more, but he or she also knows that the price comes with service and quality. With all the recent mergers however, the consumer is left wondering if the new department store has the same standards as the one they always trusted.

Wanamaker's became Hecht's, which is now Macy's, and May bought Zion, which became Meir & Frank. May and Federated merged and then they joined Macy's, too. Dayton-Hudson merged with Marshall Field's and purchased Mervyn, which became owned by Target, Inc. In 2008, Mervyn filed for bankruptcy and then closed, while Target stores continued profitably. As soon as you turn around, there is another sell-off or acquisition. Andrea Chang and David Yi suggested in July 2007 that Macy's was in a possible buyout position from Kohlberg Kravis Roberts & Co. (*Los Angeles Times,* July 19, 2007). The article explained that customer dissatisfaction since merging with Robinsons-May had hurt its retail sales.

The important thing to know is that department stores will shy away from garments that are sold to discounters because they cannot compete in those price wars. This is the market for brand names that shoppers trust for quality. Perceived value is vital to this market. JCPenney would fit into this market but they would be at the lowest end. Kohl's would like to be considered a department store, but its merchandise mix and pricing, like Mervyn prior to its bankruptcy, puts it in competition with JCPenney more than Macy's. When the economy is soft, the retailers in the moderate market are financially vulnerable because getting the best price becomes most important for consumers.

Many manufacturers make **label lines** for moderate stores and ship different fabrication but similar styling to what they would ship to discounters. Department stores also use their own labels and have manufacturers contract to do specific styling for them. In-house merchandise is apparel that the retailer will have made directly by the sewing factories, with no manufacturing middleman. Department stores in the United States have turned into space providers to huge apparel conglomerates that stock **apparel real estate**, which is the name for floor or rack space reserved for the major designer labels. The quantity of racks and display space rises and falls on the percentage gains or losses in sales at the end of the year.

The competition for manufacturers targeting the moderate market would include: the department store product development in-house sourcing, all brand names, and volume manufacturers doing upscale styling. When the economy weakens, the moderate customers shop at discount stores. This has a negative effect on the moderate retailers.

Mass Markets

Volume discounters, mass merchandisers, or discount department stores that compete against each other with the lowest prices possible comprise the last retailing segment. The stores in this group would include Wal-Mart, Kmart, Sears, Costco, and Target.

Walmart is the largest retailer in the world, with over 100 million customers shopping their

FIG 2.12a, b, c. (a) Top. CLOTHING BOUTIQUES LIKE POPULAR IN CALABASAS, CA, OFFER UPSCALE APPAREL THAT IS CAREFULLY MERCHANDISED TO SHOWCASE TRENDY CLOTHING. (b) Middle. TARGET SHOWS TRENDY CLOTHING TOO AT MUCH LOWER PRICES BUT IT IS MERCHANDISED WITH AN EMPHASIS ON PRICE. SINCE CUSTOMER SERVICE IS LIMITED IN THE STORE THE SIGN SHOWS HOW GARMENTS MIGHT LOOK WHEN WORN. (c) Bottom. THE CLOTHES SHOWN IN MACY'S TRY FOR SOME UNIQUE DISPLAY BUT ACTUALLY RELY ON RACK ASSORTMENTS.

U.S. stores weekly. To understand the impact on a manufacturer's business, consider this possible scenario: A group of four different dressy Easter dresses are shown to Wal-Mart for $10.00 per dress. Wal-Mart buys two dozen of each style dress in assorted sizes and colors for just 1/4 of their stores. Four dresses × $10.00 × 24 each × 1,675 stores. The dollar amount of that one order should be $1,608,000. If Wal-Mart decides to purchase the dresses, they will only pay $9.60 for each instead of the full price, which is their normal practice. Thus, more than $64,320 comes off the top of the purchase price. How does the manufacturer make a reasonable markup with that price reduction? They try to make deals with fabric and trim sources to sharpen those costs and then the remaining reduction in price comes out of the labor paid to the sewing contractors. The manufacturer is in a bind, needing to accept the large order, just as the fabric and trim companies also need the business. No one wants to turn down the enormous business orders even at very low markups, but the end result is that the production department has to put the construction of these garments in the hands of the lowest-cost sewing contractors. Most recently, those factories have been found in Asia, particularly China.

This is the category of retailing that is the most competitively priced. Due to the enormous quantities of ordered apparel, it is the riskiest. If a manufacturer has an order for 5,000 dozen garments, and they are late with delivery and the order is cancelled, there are very few places to sell off 60,000 garments. Although this is the lowest-priced category, the quality requirements are stiff. All discounters have rigid measurements and construction standards that must be met. All the clothing is tested for correct wash/dry instructions. This is an area of manufacturing that leaves very little room for error.

The large discount chains went through some consolidation in the late 1970s and 1980s, similar to what the department stores have experienced since 1990. There used to be many discount chains that were vital in their regions, but strong competition from the other discount-ers in price wars, specifically Wal-Mart and Kmart, drove them out of business, or bought them out to acquire the real estate. The Kmart and Sears consolidation is an example of this. Store names like Jamesway, TG&Y, Treasury Stores, and Hartzfield-Zody's are examples of giant corporations that no longer exist to offer competition in this category.

A new development at this level is also emerging to great success. In recent years, well-known designers from upstairs markets have aligned themselves with discounters. Isaac Mizrahi has gone from a Chanel-backed, high-end designer to doing a line for Target. His line has been such a hit that designer Johnson Hartig with partner Cindy Greene, both of Libertine, are selling a mass-market line for Target, too. Martha Stewart housewares sell well for Kmart. Lands' End has aligned itself with Sears.

Target is one of the few discounters that has successfully bridged the economic strata to sell customers who shop at Neiman Marcus and Nordstrom the lower-price-point clothing offered in its stores. This has pulled dollars from both the upstairs market and more dramatically from the moderately priced stores. In the global marketplace, manufacturers find unlimited customers but fierce competition at every level.

The competition for this market is fierce: besides the manufacturing sector in the United States that designs specifically for mass merchants, the biggest competition in this category is imported goods from all around the world. Online sales at bargain prices also affect this market. Companies like Marshalls and T.J. Maxx that buy the manufacturers' **overcuts**, and large outlet store malls, also siphon off dollars in this very competitive arena. Costco offers competition in apparel sales. They do not offer wide selection but often have deep discounts in basic clothing and trend-setting items.

KNOWING THE TARGETED CONSUMER

When a designer takes the time to know exactly who her company's consumers are, what they like and dislike, what their budget allows on girls' and junior apparel, and how their lifestyle impacts their need for clothing, the job of designing the line becomes infinitely easier. The following questions will be answered. WHO is wearing the clothes? WHERE will the clothes be worn? HOW much can they spend? When those answers are clear, the designer is ready to start assembling the appropriate information for forecasting the WHAT. The WHAT is which trend will be the big moneymaker for the next season. The designer now needs to do the market research to find inspiration for the line that is on the verge of being created.

Designer's Diary

Dear Diary,

Work has become my main focus. After I leave the office, I have to go to malls and stores around town and shop my line to see what looks good and then compare that to all the other items in the girls department. I make sure to see all girls' and juniors' assortments in all the malls and, let me tell you, there are a lot of clothes. With so many styles offered, it is a wonder girls can ever make a choice. I have to be so particular with my designs, even down to the last detail. Oh, I noticed that Smarty Girl only uses logo buttons—even when they don't show!

And, I found it hard to believe one of *our* outfits (not my design) was displayed at the bottom of a T-stand so low down, the only customer who could possibly see it would be a dog on a leash or a two-year-old. Having our style placed at eye level would make it sell more. I am going to mention this to the marketing manager at our next sales meeting.

Designer's Dictionary

apparel real estate large brand, upstairs, or couture lines have a designated amount of square footage in retail space. It is sometimes left to the fashion house to determine which styles the retailer will be showcasing in the stores. The retail space grows or shrinks according to how well the line is selling.

brand a manufacturer or distributor-assigned name, mark, or label assigned to a product in order to encourage consumer recognition of the product. (Calasibetta, Tortora, Abling 2002, p. 44).

label lines a manufacturing company may have known brand identification and use a different label in its goods when shipping retailers specially ordered apparel. The apparel may look like the brand item but by not carrying the brand label, it is less expensive.

overcuts the quantity of leftover garments after the orders for the style have been filled.

retro the return to the fashion look of earlier decades (abbreviated use of the word retrospective). Used when fashions from the past eras are updated and used as current styles (Calasibetta, Tortora, Abling 2002, p. 388).

tween term used as name for the size-7-to-14-range girl who is between the age of a little girl and a teenager. Interchangeable with Bubble Gum Junior, Big Girl, and even preteen.

upstairs retailer A retailer that has high-quality and expensive merchandise. This term is synonymous with high-end merchants.

1. Know your consumer. Spend some time in a public place and discreetly watch girls interact with their parents and friends. Get a feel for how they dress, how they move physically, and how play clothing fits. Needless to say, do not approach young children without speaking to their parents to gain their approval. Sketch five little girl figures in the 4–6x range to set the proportions in your mind.

2. This is an exercise in comparative shopping. Look in the daily newspaper and cut out an ad showing junior apparel. Sketch the garments on a blank sheet of paper. Cut out the ad garment and attach it beside your sketch. Now go to three different stores and see if you can find that garment or something very similar. Take the same sketch to the 7–14 department, and see if the style has already been adopted in this size range. Sketch the similar garments and note the stores and prices. Discuss in class the differences of the versions at varied price points and the style changes made to make it appropriate for younger girls.

3. This is a variation on the second exercise. Cut out ads in all three size ranges, 4 to 6x, 7 to 14, and juniors, from the upstairs mar-

ket. If you do not get mail catalogues, go online to specific stores like Neiman-Marcus or Saks Firth Avenue and find the offered garments in the particular size ranges. Sketch one garment from each range, attach a print out or cut out of that garment to your paper. Now go to a moderate store and a mass-market store. Find the closest garments to your ads, sketch them, and note their price points. Discuss the style changes that happen because of price considerations.

4. Know more about the teenage shopper. Go to the local theater on a Friday night or a mall on a Saturday afternoon. Observe preteen and teenage girls interacting. Notice their clothing. Go into junior stores and watch them shop. Sketch five junior figures.

5. To understand the 7–14-size-range consumer, you must see girls in the age range from 6 to 12. See if you can volunteer at an elementary school in a reading program and then try to volunteer at a middle school in another capacity. Get a feel for the different ages, development, tastes, and style sense of the girls who wear clothing in this department. Discuss your findings in class.

Now you have an overview of the different types of retailing operations. You have also observed and understood the characteristics of little girls, big girls, and teenage customers. You have translated your observation skills into sketches that attempt to capture the proper proportions of different size ranges. You also may be thinking about clothes you'd like to design.

1. Read Chapter 2.
2. Become familiar with the size, actions, and abilities of girls' wear customers.
3. Visit stores to compare prices and quality of girls' apparel.
4. Complete the chapter activities.
5. Expand your vocabulary with the Designer's Dictionary.

Box 2.2

Teen Chic Is Cheap

by Liz Gunnison | September 12, 2008
for Condé Nast Portfolio.com

As parents and employers feel the pinch of the recession, the squeeze is trickling down to teens—who are reinventing their tastes.

Jeannie Lukin, 19, has no trouble pinpointing where she has cut back her spending this summer.

"Shopping," Lukin says, without hesitation. "I have enough clothes. At this point it's definitely more of a want than a need."

Lukin, who has been a longtime fan of brands like J. Crew and Polo Ralph Lauren, has had to become a savvier shopper. Now, when shopping in her hometown near Albany or at school in Poughkeepsie, New York, she heads for the discount racks first, explores cheaper alternatives like American Eagle, or skips the trip to the mall altogether.

Wary of high gas prices, Lukin made the 90-minute drive home from the camp where she worked this summer only twice. But fuel still managed to cut into her cash; to compensate, she has started eating out less.

Lukin is not alone. Teens across the nation have spent their summer vacations battling high gas prices, competing for jobs in a weak part-time employment market, and making do with smaller contributions from cost-conscious parents.

All of which has led teenagers, in the past considered "recession-proof" spenders, to confront the impact of a slowing economy. According to a survey conducted by BIGresearch in July, 60 percent of teenagers said they had become more frugal in the last six months—compared with only 50 percent of adults.

"Unequivocally, teen spending is very weak," says Adrienne Tennant, a senior analyst at Friedman, Billings, Ramsey. "Usually teens are a resilient portion of the economy because all spending is discretionary, but this time around, gas prices are clearly eating up budgets."

As young adults are forced to make spending trade-offs, it's provided a window into their priorities. The takeaway? Clothing, once the sinkhole of teen pocket money, is losing its allure.

In April, Piper Jaffray released a semi-annual survey of teens that said that teen spending on fashion was down a whopping 20 percent from a year earlier.

By August, major teen retailer Abercrombie & Fitch saw its same-store sales fall 11 percent, and American Eagle ended the month down 5 percent. Pacific Sunwear saw a 6 percent drop for the month, while Limited Brands fell 7 percent. Comparable store sales at Gap decreased by 8 percent.

Retailers tend to count on a big boost in August when high school and college students restock their wardrobes for the fall, but this year, that lift hasn't materialized. Teenagers are trading down to less expensive retailers, buying fewer items, and waiting for sales and bargains.

Source: www.portfolio.com/news-markets/national-news/portfolio/2008/09/12/Teen-Spending-Going-Cheap

Chapter 3

Inspiration for Design

There are influences for fashion in society that need to be reflected in every new line, and the designer needs to be conscious of what is going on around the world in order to have his or her line reflect the latest trends. There are opportunities to monitor events that help create fashion trends including street culture, television, art, movies, music, and world events. (See Figures 3.1a, 3.1b, and 3.1c.)

PREPARING FOR A NEW LINE

Before the first sketch can be drawn for a new line, a designer must organize all the different inspirations that have been identified from her personal cultural exploration. Identifying those most valuable tidbits that might inspire great design is the hardest part of preparation, but after some practice, this process becomes second nature.

THE RANGE OF DESIGN INFLUENCES

Will unemployed starlets going to and coming from rehab visits affect the way juniors dress? The *Los Angeles Times* ran a piece called "Hooked on Look" (July 28, 2007) that suggested street style as a possible trend after several young women were photographed coming home from rehabilitation facilities in slim jeans, head scarves, and bangle bracelets. It was necessary for every junior designer and 7–14 designer to wonder about this issue and either decide to follow up with a group of head scarves **swift tagged** to little T-shirts, file the article for later consideration, or choose to ignore the information. The important thing was for every designer to be aware of the possible influence of this trend. In this particular case, bangle bracelets were already a trend as were the skinny jeans, so only the headscarf wrapped around hair in disarray needed consideration. It is possible that the combination of the three items together, jeans, bangles, and bandana, gave additional shelf life to this look.

It is the job of the designer to come to work with all the stimuli from the world floating around in the subconscious mind. Once the designer walks into the design room, he or she needs to be able to integrate and

FIG. 3.1a, b, c. (a) Top left. THE MERCHANDIS-ING AT KOHL'S DEPARTMENT STORE SHOW THE POWER OF HANNAH MONTANA TO SELL GIRLS FASHION TOPS. (b) Above. *HIGH SCHOOL MUSICAL* CHARACTERS ARE SHOWN IN ON A JERRY LEIGH OF CALIFORNIA SCREENED T-SHIRT. (c) Left. A TEEN SHOWS A T-SHIRT THAT PROMOTES VOTING.

communicate that information in order to create new apparel. Employers will go shopping with their design staff on occasion in order to get inspiration and direction, but it is essential that all designers be culturally exposed and knowledgeable regarding all facets of culture that could impact their lines.

The designers of girls' wear in 2008 needed to know if *Gossip Girl* would be the next television show to be a big influence on teens. "While many television shows like *Sex and the City* have captured the hearts of fashion's In crowd in the past, none have done so with the impact on the teen set and its emerging buying influence as *Gossip Girl* has, says Gloria Baume, the fashion director of *Teen Vogue* (azcentral.com). Finding out about cultural events, news events, and trends in the arts, and issues that may create ripples in the fashion world is vital to properly assessing upcoming trends.

World and Business Events

Common sense dictates that all designers need to know what is happening in the world. Major events bring intense exposure to a particular part of the globe, and that scrutiny can give designers trend inspirations. Problems like floods or hurricanes can affect not just the economy of the injured country but also delay production in our global economy. Financial pages in all major papers cover events and trends in the clothing industry. Knowing which stores are doing well and which are suffering economically is invaluable to a designer who shops the stores regularly and by doing so can judge correctly why one is suffering. Information is power.

In past eras, major world events like war or catastrophe caused predictable fashion changes. Skirts often get longer when countries are at war or in an economic slump. This observation is not as true as it has been in the past, but world events continue to affect consumer behavior. When interest rates are high, people who use credit cards, usually the middle and lower classes, often slow or stop their buying. If gas prices soar, then the available expendable money also becomes weak and purchases that are emotional like a new pair of jeans or hot red shoes become less frequent. High petroleum prices also directly impact the prices of synthetic fabrics. Middle-class shoppers will shop at discount stores in times of economic downturn, leaving department stores with fewer customers and more promotional sales.

At the beginning of the war in Iraq when a greater number of Americans supported the war, camouflage prints started appearing across the marketplace in cargo pants and T-shirts and later in the accessory market. As the war lingered and public support decreased so did the camouflage trend.

In December of 2004, ponchos were popular in ladies' wear, and strong sales filtered down to the girls' market. By February of the same year store sales of ponchos had reached a saturation point. In many stores, ponchos were on the markdown racks. When Martha Stewart was released from jail March 5, 2005, after serving time for insider trading, she was photographed in a crocheted gray yarn poncho with a scalloped border. Because she was big news, the photo-

graph was shown around the country. The yarn company that supplied the yarn Martha wore experienced increased sales when consumers wanted to duplicate her look. Poncho sales in all departments, including girls' wear, were reinvigorated. Savvy designers and merchandisers caught the news, and made money, reintroducing ponchos as the new *must have* accessory.

The family of the president of the United States also bears watching. When Michelle Obama wore a black and white print dress on a morning television show during the 2008 presidential campaign, the dress sold out in the stores that carried it. There is no doubt designers will watch Michelle Obama's fashion tastes, as well as those of her two daughters during her husband's presidency. With a younger first lady and girls in the 7–14 and junior size ranges, the fashion imprint from the Obamas could be sensational for the manufacturing sector's customer base.

Current events are covered on television, in the print media, and on the Internet. Taking in a good mix of all media is the best way to stay up on what is going on in the world. Lifestyle sections in newspapers have apparel coverage that projects a different viewpoint than business or news sections, and these pages should always be reviewed.

Street Culture: Hippie, Surf, and Grunge

Three cases of street culture changing the course of junior and girls' clothing are prominent examples of the importance of being aware of youth movements. The hippie influence in the late 1960s and 1970s dramatically changed the fashion world. Their street attire—embroidered jeans, fringe, shawls, and tie dye—had a profound effect and led to the huge junior manufacturing segment. Hippie trends like bellbottoms and peasant styles are brought back in retro styling every few fashion cycles.

The surf/skateboard cultural phenomenon has also greatly influenced junior dressing. This trend started in the boys' market and now generates huge profits for surf shops offering junior versions of the California beach style. Huntington Beach, California, is often referred to as Surf City, USA, and, when the skateboard culture and surfers chose to wear plaid underwear under their swimsuits, girls all over the United States gave up their regular lingerie for boys' plaid boxers. Hoodies were also introduced from the California beach as were many other ideas since 1970 including neon bright colors, ripped cut-offs, and casual tank tops with screen printing.

The grunge look also came from the streets via Seattle. Plaid flannel shirts made a big hit, first in the young mans' market, then sold extremely well from juniors all the way down to the 4–6x girls' range. Even though this was a trend, not a lasting basic, and probably not one that will be recycled over and over like the hippie influence, it came from the streets and made profits for the designers who were savvy at the time. The most likely place to see plaid flannel shirts now is on college campuses. (See Figures 3.2a, 3.2b, and 3.2c.)

The way a designer stays current with the street culture is to be savvy to which street scene is important to the current hip youth culture. By going to street fairs and other popular hangouts of young groups, and through careful observation, a designer will notice many things. For example, the new uses of accessories or repetition of prints, plaids, colors, and even the

FIG. 3.2a, b, c. (a) Left. GRUNGE, WESTERN, OUTDOORS, AND INDUSTRIAL CLOTHING OFTEN FIND POPULARITY IN THE GIRLS' MARKET AS SHOWN HERE WITH DENIM SEPARATES. (b) Bottom left. SKATE AND BEACH SCENES HAVE BEEN HUGE INFLUENCES ON TEEN CLOTHING. (c) Below. THE HIP STREET SCENE TEENS ARE THE FIRST TO TEST NEW TRENDS LIKE AMMO BELTS OR THORNY BANGLE BRACELETS.

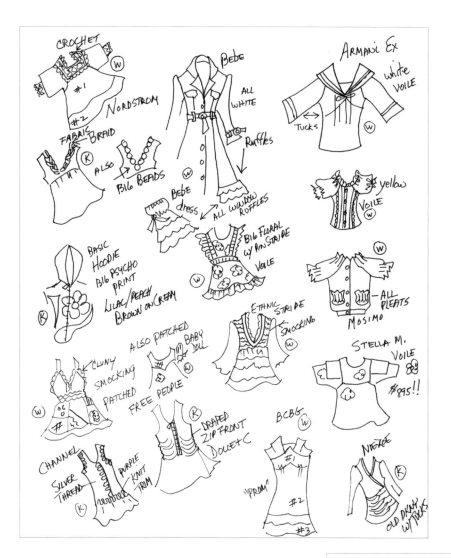

FIG. 3.10a, b. (a) Left. THE SKETCHES HERE ARE TYPICAL OF A DESIGNER'S TREND SHOPPING DAY. IT IS HELPFUL TO NOTE WHERE THE STYLE WAS SEEN AND SOME DETAILS TO JOG THE MEMORY. (b) Below. THE THREE COLORED FIGURES ARE INTERPRETATIONS FOR THE GIRLS MARKET FROM THE SHOPPING NOTES.

this market is for an overview. Recognizing colors, textures, fabrications, and trims enables the designer to predict upcoming trends for the target market. Treatments such as pleating, tucking, and lace inserts can be copied in the girls' and junior lines.

The easiest way to remember the impressions from each store or department is to sit and sketch immediately after walking through the areas of interest. Most stores do not appreciate anyone sketching on their premises, so bear that in mind, and exit the store to record in detail whatever made a strong impact. If the sketches are done quickly and key words denoting specific details are written down, the designer can redraw later and with practice recall the most important facts. **Pin sketches** or flats work best for fast reminders. (See Figures 3.10a and 3.10b.)

FIG. 3.11. THE DESIGNER IS COMPARING T-SHIRTS TO UNDERSTAND WHY ONE IS OUTPERFORMING THE OTHER IN SALES.

Shopping the Competition

Designers need to see what their competitors are doing so that they can make sure their line is the strongest it can be. Assuming that two lines of junior clothing are selling at the same price to the same customers, it is interesting to see each designer's interpretation of the same influence. (See Figure 3.11.) If your line is not performing as well in the stores as another, similar line, perhaps the problem is the fit. If not the fit, then quality could be an issue. Perhaps a garment's construction is cleaner inside, or the process of construction has made the garment easier to sew, thereby lowering the labor cost and making the competing garment sell at a lower price. All of these things need to be considered and discussed with the appropriate department in your company. Comparative shopping is one way to get all the information necessary for improving your bottom line.

Garments are sold either by the dozen or by the half dozen, like eggs. Within a dozen pieces of a particular style, for example a junior top, the store will want a size breakdown. This breakdown is particular to each retail store, but for this explanation, junior tops would be shipped two smalls, six mediums, and four larges to each dozen. If a designer is shopping competitive styles in a store that appears to receive top styles by the dozen, and the designer notices only two pieces on a rack and the merchandise looks new and fresh, then the store has sold 10 pieces. If a sales clerk can specify how long the garments have been on the selling floor, then the speed at which the garments are selling can be figured out. Now that the competitive shopping designer knows that this top is selling well, he or she can try to figure out if it is the fabric, the fit, or the style that is motivating customers to make a purchase.

In another example, a style could be on the rack offered in three different color choices. Two of those colors are nearly sold out. One color choice still has several pieces marked down. This may be the first concrete indication that a particular color is no longer popular among consumers. Obtaining style information in the store is called **reading a rack**.

This example could also hold true for sizes. If a markdown rack has only size S of a top in juniors, then we can draw the conclusion that it was cut too small and the small consumers had to size up to the mediums. If the style's designer was shopping the stores and saw this situation, it would be prudent to review the production grading on the style and refit it for future production.

Shopping the competition needs to be done routinely. Coming back to the same store in 10 days might inform the buyer that the style reordered. Another 10 days may show that the style is now oversaturated. Designers who routinely shop their prospective customers can get a definite feel for what sells best for that store and design specifically for that retailer.

Internet Exploration

Using the Internet is like having a library and a shopping mall at your fingertips. The search engine Google can put you in touch with any design trend, era, or particular designer. The Web service ask.com will answer questions like, "What is a pleat?" The site wwd.com covers the spectrum in apparel from retail sales, business changes, and lifestyles. The many and varied links to apparel and the history of apparel can be very informative. Most of the online Internet servers like MSN have news archives that keep visitors abreast of current events. Great design details of couture fashions can be researched online. Even eBay shows antique and collectible clothing that can be scanned for tailoring elements and notions.

Shopping stores and lines visually, not actually purchasing, can be done online as well. Using the Internet can save time when one simply wants a quick overview of something. However, surfing the Internet does not take the place of shopping the stores, feeling the textures, and getting a sense of what is selling.

Professional Market Services and Trend Publications

There are trend publications that can be purchased by subscription available to manufactur-

ers that do research and shop trends for apparel design. These books may project as far as 18 to 24 months into the future and give color, fabrication, or trend forecasting. Many services have photos of garments in **directional stores** all over the world, and the reports are actually done by French, Italian, and other European companies.

In order to get a complete overview of these offerings, interested manufacturers can call trade representatives of the publications and see which service best suits their needs. Design service sellers, like Trudy Adler in the Los Angeles Mart, have many selections ranging from color direction systems like *Colorplay* and *Fabric Swatch Book* to specific design services just for the junior and girls market such as *Girl Up + 17* and *Planet Kids*. *The Fashion Box* series service has several versions keyed to men, women, or knits. (See Figure 3.12.)

One design service, Carlin International of Paris, carries 16 separate books that include major trends, color, fabric, and silhouettes. Each of the books comes out each season, and each book is directed specifically to very narrow markets.

Determining which of these services is necessary for the company falls to the management of the manufacturer because all these professional services are expensive, costing several thousand of dollars a year. Some members of management believe that this direction should come from the designer and not a service, but most large companies subscribe to at least one of the publications. Small companies have been known to pool their resources and share a service when they are in noncompetitive markets.

By using the color services of companies like Pantone, manufacturing companies can plan the purchase of basic fabrications and be coordinated with their big customers like JC Penney or Macy's. Since catalogue sales divisions work well ahead of the other divisions, advance color direction can be essential to success in this category. Some color services, like Color Association, offer comments from professionals justifying why the color direction will be in certain shades. Other color forecasting companies, which would include Color Portfolio and Color Marketing

DELICATE TIES & STITCHED BANDINGS

"TINKER"

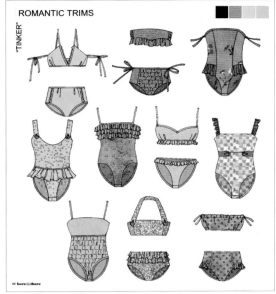

ROMANTIC TRIMS

"TINKER"

FANCIFUL BED JACKETS

"TINKER"

ROMANTIC LAYERS

"TINKER"

GIRLY CARDIGANS & PULLOVERS

"TINKER"

ELEGANT DRAPING & TWISTING

"TINKER"

FIG. 3.12. THE SKETCHES PROVIDED BY TREND PUBLICATIONS CAN INSPIRE A DESIGNER AND GIVE DIRECTION.

Group (CMG), work with large brand name apparel manufacturers, and the volume apparel companies follow their fashion leads and want the same color direction.

These services can be utilized for general information, for specific styling, and for direct knockoffs. Since the services are pricey, an increase in direct sales must justify their cost. Designers must be careful not to design so closely to the garments presented that every junior or girls' line using the service looks exactly alike. That is one of the biggest downsides of using such a service. Before purchasing a subscription for market research, the designer is be wise to make sure the service information is varied enough to be useful, even if the competition is using the same marketing research firm.

Collecting and Interpreting Inspirational Information

Because a diligent designer is exposed from all directions with ideas, trend directions, articles, and miscellaneous materials, it is necessary to keep this vast information organized and easily available. The easiest way to do this is to set up a filing system. The best thing to do is to scan the materials and then store them on a computer. If this option is too high tech, several alternatives also work well.

Sketches and Notations

It is often a quick sketch of a garment that is seen in a store that interests a designer and goes into his or her "possible influence" file. If there is time, the sketch should be redrawn more carefully and key words noted about color, fabrication, and where the item was seen. Measurements that might affect the proportion of the garment can also be estimated. If the sleeve was ¾ instead of long, or the hem length was unusual, a notation of that information may be the difference later of a great addition to the line or a reject.

Three-Ring Binders vs. Accordion Files

Three-ring notebooks can contain sketches, collected photos, and other visual items. Leaf-

ing through the notebook regularly will inspire creativity. Dividers can be labeled by category, for example blouse or pant, or by treatment, such as pleats, tucks, or embroidery. Since this is a permanent collection of information, plastic covers on the pages will protect the paper. Once the binder is full, start another one. You might eventually have an entire notebook library of pant treatments or embroidery techniques.

Using a single binder just for the ideas that were picked up then used for actual garments that were sold is another useful tool. Having the source of the original sketch idea or photo will remind the designer of what resources have been helpful over the course of the line or year. Pages can be easily added, removed, and rearranged. The binder can even contain fabric swatches and trims that you've liked.

Accordion files work great for news articles or written reports. The important thing with this grouping is to make a master list of information like a table of contents and store that in the sketch idea notebook or on the computer, so that there is a constant reminder of what info you have stored in the accordion file. An **alphanumeric** list with simple key words and the location in the file will make the eventual search easy. An example of this would be, "#1 cowboy/surf set," and the article would be filed under C. Instantly you will find that article filed under C, presumably for cowboy, in the file and the short description tells you that it is a possible trend for the surf market.

The accordion file should be cleaned out yearly. If the surf set is to be influenced by a western look then it will happen within that first year of your reading about it or not at all. Business trend articles need key words to explain their subjects. When the end of the year comes around, it is interesting to reflect upon which business news actually affected company sales or profits.

FORECASTING

Once a designer has developed a routine of checking sources for the necessary input including all the previously covered areas, current events, social influences, and the marketplace, developing a plan for a line becomes the creative outlet for all the various stimuli. Line forecasting is the entire process by which the designer studies the marketplace and turns those ideas into new designs. The designer is like a sponge, soaking up all the worldly inspiration and turning those ideas into apparel. The line becomes the embodiment of the entire scope of inspiration from all sources that the designer has consciously followed. This is why being exposed to business trends, shopping, TV, music, current events, subcultures, and even the nature of family relationships is necessary.

Junior apparel has so many layers of creative possibilities, that designing girls' and junior apparel is fun because the line can take off in many directions and appeal to many diverse tastes. One line can have preppy looks hanging right next to retro influences from the 1950s.

Since the couture market has a trickle-down effect on all apparel, the junior market will emulate some of those trends. If couture goes romantic, fabric houses will offer those looks to the designers of ready-to-wear in order for that trend to filter down. The designer's job is to wade through all the stimuli and choose the looks that are best suited to sell to their own **customer base**.

Some excellent forecasting books on the market go into great depth and explain how sophisticated this process has become. The volume designer of girls' and junior apparel needs to use forecasting tools as much as boutique and expensive apparel designers do, because large chains program garments out months in advance.

Forecasting for 4–6x and 7–14

Since the 7–14 girls' size range watches and copies the junior market so closely, the designer of girls' wear must do all the same investigative routines as a junior designer must do. There is a delay factor built in, because the younger girls like to emulate teens once the styles are considered chic. This delay, which may be only a few weeks, allows buyers to copy the most successful trends and edit out some of the less saleable merchandise.

The girls' 4–6x size range uses only the versions of the junior and 7–14 trends that are age appropriate but this size range also has the styling specific to little girls. These additional garments may mean taking old standby silhouettes and refabricating them into the colors, patterns, and textures of the current junior trends.

Color forecasting for this category is interesting. If the color story for the season is bright, then the same colors work here as they do in junior and tween sizes. If the color story for the season is ice cream colors, pastels, or primary colors, the same color story will sell. However, if the color stories are muted, then adjustments have to be made. Gray sells better if paired with pastel pink. Black sells well with hot pink, red, bright yellow, or white accents. Even when the seasonal color story is neutrals like ecru, beige, olive green, or bamboo, the 4–6x size range needs something to make it less monotone like a baby blue, pink, or maize.

LINE PREPARATION TIMING

Research that goes into the development of an apparel line is not done just before the new line's inception. It is a constant and gradual accumulation of tidbits of information. Some tidbits are of no use and are left behind. Other ideas were carefully filed and brought out at the proper time. Once a designer is trained to stay abreast of the news and become socially involved, as well as cognizant of the world and its multicultural influences, then the actual apparel research to discover color stories and style directions becomes manageable. When the manageable information is synthesized into actual design direction, the designer is able to take the next step and begin to formulate the line.

Dear Diary,

Things aren't going too smoothly. I'm waiting for the other Manolo Blahnik to drop. Like I can afford them anyway! The designer who quit didn't stay the two weeks to finish up. Last Tuesday she just didn't show up! No goodbye or good luck, nothing. She cleaned out her desk with only one day's notice to show me what needed finishing. I'm on my own.

Anyway, I have been working along with the production patternmaker because the first patterns from that designer's group were consistently smaller than the store specs. That means the yardages all went up. We had to change the fit but not use more fabric. One salesman had a snit and was screaming. Then he had to call the store and get more money. I am learning the hard way what not to do! Carmen, my new friend, is the production patternmaker. She is the one who said I was in over my head. She was right, but I've certainly learned a lot fast. We worked well together on this mess. Of course, it was easy for me to pick new trims for the garments because I didn't like the original trim.

I'm off to a fabric showroom for a presentation. The reps put on a show each season for customers. They show new colors, and the fabric designer comes in from New York City and shows the garments she bought in Europe that influenced her new knits. Should be fun. I've yet to design a single garment, and it has been two weeks.

Designer's Dictionary

alphanumeric consisting of letters, numbers, and sometimes other symbols.

customer base the group that purchases a majority of the clothing manufactured by a company. For instance, the customer base for junior clothing is teenagers. Outside that customer base, other customers may include 20-year-olds, or even 40-somethings, but the customer base is designed for a narrower group. A customer base may be a narrow group, such as teenagers attending private school. A uniform company's customer base may be teens who wear navy pleated skirts to Catholic high schools.

directional stores retail establishments that are known to carry clothing that is trendy or even ahead of the trends. These stores have earned the reputation of having clothes that manufacturers shop to see early trend direction.

knockoff this term is used as a verb meaning to copy. If you knock a style off you are copying the important features of the style. This term is also used as a noun meaning a copy. The style that has been copied from another garment is a "knockoff."

pin sketches these are the small garment sketches that just show style lines. The garment sketched is not on a body. Synonymous with flat sketch, or flats.

reading a rack method of determining which garments, of what size and color, are selling in a store.

swift tagged small plastic string that connects price tags or small attachments to a garment. The swift tagger is a handheld device that punches through the fabric for attachments without damaging the garment, if done correctly.

Activities

1. Find three news articles from three different sources like general news magazines, newspapers, and either Internet news or a fashion magazine that you think will have an impact on apparel. Bring them to class for a roundtable discussion.
2. Cut out three different ads for couture clothing that have some wonderful detail that you think may influence the garments in the junior market and filter down into the girls' market. Now sketch two garments in juniors, one in the 7–14 range, and one in the 4–6x range using these details.
3. Using a current movie or a current television show as inspiration, draw three garments in each size category, 4–6x, 7–14, and junior, that may be inspired by a new trend in the show. Discuss in class how the student choices for trend direction could affect the apparel market in coming seasons.

Weekly Planner

Now you understand the process of letting miscellaneous stimuli inspire you and using observations and forecasts to project trends and direct styles for a girls' line of apparel.

1. Read Chapter 3.
2. Accumulate a list of at least 10 important movies, television shows, couture garments, and/or any other influences and add them to your file for your line development. Organize them alphabetically by keyword, or devise your own system.
3. Discuss the best fashion influences in class and discard any that were determined not to be potentially profitable.
4. Visit a large department store and read the racks of the girls' apparel departments. Write notes on your observations, and use the principles from this chapter to evaluate the benefits and drawbacks of the retail mix and visual presentations you saw.
5. Complete the chapter activities.
6. Learn the words from the Designer's Dictionary.

Box 3.1

FEATURES DESK

Your Trendy Friend

You can't borrow its shoes, but MySpace Fashion
tells what cool kids are wearing.

By Emili Vesilind, *Times* Staff Writer

SAMANTHA RONSON is trouncing around the hip, West Hollywood boutique, Brooklyn Projects, in vintage Nike Air Jordans and a faded Guns N' Roses T-shirt, trying on clothes for a small video crew. The Hollywood DJ is the latest celebrity to collaborate on a fashion-themed video spot called "The Fit," scheduled to air on MySpace Fashion.

Yes, several weeks ago, MySpace added fashion to its expanding menu.

Designed by the social networking behemoth to be a virtual clubhouse for industry professionals (designers, retailers, stylists, etc.) and those who follow them, MySpace Fashion functions similarly to MySpace Music, featuring videos, photos, and a slew of links to other fashion-themed MySpace pages, including designers' websites and fashion blogs. Users can also add the profile to their stable of "friends," MySpace-speak for connections, and then be updated when new content hits the page.

For avid users of the Web site, the wrangling of buddies borders on a competitive sport: The more online friends you accrue, the more loved you feel in real life. And MySpace is betting that fashion companies will be keen on racking up thousands of close, personal friends—the kind you blast with advertising bulletins and include on marketing reports.

(The music industry has already embraced this format, with almost every label and music artist in the stratosphere corralling fans via MySpace.)

Though the stated goal of MySpace Fashion is to "provide a bridge between amateur and more established designers," its brass-tacks mission is to forge collaborations with mass-fashion retailers and generate advertising dollars for the company, which was bought by Rupert Murdoch's News Corp. in 2005. The company works with such sponsors as Victoria's Secret, JC Penney, Hollister Co., Armani Exchange and H&M to create "branded communities," or souped-up MySpace pages. The concept probably isn't a hard sell: MySpace has more than 115 million users monthly.

Not that MySpace Fashion is all mass, no flash. Its sleek, magazine-like facade is easy to navigate and features fashion news (courtesy of sponsor *InStyle* magazine), links to up-and coming designers, and video footage from New York Fashion Week and style events, including the recent Fashion Rocks concert.

And then there's "The Fit."

As a highly sought-after A-list DJ with her own quirky sense of style, Ronson is an offbeat and yet somehow perfect choice for MySpace Fashion to feature in a video.

"In real life, I like wearing fun clothes,"
says Bynes with a straight face.

Past video subjects have included Hilary Duff, Amanda Bynes, and Fall Out Boy's Pete Wentz, among others, getting dolled up with their stylists or shopping at their favorite stores. The content is perhaps too vapid for adults ("In real life, I like wearing fun clothes," says Bynes with a straight face) but could easily hook teens who are already fans of the celebs.

Ronson, twin sister of designer Charlotte Ronson, and party pal to the likes of Lindsay Lohan and Nicole Richie, filmed her spots for "The Fit" at various stores in Los Angeles, including Tracey Ross, Brooklyn Projects, and Dior Homme.

"I'm addicted to MySpace, and I'm a crazy blogger," she said.

"Also, I have friends who have stores and fashion lines, and I like to promote my friends."

Indeed, Ronson chatted with friend and retailer Tracey Ross on camera and cooed over a charcoal, wool swing coat designed by—who else?—her sister.

But there's no shame in plugging your friends here. It is MySpace, after all.

Source: *Los Angeles Times*, Sunday, September 30, 2007. Home Edition; Image, Part P, pg. 4, Features Desk.

Chapter 4

Foundation of the New Line

In the garment industry, a line is an assortment of garments made up in several groups that are different one from another but in their entirety tell a complete fashion "story" for the season. Each group could be distinctive from the other groups by color, fabrication, **trims** used, or any other design element. The single most important rule is that a complete group must hang together as a unit, fit into the larger scope of the line, and fit into the manufacturer's clothing point of view.

For example, a brand name like Ralph Lauren might have a group of madras plaid tops, a group of knit polo shirts, and a group of button-down shirts in a girls' 7 to 14 size range. That line would never have a group of satin frilly tops to wear with netting skirts that projected a trashy bohemian fad. Such a group would not fit into the brand's classic and traditional sales expectations and wouldn't hang well with the rest of the line, either. It would be out of place, out of character, and out of touch with the rest of the brand. Sales representatives will often report to their bosses or back to the designer that a line "shows well." This compliment from the seller means that all the groups flow nicely into each other.

The type of garment slated for the line depends upon the scope of the manufacturer's customer base. A company that is a **dress house** will offer dresses. The Perfect Pear is a company that concentrates its business on special occasion clothing. On its Web pages, the customer will find pageant dresses, flower girls' dresses, *Quinceañera* dresses, sweet 16 dresses, and prom dresses, and an assortment of other dressy offerings, but they do not sell jeans or short shorts. They are considered a dress house, and they market their merchandise for special occasions. A coordinate group manufacturer may show tops, pants, skirts, vests, or any combination of separate pieces that are important that season, but they will not show taffeta prom dresses. If the separates company sells an assortment of styles, each group in the line will offer all the garment choices and coordinate those choices with each other and with other groups to give a wider range of choices to the buyers.

There are girls' manufacturers that do sell a wide variety of styles. The way this is done is to have several lines within the company. There could be a dress line with a label, name, and identity that is completely different from the label, name, and identity of the coordinates line. Usually when there are diverse lines within the company, a designer and design staff work separately on each line. Often these design rooms are set up in different spaces, perhaps even in different buildings, and they are completely independent of each other. The companies also have the option of setting up each line by size. A large girls' dress house may employ design staff teams to concentrate on each size range offered. Alternatively, the design staff might be assigned to the specific type of dress group that fits into the larger selection. Perhaps there is a designer for prom dresses and a designer for flower girl dresses. Different companies set up their design departments to perform different tasks.

There is no set number of garments in a line, and one manufacturer may present more groups than another. One season may have more garments in the line than another season by the same designer. A designer is like a painter who starts a work of art and does not finish until his or her vision appears on the canvas. The line is the designer's canvas, and it is finished when the last group has been sewn, pressed, priced, tagged, and hung on showroom hangers ready to be presented.

CHECKOUTS AND REORDERS
In the girls' and junior markets, the seasonal fashion story is a combination of inspirations that we discussed in Chapter 3 plus another key factor. This factor is the **sell-through** percentages of the previous lines. Sell-through information indicates how many garments sold and how quickly customers bought them. When a garment performs very well at retail, buyers have the opportunity to bring in more of the same style, or **reorder** for a fast selling style, which is called a **checkout**. Checkout styles that reorder are the most profitable garments a manufac-

turer can ship. The design, pattern, and markers are already made and paid for during the first production cycle. The factories have figured out the speediest method of construction and have eliminated any problems with trims and quality. Reorder business is vital to the bottom line because it raises the percentage of profit for the company.

There are situations where a style shipped to the store sells incredibly well but the rest of the department's mix is not as successful. The buyer does not have the budget to bring in more of the style that is hot at that time, but would entertain the idea of buying it for the next season in some updated version. The new shipment of the style is not technically a reorder, but the benefit to the bottom line is the same. If the style is not altered in any way but is simply **recut** in new fabric that is the same width as the original fabric, there is no cost for a pattern, or new cost for a marker so the profit margin goes up.

Reorder Designation
Designers are always aware of which garments reorder in their own company after the initial shipping because it is the big buzz in the office as soon as a salesperson gets the new order. Creating a checkout is the most exciting part of the designer's job. It is the reward for putting together the right style in the right fabric at the right time, for the right customer, at the right price. All styles have their own style numbers assigned and, most large retailers send electronic updates to their vendors with current selling information. Quick Response Systems alert vendors immediately when more goods are needed. There is software available that is called Enhanced Retail Solution that will provide the manufacturer with sell-through numbers by both style and color, give stock positions on the retail floor, and figure out the timing and quantity required for restocking the racks.

Designers should also go into the stores to see how their garments appear on the merchandise floor and observe how fast they are moving from the racks to the consumers' shopping bag in smaller boutique stores.

some floral bouquets on top of it to form a new print motif. Two areas of strong retailing information may evolve into this new direction and give an old fabric a new look, thus extending the life of a checkout garment. In the upcoming season, a creative designer may have to invent a new detail to take the theme of the line into the next phase. Perhaps, instead of using big butterflies, a print with little butterflies in the background with birds as the primary item of interest would be a good way to take the reorder fabric to the next season.

Conversational prints, those that have small or large figures or themes, like the butterflies that so often appear in feminine patterns, may retail well enough to reorder. When these particular prints are selling well, it is amazing how much the consumer can purchase of the same print that has simply been recolored.

The designer should go back to the original print or knit resource as the starting point when considering an update on a checkout fabric. The knit fabric designer may have anticipated the need for a follow up on the reordering fabric and provided several new versions of the same goods for purchase. The woven fabric company that produced the reorder print may already offer it in new colors, or in a print, that sends a similar theme forward to the new season. Shopping the entire market for similar fabrics is necessary so that the best fabric selection is insured. Loyalty to the original fabric source is a courtesy that will be repaid when the fabric seller recognizes the company's checkout potential and shows the designer his latest goods first. Business relationships can be just as vital to maintaining a presence in the marketplace as having an excellent product.

Silhouette

When a style reorders and it is retailing in all sorts of fabrics, textures, and colors across the market, it can be assumed that the *silhouette* is the factor that is driving the style for multiple sales. Silhouette is a fancy name for what in the garment business is usually referred to as the **body**. The body can be a camp shirt, a tunic, bell-

bottomed jeans, or any style that is trendy this season and performing better than other styles in the stores. The checkout body can be a brand new silhouette, or a revision from decades past that is currently "on fire," which is hyperbole from sales staff about the selling status. The important thing is that the body appeals to the masses. (See Figure 4.4.)

Any specific style that has its own personality within the larger categories of tops, bottoms, and dresses will be named by the marketplace as soon as it starts selling well and reordering. Sometimes the body name reflects the name of the firm that first shipped the style or made it a

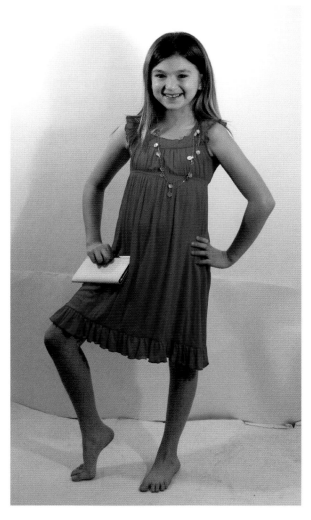

FIG. 4.4. THE SILHOUETTE WORN BY THE MODEL IS PERFECT IN ITS SIMPLICITY. IT ALSO EASILY FITS DIFFERENT SIZES AND SHAPES AND IS FEMININE WITHOUT BEING FUSSY.

FIG. 4.5. THESE JEANS USE TRIM AS THE DESIGN FEATURE THAT WILL MOTIVATE CONSUMERS TO PURCHASE THEM. THE CREATIVE USE OF TRIM MAKES THE GARMENTS APPEAR TO BE ONE OF A KIND OR HANDMADE.

long-lasting trend, like the "Polo" shirt, or a style will be named after an inspiration of the style like the "Marilyn dress" after Marilyn Monroe for the off-the-shoulder draped garments she often wore. Other garments may be named after an influence that is commonly recognized, like a gypsy skirt or tap shorts.

If a particular company's version of a silhouette, or body, is retailing better than the competition, further examination needs to take place. It may be that the fit of this checkout is the best available fit in the stores, and that should tell the designers mimicking that style not to mess with the actual fit or proportions of the garment in any way.

When a particular body is selling well, one important factor to judge is the *life* of the style. How long will this silhouette be hot? Is it a silhouette that can be adapted to the next weather cycle, or should it be revisited next year for the same season? The first inclination may be to alter this style, but if the style can be refabricated exactly as is, then it will be a more profitable reorder.

When silhouettes are the driving force for sales, and they have at least another season's life to them while the competition is fierce, the designer needs to be creative in the revisions. Trim could be added to a garment cut in basic

or less-expensive fabric, two-toning could be applied to the garment instead of using just one color, or decorative stitching might be used in a creative way to continue the retail selling success. The variations are endless. Subtle tweaking often works well.

Another way to freshen up a checkout silhouette is to take a garment that is cut in one print or solid and cut two coordinating, or two complimentary fabrics into the garment. The garment could also be recut in several prints of the same color story, contrasting colors, or any number of combinations. In these last two cases, it should be noted that the same weight, content, and quality of fabric should be used for the revision.

When recutting, the cost needs to be taken into account. Remember that the original garment retailed for a specific price point, and unless the designer is taking the garment into a different classification, like school dress into dressy dress, the consumer may not want to pay a higher price for the new version in the new season. Additionally, price can be a major factor at retail, because when a body becomes popular, manufacturers tend to cut and sew that body in leftover piece goods at promotional prices. A rule of thumb is that the longer the trend stays hot the more the prices fall.

There are two different steps that need to be taken with silhouette reorders. The first is to replicate the body in new fabrications. The second is to alter the silhouette just enough to keep the style recognizable to the consumer but give it a fresh approach. For argument's sake, let's say you are dealing with a princess line, short-sleeved dress. One reworked sample would be exactly the same body as the reorder but in new colorations or a new but very similar fabric. Another copy could be offered in a different fabric changing to a solid if the original was print or vice versa. Another sample for the line could be a princess line that develops into a flare at the bottom of the skirt so that it is not a straight skirt but a flared hemline. If the designer has observed indications of flared skirts coming into style then taking a reorder dress body and altering it in a new direction might be the perfect continuance of a reorder silhouette.

Trim

When trims are the hook for checkouts, then recoloration of the garment should be the first revision, followed by the substitution of similar but more interesting trims. The jeans shown in Figure 4.5 could be made using white denim so that the trimmings remain the same. The screen print behind the beading could be done in pastels.

Different silhouettes can be used, different fabrics can be brought in, or different placement of the exact same trim can be employed but the price points on trim garments need to be kept constant. Garments that have dyed-to-match trims can be treated like the garments that need fabric substitutions and are one of the easiest categories to update.

By using fringe as the selling hook for a checkout garment, a designer could introduce the fringe on a similar garment but use it on the yoke front instead of on the sleeves, thus expanding the group. If the checkout garment was first shown in a group of all fringed garments, then that group could also be revisited for additional ideas. A good salesperson might also send photos of the entire fringe group to the retailers

who are getting the checkout information, in case the retailers want to add to their stock of the designer's original line.

New colors adjusted to the coming season, and sleeve-length changes to match weather are usually all that are necessary. After dealing with the checkout body recoloration, more styles can be introduced with the same trim, and the designer can experiment with new trims to see if trims in general are hot.

It cannot be stressed enough that the girls' and junior markets are trendy markets, and fads come and go at a fast pace, so the best designers in this field must stay on top of all the current trends. In addition, the designer must capture the trend in the best or most suitable way for the consumer.

If the best way is a conservative, less creative version of a very trendy item, then the designer must anticipate this and have some more basic versions in the line hanging beside the more outrageous samples. With that in mind, the smartest designers will incorporate past successes with new ideas, so that the line always looks fresh and happening. To get orders on the line, the salesperson has to show *staples,* garments that are basic and proven, with the new creations. In the girls' market, it is not unusual for buyers to love the new items in the line that are the trendiest, and even respect the designer's creative abilities, yet write orders on the more conservative garments that may be more suitable to the buyer's own customer base, until there is accumulated retail information assuring that a trend will be accepted by the consumer. That information could come from the junior department in their own store.

It is also important to note that any checkout garment that reorders several times will finally drop dead. There is a fine line between using past successes and looking stale. It is the designer's job to tackle the job of making the line current while milking all the sales possible out of the tried and true garments that have made money for the company in past seasons. A talented designer can reinvigorate old styles in such a manner that buyers may not even

FIG. 4.6. WHEN A STYLE SELLS AS WELL AS THIS TOP DID FOR SPRING, THEN IT NEEDS TO BE TRANSLATED INTO A GROUP FOR BACK TO SCHOOL. HERE THE IMPORTANT DETAILS ARE THE PEASANT STYLE AND THE ETHNIC FEELING TO THE PRINT.

recognize that they've purchased it in another form.

MAKING GARMENT SEASONAL CHANGES

Changing a reorder garment from the current season into the next line is more challenging than it first appears. The supposition of the designer is that the checkout garment is perfect in all respects except for seasonal color adjustments and the appropriateness of the garment for either warmer or colder conditions. If the garment is a top in the junior or girls' market that has short sleeves, and the weather changes demand long sleeves, a simple sleeve-length change is all that has to be done. Lengthening the sleeve doesn't have to mean simply adding inches. The variety of ways to lengthen the

sleeves is the creative part of the designer's approach to satisfying the need for more coverage. The key is to keep price points as close as possible to the original cost.

To make adjustments on a garment that needs to go from fall to spring/summer, simply shorten sleeves to a sleeve style that is current with the trends. Carefully select fabrics to keep the essence of the checkout as similar as possible to the past reordering fabric. (See Figure 4.6.)

Adding mock two-piece looks to a reorder silhouette is another way of taking spring body and making it appropriate for fall. Cap or extended shoulders can have secondary, mock sleeves attached. Just adding contrasting knit sleeves and a mock T-shirt to make the original garment look as though a T-shirt is being

1. Look through fashion periodicals, catalogs, and newspaper ads to find current bodies that are selling. Go to stores, and ask clerks to recommend the season's best-selling styles. Determine three best-selling garments for the season. Sketch the selected garments in the center of an 8″ × 10″ piece of blank paper. Going clockwise around the original sketch, change the garment as needed and redraw to adjust for a different weather season, a new fabric, or new use of trim, and now alter the body in some manner to create a newly inspired garment.

2. Pretend that basic camp shirts are selling well. Sketch a basic camp shirt in the middle of a blank page as in #1. Sketch more camp shirts around the page, each one showing minor style changes that could reinvent the style for the next season.

3. Using three different trendy styles from design source material researched in activity #1, sketch each body on three separate pages. Now find four different fabrics swatches from classroom cuttings, retails stores, or personal collections for each body. Staple the swatches to the bottom of the page and redraw the garments with the new fabric in mind, adjusting any style features that need change to best complement the new fabric.

The objective of Chapter 4 is to make certain that you understand how the development of a new line is based on factual data about retail sales. Second, you need to be able to logically organize the information available to you to form a plan for the new line. Finally, the fun part comes when you design creatively using seasonal fabrics, silhouettes, and trims, aiming for the payoff of a repeat selling garment.

1. Read Chapter 4.
2. Complete the chapter activities.
3. Learn the terms in Designer's Dictionary.
4. Organize all the input accumulated from Chapters 3 and 4 to formulate a line. Using the checkout/reorder considerations, plan how those garments may be changed to go forward in the line. Take into account seasonal changes.

Box 4.1

Hogwarts Chic

By Melissa Magsaysay, *Times* Staff Writer

PRIVATE SCHOOL is having a fashion moment. Buttoned blazers, knee socks, crested sweaters, university-striped scarves, rep ties—all those stodgy restrictions of self-expression are looking like high style this fall. From the Balenciaga runway to the pages of the J. Crew catalog, designers are turning the preppy uniform into something actually cool and wearable. Why do we feel so ready for it, after a summer of free-flowing style? Maybe it's the Harry Potter effect. Call it "Hogwarts Chic."

Source: *Los Angeles Times* — Sunday, September 9, 2007. Home Edition; Image, Part P, pg. 8, Features Desk.

Chapter 5

Considerations for Fabric Selection

The **designer** who knows how to select fabric and use it effectively to create a sample line of girls' clothing is starting out yards ahead of the closest competition. In order to understand how to select fabric for a new line, the designer in the girls' and junior markets must first understand how the important elements of the garment factor into the customer's decision to purchase girls' apparel.

UNDERSTANDING THE SHOPPER FIRST

When a shopper sees a rack of assorted garments for girls in a store, the first thing that catches her eye is the color. Next, the shopper notices if the fabric is appealing, and she makes a few quick determinations as to whether the fabric is solid or print, knit or woven. If the shopper's first impression of the color and the appearance of the fabric are favorable, his or her next instinct is to feel the material. Now the shopper consciously feels the hand of the goods. Hand is a word used to describe the feel and the texture of material when it is touched. Is the fabric soft and clinging, or stiff? Would it feel snug and warm, or simply heavy? The shopper weighs the appearance and the hand, and she decides if the garment whether or not to examine the garment further. These details are considered in a matter of seconds as the customer sorts through the rack and pulls out the sleeve of a garment to get a quick glance at it.

The consumer's past experience comes into play at this point because she may realize from previous experience that this particular material needs to be dry-cleaned, shrinks, feels too warm when worn, or wrinkles badly like linen. Even a very young girl will have a strong opinion and express it immediately if she hates the fabric for any reason—especially if in the past a garment was uncomfortable or scratchy.

ESSENTIAL GARMENT DESIGN FEATURES

There are essentially four garment features that compel a customer to purchase an item of clothing, excluding price and trim. For this explanation, we will assume the customer has need for the garment and money to spend. These compelling features are color, style, fit, and fabric. These features are dependent upon each other and are almost equally important. All four features need to match the shopper's expectation in order for the shopper to purchase the item. In this scenario, the price of the garment is being ignored for the moment. The shopper does not know the price of the garment unless or until he or she looks closely enough at it to examine the price tag. Trim is left off this list intentionally because although it is important to the garment's appearance, it is really the icing on the cake. The garment must satisfy the consumer in all other ways. It is a very unusual customer who will purchase a nicely trimmed garment in an ugly color, a garment sewn in an out-of-style body, or a garment that doesn't fit, just because the trim is attractive.

Color

The color of the garment is what makes a strong first impression. This is especially true when a long rack has many shades of the same color, and some of them look faded or **off-cast**. If the consumer wants a pretty pastel pink dress for a little girl, neon orange is not going to make her happy. Nor will the consumer choose a dirty pink garment when a competitor has a light pink item hanging next to the garment in question. Because color is what first catches the eye, a designer must establish a color story before beginning to look for fabrics for the line. Sometimes the theme chosen for the line will dictate the color direction. If the designer were creating a group of Popsicle Brights for spring sportswear, then the colors of fresh fruit sorbet would complement that idea. In the girls' and junior markets, clean, clear colors sell better than colors that have been dirtied with gray or yellow casts. Even black sells better if it is pure black, rather than black off-cast with brown undertones.

Sometimes a retail buyer will give the color direction to their vendors directly from their **in-house** product development department. Buyers who purchase apparel for large stores or departments within those stores often pick their own seasonal color stories, and they will send swatches of their preferred colors to the companies with which they do substantial business. That way, apparel designers can choose fabrics that fit into that buyer's color scheme. The difference in color hues from one store to another may be so minor that the bolts of fabric to be used on orders are actually named after the store to eliminate the possible error of cutting "Macy's blue" instead of "Bloomingdale's blue."

The colors chosen also need to be appropriate for the garment and season. Even if winter white is the rage, it is not the best color for a girls' back-to-school wool coat. Common sense must be used when selecting colors for girls.

Silhouette

A garment has to have some form of construction in order to cover the body effectively, and the silhouette gives it that shape. The silhouette also gives the garment personality when it is combined with the color and fabric. Each silhouette, commonly referred to as a style, is then categorized by the intended purpose of the garment. A shopper has to figure out from the type of fabric used in the silhouette whether the garment is appropriate for her specific needs. The consumer who needs a party dress is not likely to purchase a nightgown for a special occasion even if has the nice A-line shape she prefers in dresses. Shoppers may or may not have a preconceived idea of the actual style they are looking for, but they do know the category they are interested in, and they know what they do not want to take into the fitting room to try on.

The silhouette entices the shopper to try on the garment after the color and fabric have favorably impressed them, but very often in girls' and junior clothing, the silhouettes are so similar from one manufacturer to another that it is the fabric that makes one garment sell more successfully than another. A silhouette that is the **hot** body for the season will tempt the shopper to try on something that she may not have normally liked, but having seen it on others in their peer group, the shopper will want to check it out. In the girls' and junior markets, popular styles are essential to the successful sale of a piece of clothing. The designer, who has hot bodies included in the line season after season, will have great success.

Fit

It is impossible to guess how many times mothers have taken cute styles into fitting rooms knowing the color, the fabric, and the style are perfect for their child, only to come back out totally disappointed because the garment didn't fit correctly. If the style is acceptable to the shopper, and it fits like a glove, the garment is on the way to the shopping bag because the color and fabric were already approved prior to trying it on. Style and fit have one thing in common: neither feature is enough to ensure the purchase of a garment. A style that does not match the shopper's tastes, or a poor fit, will kill any chance for the garment to sell. The younger the consumer, the more comfort comes into play. Proper fit is paramount to juniors due to teen body image issues, but they are even less demanding than young girls who simply will not wear clothing that scratches or feels tight and uncomfortable against their tender skin.

The correct fit for junior clothing is dependent on the teenage perception of how garments should be worn on the body, and this perception changes from season to season. If the trend is baggy pants worn low on the hips, teens will not purchase tight, waist-hugging trousers. Fit in junior clothing is a personal teen preference and an issue the designer has to analyze to stay current.

Fabric

The last design feature is fabric. A pretty little size 5 dress with a princess-line bodice and a bouffant skirt that fits perfectly in the child's favorite color will not be selected if the fabric is stiff and scratches the inside of the girl's neck. In this case, the wrong fabrication is the deal breaker.

This same scenario could take place with a junior top. If a **baby doll top** is the current fad in juniors, and a consumer wishes to buy one to wear over black pants, she will not be satisfied until she finds the right silhouette, in the right color. Her shopping focus is narrow. When the shopper locates two adorable baby doll tops on the rack that will go with the black pants, she will try them on. If both fit perfectly she has found the right silhouette and the correct color, and she needs to make a choice. If one top is soft and flowing with a graceful drape, and the other style is very thick where the fabric is shirred into the bodice and the gathers are clumpy, this garment is left in the dressing room while the first one is purchased. The fabric for the rejected garment was too heavy for the seam lines of the style. The designer had not taken into consideration that the silhouette and fabric did not complement each other. In this case, the fabric as a design feature was inappropriate for the silhouette.

Unique print patterns on woven fabric or unusual textures on knits can turn simple silhouettes into hot items that sell extremely well at retail. A designer who is able to use unusual fabrics while cutting them economically into junior and girls' tops is an asset to any manufacturer in this market. (See Figure 5.1.) A garment's fabric

FIG. 5.1. THIS WALL OF COLOR SWATCHES IS CAREFULLY TAGGED WITH COLOR NAMES AND DYE LOTS.

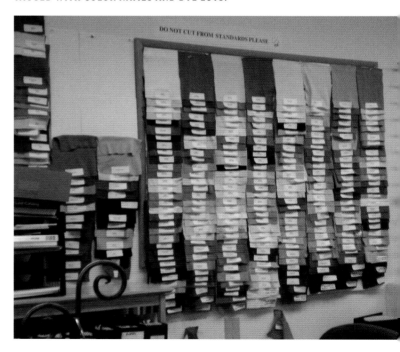

FIG. 5.2. CHOOSING FABRIC IS AN
IMPORTANT PART OF DESIGNING
SUCCESSFULLY. FABRIC GIVES THE
GARMENT THE PERSONALITY THAT
APPEALS TO DIFFERENT CONSUMERS.

sets its personality. Fabric tells the mood of the garment. Perfect fabric choice lets the garment tell a story. Large, hot pink polka dots might invoke smiles, while gray tweed could remind a girl that she is in school to study and learn. (See Figure 5.2.)

FABRIC REQUIREMENTS

There are so many factors to consider in fabric selection that each designer's personal imprint can be seen easily in their choices of fabric for garments of similar bodies for sale in stores. A knit garment can be made into something funky, tailored, or pretty simply by the designer's choice in material. Once the desired *look* is conceived, the choice of fabric needs to be narrowed by individual assets of one knit over another. Is the content the same? For example, polyester knits are brightly colored, but they

don't breathe; cotton is a natural fiber and comfortable but it shrinks; and silk knits can snag. The different characteristics in the yarns' contents need to be considered.

Again, using a knit fabric as the designer's choice for a new garment, how will the knit sew into the bodies the designer has in mind? Will one knit drape, pleat, or stretch on the hanger more or less than another? The weight of the fabric must also be considered and compared in terms of how the designer will use the material in the garments.

Several criteria must be considered before selecting fabric for a line, and there are several questions to ask before sampling. Is the fabric affordable? No matter what price range line you are designing, the cost is always relevant. Is the fabric appropriate for the garment that the designer has in mind? Active clothing demands material that can handle the stress of movement. What is the durability of the fabric? Clothing that children wear to school needs to hold up to many wash cycles. Is the fabric age-appropriate and weather compatible? What are the care instructions given for this fabric? How difficult will this fabric be to sew in production? Each of these questions is legitimate and important.

For example, assuming there are many fabrics in a knit category for junior tops that are affordable, durable, age-appropriate, and suitable to a particular style, a designer has to pay attention to the qualities that differentiate one knit from another. When a designer is armed with this insight, the process of choosing which fabric is the best for a garment becomes a manageable task.

Salability

Is the fabric stylish and salable? Does the fabric fall into the categories of fabrics that are currently checking out? Will the fabric that sold well last year in the same season sell well again? What fabric is forecast to make a big splash this season? Remember that the question of attractiveness is from the junior or girl's point of view. Much of this information is gathered before sourcing the fabric. With experience, designers should come to know their customers' preferences in fabrics and choose accordingly. Whether a fabric is attractive or not, universally, is not enough reason to sample it for a line of junior or girls' clothing. The fabric must meet the criteria proposed by the designer's vision for the new sample line. The designer must be focused on the consumer's taste in current trends in order to select the best material.

The trends in the marketplace will help narrow the types of fabric in demand. The fabric companies will offer fabric to meet most trend directions. If Hawaiian prints are a trend for the season, then a designer needs to show that trend in the line. The designer must also pick the most outstanding tropical floral prints that are available in the market and then tailor them to the consumers' preferences. The ability to "capture the taste" of the consumer makes one designer's fabrications outshine other lines and sell well at retail.

The designer who learns to track what sells best, season after season, will be better equipped to use both basic and unusual fabrics effectively. The actual fabrics may change radically, but the information learned can be applied in general terms. Sometimes the tracking involved with the Enhanced Retail Solution software or Quick Response will give a designer insight into a particular region where, for example, 4–6x dressy dresses sell poorly in deep purple but retail well in pastels. Demographics can influence color choices, style preferences, and fit preferences, just as they influence pricing. Retail buyers attempt to purchase merchandise while factoring in regional differences so the purchase orders from previous seasons will reflect some color guidance in the garment-by-color distribution.

Age-Appropriate Fabric

Some of the questions a designer needs to answer are **subjective**, but **objective** reasoning can be used to clarify which fabric is more appropriate. Whether a particular fabric is age-appropriate is one of those subjective questions that may vary with different situations and with different categories of clothing. Popular junior fabrications can be translated into the 7–14 girls' market, and a simpler version will work for 4–6x girls. Printed fabrics that copy junior prints can be created for the girls' market. Hot junior knits can be made into simpler garments for girls' clothing when price points are an issue, by altering the fit and raising necklines.

Transparency in fabric is never appropriate for young girls on the body of the garment unless it is lined. See-through sleeves are fine, as are see-through collars. If you have a question about whether it is inappropriate the best answer is that it probably is. If you have questioned it, parents will question it, too. There is a standard of modesty in the girls' market and the best way to stay informed of those standards is to go online and read about dress codes at public schools in the midwestern United States. The designer can work around some modesty issues by using linings and built in tank T-shirts, but the question of age-appropriateness in clothing must be considered and addressed in order for a line to be successfully marketed around the entire United States. Regional differences exist and must be addressed.

A girls' wear designer can also use objective reasoning on the subjective issue of sexiness in junior and tween clothing. Objectively, the designer can see the sales potential in top items that bare more skin than one might like to see a teenager wear to school. For example, when in style, little halter-tops can make a season profitable. These hot items should be included in the line, designed as carefully as any other tops, and then submitted for sale to the buyer who will allow the consumer and her parents make the rules of where and when the halter tops can be worn. Modesty is a gray area in junior apparel in our present culture. What is shocking to adults may be perfectly acceptable to teens, but diversifying the line with many styles is a way to capture sales in all trends and still offer suitable clothing at both ends of the modesty scale. The retailers will pick and choose for their own consumers regionally, the teens and tweens will pick what they feel comfortable wearing and think they can get away with, and the parents will supervise with their pocketbooks by refusing to pay for any garments they find inappropriate.

Fabric Durability and Suitability

Durability is a question of the strength of fabric versus the activity the consumer expects to do while wearing the garment. A mother purchasing overalls for a 4–6x girl expects her child to be able to roughhouse and play games. The material needs to be durable enough to last at least one full season under tough conditions. Common sense would eliminate sheer, thin, loosely woven fabrics and demand denim, corduroy, or another weightier fabrication.

The durability of the fabrication must match the designer's choice of proposed construction of the garment. Play clothes, exercise apparel,

and denim jeans all have a perceived use, and demand fabric and seaming that can hold up to the activities the consumer expects to wear them for, and for the multiple washings that will be necessary after use.

One issue of suitability is comparing the fabric choice to the style the designer intends to cut it in. For a complex garment that has a lot of needlework, the designer must consider how well the fabric will handle the seaming, not only in appearance but also in ease of construction for production. If a knit snags easily, then putting that knit into lots of different processes for production is not suitable.

The suitability issue is more complex because there is a dichotomy of artistic use of the *opposites attract* creative option that works extremely well in fashion. One would not think that satin was suitable for overalls, but both satin, lined lace, and velveteen have all sold well in the girls' clothing market in seasons where those fabrications were the hot material, and the overall was a trendy body already. This is a tricky design opportunity that can be very successful, but normal suitability issues have to be creatively ignored. When a particular fabric is in demand, some creative uses in non-traditional pairing of fabric and style can work in funky ways that might not normally. In the girls' market, this situation will only present itself after the junior market has had checkout garment sales in the fabric, and if the style in question, for girls, like an overall, is checking out in conventional material. For example, if corduroy overalls are already selling well, and satin is hot in the junior market, a satin overalls suit might be well received in the girls' market.

Suitability, when it is regularly applied, is a simple common sense answer for designing apparel. A 7–14 range sundress is to be worn when it is warm weather. Common sense dictates that heavier fabrics like faux fur or wool are not the best choices for a sundress. A designer would be foolish to offer unlined voile skirts for juniors for the fall season. Such a choice would not be suitable, probably would not sell, and certainly would not be designed using common sense.

Comfort Issues

Juniors will wear tight, constricting garments in trendy fabrics, and they will tolerate some discomfort in their quest to be cool. The 7–14 range of consumers will expect clothes to be fairly comfortable, but the girls in the 4–6x range *demand* comfortable clothing. Little girls don't like tight necks, scratchy surfaces, or garments that confine them when they move. Designers need to feel the coarseness of the fabric against their skin to make sure that the hand of the material is acceptable to their customers. It is not just the fit of the garment that needs to be taken into consideration. The fabric needs to be compatible with the style it is going to be cut into. The designer must determine if seams may scratch, if fabric may bunch, and if they might be too thick at pressure points. If you're considering using a fabric that doesn't have a pleasant hand then you need to consider the cost of completely lining the garment so that the wearer will be comfortable when the clothing is worn.

Easy Care

Fabrics that are machine washable are preferred in the girls' and junior markets. The normal exceptions to this are special occasion and dressy apparel. Cost of dry-cleaning in these markets is prohibitive for play and school clothing, except in the very high-end apparel lines. Parents are looking for wash-and-wear fabrics that are easily maintained. Teenagers who have to do their own laundry also want the convenience of easy-upkeep garments. There are so many fabrics available that meet these criteria that it is not difficult to find the appropriate material that fits the trend vision and the laundering requirements. Hand-wash and hang-dry materials will also sell in the junior and girls' market.

As with most situations, there are exceptions to the rule. Sometimes in the junior market, a fabric will be so sought after because of the look, drape, or stretch of the garment, that dry-cleaning labels have no negative effect on sales. The slowing influence on sales of dry-clean-only garments is less on upstairs or boutique clothing than it is for mass-market lines. If the care instructions indicate that a garment can be dry-cleaned, and it does not hold up well, fades, or shrinks when the customer cleans it while following the label directions, the manufacturer faces garment returns in all price categories.

The dry-cleaning solutions for use in home machines has helped make the sale of dry-clean-only garments less of an issue in sales, but with the attention of save-the-planet and green campaigns, this may introduce another factor against dry-cleaning garments altogether.

PICKING THE PERFECT FABRIC

One of the most difficult balancing acts for a designer is to rely on personal taste in some instances, and ignore it in others. Some designers have an innate sense of proportion, or a flair for draping. Some designers have a talent for combining different fabrics or selecting the perfect floral print for the season. The talent to choose fabrics correctly season after season comes from consciously monitoring past successes and learning from mistakes. Personal taste is subjective, and it helps to have some experience under your belt when using personal taste to select fabrics. In the girls' 4–6x market, a designer may use personal taste to guide fabric selection of pretty prints, but in the junior market, the choice must be much more informed. If the juniors want retro prints in dresses, all the contemporary prints that a designer may find appealing will sit on the rack and turn into **markdowns**.

Assuming there are many fabrics in a knit category that are affordable, durable, age-appropriate, and suitable to a particular body, a designer has to pay attention to the objective qualities that differentiate one knit from another. How will a particular knit drape, pleat, or stretch compare with another knit?

Texture and surface interest need to be compared. Does the shininess of the knit detract from or enhance the style? If the knit is to be coordinated with another fabric, like a plaid wool skirt paired with a knit long-sleeved tee, do the surfaces or textures combine well? Before spending company money on a fabric sample, the designer must consider many issues.

Probably the most subjective part of choosing fabric is determining which fabric is the prettiest, the most beautiful, or the most attractive. This is really a case of personal design tastes, but designers in the girls' and junior markets have to be able to select fabrics that will stand out against all the other choices when the fabrics are viewed competitively on a rack. If just one little sleeve is poking out of a rack of 4–6x tops, will it be interesting enough, bright enough, or pretty enough, to get the shopper to take the garment off the rack and examine it further?

One way to stay ahead of the competition in picking the prints with the best chance to sell is to look for something slightly different in a specific category. Tropical prints are usually big, bold, floral prints, with or without animal motifs among the flowers. A tropical floral print with birds hidden among the leaves, or a skin print in the background might set the garment apart from similar looks on the rack.

The seasons that have specific hot fabrics are the easiest for a designer to make selections for—and can sometimes be the most exacting, too. The consumer has already spoken by purchasing a particular fabric and reordering it, and the sales are continuing. The designer's job is to come up with the best silhouettes in the correct colors. If it is a print season, finding the print that appeals best to the junior or young girl consumer becomes the designer's quest. Deciding which fabrics are perfect fabrics for a style group is left to the creative genius of the designer. The subjective selections of fabric that the designer makes, can be influenced by some objective reasoning by taking three issues into consideration: current and past fabric trends, collective consumer personality, and **scale/repeat**.

Fabric Trends

Fabric goes in and out of favor just as hemlines rise and fall. The designer in the girls' and junior markets must follow style trends in fabric the same way they follow silhouette trends. By

process of elimination, all the fabric that is not currently important should be put on the "do not sample" list.

At this point, the designer has a line plan and a rough list of the types of fabric he or she needs in order to start creating the samples for the line. The listed fabrics are the ones that fit the individual group trends, the refabrication for checkout bodies, and fabrics that sold exceptionally well the same season during the prior year. Only those fabrics that fit within the planned groups should be considered. A possible exception might be a fantastic fabric discovered in the sampling process that will complement the other groups and add an additional grouping to the line. These unplanned fabrics need to be innovative, unique, and immediately inspirational to the designer. The designer needs to objectively review all the fabrics that he or she is drawn to subjectively and make sure that each fabric fulfills a need in the groupings that are planned. The fabrics that are nice but don't fit among the other fabrics or don't help realize the theme of the line need to be left out. However, if you really like a fabric, and it's not hot at the moment, note it in your binder or accordion file for another line, another season, another year.

Collective Consumer Personality

Collective consumer personality is the general frame of mind of the shopper relative to what else is going on culturally and this can help the designer stay on track with fabric trends. For example, if 4–6x girls are going crazy over American Girl dolls instead of Barbie or Bratz dolls, the mood at the moment is conservative. The little girls may be much more receptive to girlish, pretty prints in traditional dresses. In the reverse case, if Bratz and Barbie dolls are the rage, then the little girls might prefer more chic clothes like vinyl mini skirts and metallic, rugby-striped T-shirts.

In the junior market, the collective consumer personality might be more fractured, but some indicators of it might be found in the accessories market. There is a relationship between shoes, handbags, jewelry, and clothing. If dainty

necklaces are in style, the prints may follow in a retro feminine vein, and knits could be thinner and slinkier. When the movie, *Pirates of the Caribbean* came out, printed fabrics with small skulls and crossbones retailed well in scarves, bandanas, and pajama bottoms for juniors. Big beaded necklaces and bangles might demand brighter and bolder fabrics to balance the accessory's impact. By observing cultural trends beyond just clothing, the designer can gain insight that will help sway the fabrication direction. (See Figure 5.3.)

Fabric Scale and Repeat

The scale of the pattern in printed fabric is another factor that the designer needs to address before sampling. It is not enough to think that a floral print is pretty. The scale of the print versus the size of the garment, or size of the section of the garment to be fabricated in a pattern has to be considered as well. A cabbage rose

FIG. 5.3a, b, c. EACH FLORAL PRINT CHANGES THE THEME THE DESIGN IS PROJECTING. THE YELLOW TROPICAL PRINT (Top left) IS CASUAL, THE IMPRESSIONISTIC PRINT (Top right) IS PLAYFUL, AND THE CABBAGE ROSE PRINT (Above) IS FEMININE.

floral print on a woven fabrication, cut into a size 5 dress, might be interesting with one rose covering the entire bodice. Using very large, seemingly out-of-scale patterns on printed fabric for garments can be a creative way of making basic silhouettes more striking, but it has to be consciously taken into consideration before sampling. The scale of a pattern also needs to conform to the current trend in printed fabrics. If small, retro swirls reminiscent of the 1940s are selling, the designer needs to consider scale as part of that appeal, and stay within the same sized scale. Giant swirls will not create the same feeling, even in the same color story.

If a girl's top measures 12 inches, from neck to hem, and the *repeat,* which is the distance from the start of a pattern to the end where it starts to repeat itself, on a striped knit is every 18 inches, the designer must make the sleeve pattern pieces or any other pattern pieces fit in the remaining 6 inches, with grading room. If the designer does not do this, the garment will have the stripe pattern in a random configuration instead of the way it was on the original sample. The size of the repeat on fabric can be used creatively, but each designer has to design accordingly and make sure sample garments are priced to account for any wasted goods. (See Figure 5.4.)

SAMPLING FABRIC

After a designer has figured out the general story or theme for the line, and outlined the basic style groups, it is time to start looking for the fabric that is going to make the designs go from imagination to reality. Preplanning provides a loose shopping list of fabric that enables the designer to stay on target while being bombarded with presentation after presentation of fabrics to sift through.

Fabric sales representatives carry extensive samples of fabrics that the company, or companies, they represent offer for sale to apparel manufacturing companies. The fabric companies come out with new lines several times a year, and the job of the sales representative is to show every designer within his sales territory

all new fabric as it has been introduced to the marketplace.

The fabric representative (or rep) comes to the designer's company and presents fabric swatches of each pattern or type of fabric, stapled to a paper header that states the name of the fabric company, the style number of the fabric, the content, and the care instructions for the fabric offered. The bottom swatch can be big enough to show the entire pattern repeat, and the swatches mounted atop this one are cut smaller so that all the color choices can be seen. These *headers* are usually packed into a huge suitcase and brought out in groups. The designer sits at a table or desk and reviews all the new fabric choices.

Shopping for the fabric is the first concrete step to getting the line ready for market. Finding the perfect fabrics for each group in the line is one of the designer's responsibilities. Shopping the entire fabric market also allows the designer to be inspired by new fabrics, and create new garments, while, working from fabric to silhouette. When this happens, the fabric will inspire a completely new group to add to the line. Designers will sometimes look at fabric lines with a design assistant in tow, enabling the assistant to become familiar with the fabric resources. This also helps to familiarize the assistant with the sample cuts that will be on order, which will make checking in the goods later a more efficient process.

Fabric companies do their own forecasting to figure out which trends will be in for the next season. Their lines reflect which trends were given priority by their designers and merchandisers. Since the fabric has to be ready for sampling prior to the apparel line market dates, there could be hot looks that some of the fabric companies didn't anticipate. The garment designers then have to search harder to find the particular fabrics they envisioned when they planned their own trend groups.

Because designers are sampling fabric at the same time they are planning the line, the new season's materials may be viewed before the designer organizes a new group. In this case, the

FIG. 5.4. THE SKETCHES SHOW
THE 4–6X GIRL AND THE JUNIOR
GIRL WEARING THE SAME
PRINTS IN DIFFERENT STYLES.
THE SCALE OF THE BIG FLORAL
WORKS IN BOTH CASES, AS DOES
THE BORDER.

fabric is selected on the merits of the material, and it will be matched to the style groups later. If the sampled material does not fit into any of the groups that the designer has planned, it might not be used at all. Sometimes the fabric is so inspirational, however; that a group will be designed late in the game if it complements the rest of the groups. Designers in the girls' and junior markets become accustomed to designing from the fabric or from the silhouette. Both skills are important and both design methods are used each season.

Shopping a line of fabric for a specific fabrication, a small floral with butterflies, for example, is a tedious job. An assistant designer is often called in to do the needle-in-a-haystack search for a designer's request. The assistant can call the fabric resources and ask if they are showing butterfly floral fabric. If, by chance, the designer is onto a new trend, this would alert the fabric companies and they would run around the market trying to interest other designers in the possible trend, creating a buzz. It is always easier to preview all the fabric lines, try to stay current with all the trendy fabric, and make notes on which **vendor** or **source** has which goods.

After a season or two of designing in the girls' and junior markets, most designers develop a list of all their preferred fabric companies. Some of these companies carry basic materials and some the more creative fabrics. It is prudent, however, for designers to be open to seeing the entire market of goods so they can be assured that they are investigating all available options at the best prices. They also need to view everything that their competition sees.

Sample Orders

If a designer likes a fabric and wants to put it in the new line, a sample order is written on the company's order book. Filling out this sample order correctly is very important to the entire design staff, and if the fabric is adopted and sold, the purchase order becomes even more essential. (See Figure 5.5.)

The obvious information included on the purchase order (PO) is the fabric company name, style number, pattern number, name and content of the fabric, the color numbers of the goods sampled, the price, the date, how many yards were sampled, and the contact number for the rep. The purchase order will also list the **cuttable width** of the fabric, which is important for pricing the initial garment. The PO must have the price of the goods, because no garment can be priced without knowing the fabric price per yard, and when the design room is in the hectic stages of trying to get the line ready for market, it is essential that all the information is readily available. The fabric order should also include the estimated time it takes to receive stock goods after they are ordered, although this can change as production increases. The purchase order needs to reflect the minimum yards that must be ordered in order for the fabric company to honor a stock order.

The last bit of information to be filled in on the PO is the **cancellation date**. The designer has to have the line ready for market and will need the sample fabric to be shipped and received in time to have garments sketched and sewn. The sample cuts can be monitored according to this cancellation date, and calls to the fabric company representative can keep track of delivery problems.

Minimum Fabric Orders

The **minimum stock order** per fabric is a very important piece of information for the design staff to have. Every fabric company has a set yardage minimum per fabric that is profitable to ship to each manufacturer. A designer needs to know what that minimum amount is in order to make certain the sampled fabric is appropriate

FIG. 5.5a, b, c. DESIGNERS MAY SEE AS MANY AS TEN FABRIC LINES IN A DAY.

for the line. Of relevance to the designer is how much fabric will be used per garment.

This is especially important if the fabric is new, but only for the trim portion of the garment. Perhaps the designer plans to use the goods for yokes, pockets, and other small sections. The usage may add up to just six inches per garment, and the minimum yardage order amount of the fabric that the company could purchase is 3,000 yards. In this case, 18,000 garments would have to be sold to use up the goods. If the apparel company does not have potential sales distribution that could handle that many garments, then problems will arise should the garment sell and go into production. The minimums might not matter to a manufacturer of girls' sportswear selling to Wal-Mart, but the minimums could be unreasonable for a small company that sells one dozen of a style to expensive boutiques. Nothing makes a sales staff madder than to sell garments that will be cancelled by the retailer, losing that potential business and the profit. Nothing annoys the production department more that a designer unconsciously designing problems into production.

Of course, there are ways around this issue, but it is a concern that must be addressed when the designer is sampling the initial fabric for the line. In the previous example, the designer could also use that trim fabric in the rest of the group on larger sections like a complete skirt or jacket, thereby using more of the goods, and increasing the chance that more sales will resolve the minimum order problem. If the fabric minimum is very high, and the fabric cost too expensive to use except as trim, then the designer's best option is to find a substitute fabric to sample that does not create production problems. Planning ahead, and considering the possibility of meeting the minimum yardage will save time, eliminate hassles, and protect the original design's integrity.

Fabric Company Reliability

Selection of fabric that best suits the designer's vision is the first issue when sampling the material, but the fabric company must also have ac-

ceptable prices and good quality, and finally, the fabric firm must ship its samples and the stock goods on time. If a fabric company has been late fulfilling shipments, the designer has to have the common sense to skip its goods in the future. If a designer persists in sampling and sewing up goods that cannot be shipped on time because of fabric cancellation dates not being met, the production department will step in and blacklist the fabric vendor.

Sample Fabric Cost Caution

One of the biggest design expenses in manufacturing is sample yardage brought in by the designer. Each time a fabric is sampled, there is a sample price that is usually a little higher than the line price, as well as charges for shipping and handling. With smart planning, some of the unnecessary expenses in sampling can be eliminated. Several other precautions will also control costs.

First, all **sample cuts** from one fabric company should be shipped together, not piecemeal. This eliminates multiple handling charges and results in cheaper freight costs. Second, the designer should keep records apart from the purchase orders, with swatches, so that the design department does not duplicate or triplicate very similar fabrics. The designer has the advantage of seeing many fabric lines, and he or she has the ability to eliminate duplication of similar themes or trend interpretations. After scanning the textile market, the designer may return to those resources that offered the best of the desired trends and sample their goods.

Lastly, designers can watch that the samples are shipped at the cheapest rate that allows the fabric to arrive when it is needed. If left to the fabric company's discretion, the garment manufacturer might be paying high airfreight cost when ground shipping would be satisfactory. When a garment manufacturer does a significant amount of business with a fabric company, all sample costs and freight costs can be negotiated. Here is another arena in which relationships and integrity contribute to manufacturing success.

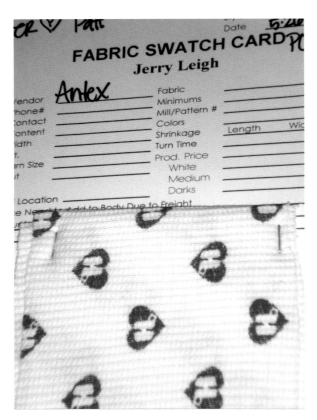

FIG. 5.6. EACH FABRIC SHOWN TO DESIGNERS HAS ALL THE INFORMATION ABOUT THE GOODS ATTACHED TO THE FABRIC.

Checking In Samples

Part of the responsibility that falls to the design room staff is to check in all the sample fabrics that the designer has ordered. In medium and large companies, a design assistant usually gets this task. Some designers, however, like to check in their own sample fabrics immediately when they are received so they are always aware of new fabric choices. The most important part of this procedure is to check the original purchase order and compare all information listed on the packing slip. If there are discrepancies in the price or width of goods, it is important to make sure the sample garments that use the fabric are priced correctly. Sometimes the fabric company will ship wrong colors, wrong patterns, or less sample yardage than the designer ordered. Any variance needs to be discussed with the designer and corrective steps taken if necessary. The packing slips should be signed off as received and given to the bookkeeping department to match up later with the fabric invoices. (See Figure 5.6.)

Different garment manufacturers have different systems for keeping track of sample yardage. Some design rooms cut off the fabric labels and keep them in a notebook for reference with the original PO. Other companies leave the samples intact until they are cut, and the fabric label is stapled to the cost sheet. Computer-savvy companies scan all the information into the computer and simply download the information as needed. The procedure is not as important as making sure all that sample yardage information is easily available when it comes time to price the new line.

DEVELOPING FABRIC DESIGNS

In addition to shopping fabric lines for materials to make up for a sample line, a designer might be involved in developing fabric that only his or her apparel company would be using. Some apparel manufacturers have in-house fabric designers who create the company's prints or knits. Other apparel companies use a mix of resources in the fabric market and develop fabrics through ideas from design staff employed to do apparel design. Designing fabric for a girls' apparel company can be a very interesting and rewarding project. It puts a very personal design stamp on the entire line.

Designing and Confining House Printed Patterns

Designers who have the option of designing their own fabric can use a textile converter to process the fabric for them with a surcharge. The apparel company hires the textile company to act as a contractor to dye, print, knit, or weave the fabric to the apparel company's specifications. Some companies manufacturing in the girls' and junior markets are large enough to develop their own print or knit patterns on fabrics. This is advantageous for the line because the fabrics and garments shown will be unique to the company. This originality eliminates the chance of print duplication in the marketplace and makes the line stand out. An example of this opportunity might be when characters like teddy bears are selling well in the junior woven

SKIN PRINTS

STRIPE

GEOMETRIC

CORDUROY

CHECK

RANDOM FLORAL

POLKA DOT

DENIM PIECED
TOGETHER

PAISLEY

PATCH

GINGHAM CHECK WITH FLORAL

STRIPE WITH FLORAL

FIG 5.9. (continued) TYPICAL FABRICS OF THE GIRLS' AND JUNIOR MARKET.

FIG. 5.10a, b. THE PRINT IN THE DRESS WORN BY CAITLIN (a) SHOWS WHY CLEAN TROPICAL PRINTS REALLY POP ON GIRLS' WEAR AND COME BACK INTO STYLE SO OFTEN. (b) THIS TWEEN MODEL SHOWS HOW EFFECTIVE A BORDER PRINT CAN BE USED IN A SIMPLE SILHOUETTE.

There is a big maturity difference between young size 7 and 8 girls who are big for their age and just out of the 4–6x range, and the girls who wear sizes 12 to 14. By recognizing the two extremes and designing garments in the same fabric group that might appeal broadly, a designer can appeal to both ends of the spectrum. Using a Burberry-type plaid, when plaids and vests are retailing in junior clothing, the designer can do a plaid skirt that appeals to all sizes and ages, and pair the skirt with two different tops. One top might have a junior influence body with a separate vest, offered as a two-piece set that would be favored by the larger sizes, and the other top could be a knit T-shirt with a mock vest with a watch fob chain attached with a small heart charm that would appeal to the younger girls. Careful merchandising of the line after it is designed will help the designer fill in the groups so that all ages are satisfied with both the styling and the fabrication. (See Figure 5.11.)

Junior Favorites

The fabrics that have general appeal to juniors are the seasonal trends that change from style to style and from fad to fad. (See Figure 5.12.) To try to generalize would limit the possibilities and disregard all the innovations that have yet to be discovered in the fabric market for the junior shopper. Junior purchases are heavy in the top area, with tops selling approximately three to one over bottoms. Emphasis must be placed on fabrications that can be worn well with whatever denim color is hot for the season. Patterned fabrics, whether knit or woven, floral or abstract, that have a touch of pale blue to coordinate with the denim have an edge in this market. Denim is considered a neutral pant fabric, and any fabric from slinky knits to stiff cottons will sell well if the teens have chosen it as their current rage.

FIG. 5.11a, b, c. THREE TWEEN GIRLS WEAR AGE-APPROPRIATE STYLES. (a) Top left. HIP AND TRENDY WITH JUNIOR INFLUENCE. (b) Top right. YOUNG AND SPORTY WITH HEARTS. (c) Bottom. HEAD-TO-TOE PREPPY GIRL FROM ENGLAND EMBODIES A RALPH LAUREN AD.

FIG. 5.12. THE INSPIRATION FOR NEW FABRIC DIRECTION CAN COME FROM THE UPSTAIRS DESIGNER MARKET. HERE THE JUNIOR DESIGNER HAS TAKEN TWO DIFFERENT DESIGNER'S FABRICATIONS AND REINTERPRETED THE PRINTS INTO NEW GARMENTS FOR THE JUNIOR MARKET.

Designer's Diary

Dear Diary,

Did you know that you could fly into a city, meet with buyers, show a group, and fly back to work without even getting a meal? That happened last Tuesday. Tracy, my line sales rep, broke her leg on Sunday and couldn't keep an appointment with JCPenney. The buyer insisted on someone else showing her the group of men's wear looks for an ad campaign, so the boss took me. He used to sell the line when he started the company but said he was out of touch with this new young group of buyers and needed me to add my design inspirations for emphasis. We caught a 6:30 a.m. plane out of Burbank, flew to Dallas, worked at 11 a.m., finished by noon and caught the 12:45 p.m. plane back. Since we were running to catch the plane, even a hot dog was out of reach. The boss laughed when they ran out of peanuts on the plane.

I am having such a hard time working in crinkled gauze for my gypsy/hippie group. It seemed like such a natural combination between hippies and gypsies, but my garments are coming out looking like scarecrows. I am certainly not a farm girl but this group could outfit Scarecrow from *The Wizard of Oz,* who had straw coming out of him and no brain. I am almost ready to scratch the group from the line because it has no personality.

The boss said the Macy's buyers called to get some delivery information on the group we showed. Can you imagine my first line getting a national ad?

Designer's Dictionary

baby doll tops tops that have short puffy sleeves, full front bodices that are eased into small front yokes creating a smock shape. These tops can be button front or pull over. Reminiscent of baby doll pajamas popular in the 1950s.

cancellation date the date by which items on order must be received or the purchase order is considered void. Used here as cancellation date of fabric purchase orders or garment purchase orders.

cuttable width fabric is sold with selvage edges running down the length of the goods. The cuttable width is the distance between those edges. Sometimes fabric comes with perforations due to a finishing process, and those perforations may cause the fabric to run or look unsightly. The cuttable width would be on the inside of the selvage and inside those perforations. The markers for the piece goods would have to be made to the narrowest width to insure the quality of the cut.

greige goods unfinished fabrics as they come from the loom. Some fabrics may be mill-finished but most are sent to converters for the finishing process. To remember the term, think "gray" from the French word, *grege,* that means raw. (Calasibetta, Tortora, Abling 2002, p. 215)

hot used here to mean selling well. Garment salespersons will call checkout garments and reorders hot when describing them to retail buyers. "I've got a hot item in the line" means "you need to see it and buy it."

in-house apparel that is produced directly by a store. Large retailers often directly contract for apparel with factories putting their own "in-house" labels. This cuts out the middle-man or apparel manufacturer, and brings in

markdowns merchandise that has been price reduced in price.

minimum stock order the amount that a company will sell of an item. In fabric, the minimum stock order is the number of yards of each color of each fabric that is acceptable to ship against a purchase order. In garments the minimum stock order is taken in dozens.

objective thinking logically, without bias. Looking at the facts without prejudice or personal feelings. Designers can be objective in choosing fabric to design into clothes that they personally would not wear or even like.

off-cast term used to describe colors that are not pure or true. Some off-cast colors are muddied from a poor mix of too much yellow or blue causing the dye color to be dusty or dirty looking when shown against cleaner dyes.

sample cuts the fabric ordered from fabric companies to make the first garment prototype for a line of clothing. It is called a sample because it is enough fabric to make up one or two *samples* to go into a group of the new line.

scale/repeat the scale is the size of the motif on a print relative to the size of the garment or section of garment that it will be used for. Repeat is the measurement of the design components of a print in total before they are repeated again down the length of the goods.

goods at a lower cost for basic business. Also called private label or private label brand.

shopping a line a designer is said to be "shopping the line" when she looks at fabric lines and has something particular in mind. Perhaps the designer is looking for retro prints so many fabric companies will come to show their entire line of fabrics and the designer will pick and choose only those retro prints needed for a group. Reviewing a fabric line is easier because the designer has nothing in mind except to find some interesting new fabric concepts to sample.

subjective letting one's feelings, prejudices, or personal opinion flavor one's thoughts and interpretations. A designer needs to be subjective when being creative and objective when considering facts. For example, if mini-skirts and halter tops are in style, then the designer must include them in the line. Objectively, if they are selling, then they will bring in new orders. Subjectively, the designer is opposed to teenage girls wearing such items to school.

vendor/source these words are used interchangeably. A vendor is a seller. For retailers, the vendor they speak of is the garment manufacturer or supplier. For apparel companies, the vendor is a fabric or trimmings company. Source is used as the provider of a commodity. A source for buttons, a source for fabric, or a source for jeans would be those companies that sell those resources.

Activities

1. Each student should bring to class 10 swatches of various assorted fabrics that could be currently selling in the junior and girls' clothing categories. The swatches should be collected into a box and mixed up thoroughly. Holding the box high so the swatches are hidden, each student then picks out 10 assorted swatches. Using the selected swatches, combine several together to come up with three different fabric stories.

2. Sketch three garments using a swatch, or a combination of swatches, as inspiration to design 7–14 sets.

3. Sketch three garments using a swatch or a combination of swatches as inspiration to design junior tops.

4. Sketch three garments using a swatch or a combination of swatches as inspiration to design 4–6x dresses.
5. Trade swatches with another student to design four additional garments in any category, using at least two different fabrics per design.

The purpose of these design exercises is to learn to design from the fabric to the silhouette and use fabrication as inspiration.

Weekly Planner

Chapter 5 gave students an overview of the role that fabric selection serves in the designing of junior and girls' apparel. The chapter discussed the process of selecting, sampling, and keeping records of the fabric and provided information about the possibility of fabric design opportunities for a girls' apparel designer. The chapter also offered information about the traditional trends in fabric for girls' apparel.

1. Read Chapter 5.
2. Complete the Chapter 5 activities.
3. Determine a color story for the mini-line.
4. Book appointments for shopping fabric stores for samples and swatches for at least six different groups that will be narrowed to four.
5. Study Designer's Dictionary, and learn new terms.
6. Present swatches to instructor and get approval.

Box 5.1

FEATURES DESK

You Know You're Hot

The '80s have been mined so thoroughly, so deeply, it's come to this: Hypercolor is back.

By Erin Weinger, *Times* Staff Writer

Generra Sportswear created the craze in '91, with heat-sensitive T-shirts that changed colors like magic. Touch a purple shirt and leave a pink fingerprint; boogie down and your green tee would be splotched with bright yellow hot spots.

Small-screen cameos on MTV and *Beverly Hills, 90210* propelled Hypercolor into style stardom. The tees sold out across the country, and fluorescent tops bearing the Hypercolor logo became a major status symbol among school-age followers. But the novelty faded as quickly as pink back to purple, Generra filed for bankruptcy, and Hypercolor became a forgotten fad.

Until now. This time around, the trend has a more fashionable spin. The L.A. line Anzevino and Florence is making a racer-back tank dress ($84) and cotton scarf ($26) that start out aqua or lavender and turn yellow or pink. British designer Henry Holland took inspiration from early '90s Vogue photos of Stephanie Seymour and Axl Rose for his heat-activated T-shirt ($110), mini-dress ($236) and denim shorts ($150), all in a neon print befitting Will Smith's reign as the Fresh Prince.

American Apparel offers a hyper spinoff with a unisex tee ($34), and bodyfaders.com has tank tops in a rainbow of changing colors ($24.95). But the most updated version is Puma's sneakers ($65)—if, of course, you don't mind your hot, sweaty feet dictating the color of your kicks.

Just remember: The gear is dyed with a heat-sensitive pigment, so it's washable in cold water—but iron it, bleach it, or dry it in a steaming-hot machine and your shirt won't last the 15 minutes this trend is destined for.

Source: *Los Angeles Times,* Sunday, July 6, 2008. Home Edition; Image, Part P, pg. 7, Features Desk.

Chapter 6

Pin Sketch to Pattern

In this chapter, we will examine how lines are organized and then sketched for patternmaking. This is the point where the designer must pull together all of the previously researched material acquired through competitive shopping, fashion forecasts, and magazines, and researching all checkouts and assemble the information into the mix of the different groups that will be in the new line. This is the active phase of designing that is exciting for most designers because they can now apply their design talents to the creation of new styles. As they begin line sketching, the first patternmaker begins the process of developing new first patterns. The sample cutter starts cutting the checkout bodies in the new fabric as assigned by the designer. The sample makers begin to sew up the first samples and give life to the designer's vision.

At the beginning of a new season, many designers are inspired by so many new ideas that the first garments coming out of the sample room are often too expensive for their market, or *ongepatshket*—Yiddish for overdesigned, gaudily decorated, with too much going on to sell (see Box 6.1). The creative juices are flowing and there is an anxious desire to rush garments into being. It is important, however, to harness this creative energy and direct it carefully into garments that will sell to the manufacturer's target customers.

By first making an inspiration board, then outlining, then **swatching** checkouts in new fabrics, then pulling together a new style line plan, the new line will be manageable and the designer will have a solid foundation to build upon until the line is complete.

INSPIRATION BOARD

Creating a board with pictures, photos, swatches, and anything else that has been gathered as inspiration for the coming season will focus the direction of the new line. This board, if prominently displayed in the design room, will also inspire the rest of the design team, and bring a cohesive element to the trends the designer has chosen that will define the different groups. This board can be any combination of inspiring elements that

Box 6.1 Designer's Yiddish Dictionary

These words were commonly used in the apparel companies where the author worked. To honor the contributions made by the Jewish immigrants to the apparel industry in New York and Los Angeles, they are included in this book.

Babushka head scarf. Hearkens back to Eastern Europe, newly popularized by startlets who wear them with large sunglasses while out and about.

Chutzpah nerve or gall. If someone is asking for more than they deserve it takes *chutzpah*. This doesn't mean brave, but it might mean brazen.

Drek nasty word meaning dirt or worse. Used as a derogatory word for apparel that is cheap or worthless.

Emes the truth. If a salesman is showing the line and telling you a garment is selling well for him, he might say "*Emes*" . . . meaning he is not lying, he is telling the truth.

Farmisht befuddled. A person who is so confused you can't rely on him or her is said to be *farmisht*.

Garmento this is actually not Yiddish but it is a term for anyone in the apparel manufacturing business. It is not an insult or a compliment . . . just a moniker.

Mitzvah a good deed.

Ongepatshket this can be spelled *ungapatchket* or *ongepotchket*. It is a wonderful word that designers may use to describe a garment that has everything but the kitchen sink sewn on the front. It means overdone, garish, and gaudy, with too many bells and whistles.

Shmatteh this means rag. The "rag business" is the apparel industry. If you sell *shmattehs* you sell rags. *Shmatteh* is also used describing a poorly designed garment. "What a ugly *schmatteh*!"

Schmooz talk or chat. Sometimes the sales staff will complain that they had to sit and *schmooz* for too long with a buyer.

Tchotchke knickknacks, toys, a random assortment of small items.

Verklempt extremely emotional or choked up. If you do something outstanding to be nice to someone, they may become *verklempt*. Also spelled *farklempt*.

Yente a gossip.

For more Yiddish words, see *The New Joys of Yiddish* (2001) by Leo Rosten. Three Rivers Press: New York.

---

create a core for the designer's creative approach to the new season. Photos of scenery, interiors, flowers, landscapes, car colors, pottery, historical costumes or any other bits, pieces, or swatches that in some way capture the trends of importance, or the mood the designer wishes to convey can be attached to the board and will further direct the new line. The board is an indicator of what has been forecast in the fashion community. The designer's own interpretation of the board's contents will stamp the sample line with its unique appearance. (See Figure 6.1.)

Designers who use inspiration boards alter them to suit their own personalities. Some boards have an extensive number of items that reflect a wide variety of input. Other designers may choose a simple moonscape photo with various colors to create a mood that they want their line to emulate. The board is a tool for the designer to use as a muse to recall the original inspirations for the season. The board also acts as a reminder to the design staff of the designer's focus for the coming season's line.

OUTLINING

Writing an outline serves as an organizing tool at this point. By listing all the trends that the designer has already chosen that are the most influential to this line's market, and by giving these trends a number in order of importance, the information becomes focused into something that is workable. Each trend can be developed into a group. If each trend is listed as a brief catch phrase or one word that captures the essence, it is easier to keep the outline concise. Words like "Gypsy" or "nautical" or even "1980s" will describe each trend well enough for this purpose. After each numerical heading, a subheading list needs to be a labeled A, B, C, and so forth, noting the design elements or trims that the designer plans to employ to implement the group. These words can be specific. For example, under the nautical group "A" might be gold anchor buttons and "B" sailor collars with ribbon trim. Jotting all this information down helps define the line structure. Additions, **knockoffs**, and alterations may morph the original outline as garments are developed, but having this early guide will make the process smoother.

FIG. 6.1. DESIGNER'S INSPIRATION BOARD.

I. Gypsy
   A. Ruffles
   B. Mixing assorted prints in different colors
   C. Thick cords for belting
II. Russian Military
   A. Gold Braid
   B. Gold Buttons
   C. Tunic lengths
   D. Stand collars

The checkout silhouettes and best-selling styles from the same season a year ago need to be incorporated into this outline. The reordering styles may need sleeve-length changes from season to season. The styles that sold well the year before may need updating, but they should not be overlooked. Refabricating checkouts is a great way to test new color stories and fabric choices without wasting the patternmaker's time. These checkouts usually have a body name that is known to the design staff and the sales department, and that name should be booked into the outline where the designer thinks it could be updated best.

This preliminary outlining procedure helps to constrain the urge to be wildly innovative, because it brings to mind exactly the types of garments that are profitable for the company. Profit is the goal in manufacturing, and designers must come to terms with making garments that sell well, not just garments that are unusually creative. Finding the correct mixture of what is saleable yet creatively interesting is the biggest challenge for the designer of girls' and juniors manufactured clothing.

The new silhouettes, or new hot bodies, that have emerged from research also need to be named and paired with an appropriate trend group. For example, a baby doll top that sold well in juniors will be incorporated into a 7–14 line, renamed "Baby Jane," and logged to go into the "Sheer and Breezy" group. Once a new body is plugged into a new trend group, more styles can be developed around the new garment's particular style features. These new styles may turn into profitable reorders and in a few seasons become **bread and butter** favorites that sell season after season with little alteration.

I. Sheer and Breezy
    A. Miniribbons hanging loose
    B. Print as lining, or sheer solid on top
    C. Baby Jane body with puffy sleeve

New bodies that are especially strong can be tweaked by changing necklines or sleeves, and then they put into the line in several different versions.

New Style Line Plan

A line plan is an organizational method that helps to unite the different trend groups in the outline into a plan of action that will lead to a varied and saleable line that hangs together in an attractive array. The point is to get a visual layout matching the accumulated ideas, along with swatches from the outline, and start putting style sketches into the groupings.

Each outline heading should be copied onto a separate page for each group. At this point, the designer may want to staple fabric swatches onto the page and sketch preliminary styles for his or her own clarification. Reorder bodies should be plugged into the most appropriate trend pages just as they were onto the outline. The sketches of the trending bodies can be plugged into whichever new group is the most compatible with the new fabrication.

The designer now has as many pages as there are groups from the outline. Each page has swatches, photos, and trimmings that are either attached or noted. Now each page is a visual plan for the trend group that immediately shows how many garments within the group actually have been designed. If each group has two skirts, a pair of pants, two dresses, and five

tops, then ten garments need to be shown on the page. If one garment, a checkout body that is being refabricated, is the only garment now sketched, the designer needs to come up with nine more original sketches in order to complete the group. The designer needs to design garments to complete that group and each style that the designer sketches for the group needs an additional sketch in order for the pattern maker to draft the first pattern.

Designers can keep their design plan on a corkboard, on a wall, in a notebook, or in a computer. It does not matter which method is used to keep the plan in place, but it is an important tool for staying organized when the rush to get a line to market creates chaos in the design room. Now the designer is ready to sketch for the pattern process.

SKETCHING FOR THE PATTERNMAKER

Once the designer has the outline smoothed out and the inspiration board up, it is time to start feeding the patternmaker sketches for the line. The patternmaker who takes the designer's sketches and makes the initial pattern is called a first patternmaker. A strong working relationship between the designer and first patternmaker is crucial to creating a new line because the designer is completely dependent upon the talent of someone else to interpret each sketch. As in all other relationships, good communication is essential. The kind of communication that is most effective in this case is sketches that make sense. Because the designer is often out of the design room doing a multitude of tasks, the sketches the designer gives to the first patternmaker need to be clear, concise, and explicit.

It is rare that the designer has the time or luxury to discuss each piece in the line. Sketches must be complete, leaving nothing unanswered as to proportion, length, or specific measurements. At first glance, the sketch should be neat with clean lines. It should be precise. This means each designer sketch should answer all questions in terms of proportion and scale. If all these details are apparent in the sketch, it enables the patternmaker to give the pattern the personality and flair, and the garment will come alive.

Pin Sketches

The first step for the designer is to redraw each new style from the different trend groups and give them to the patternmaker with swatches so that a pattern can be drafted and a sample garment cut and sewn. First patternmakers work from a *pin sketch* that the designer gives them in order to start the sample line process. This is a type of sketch that shows the detailed seam lines and the cut and proportion of the garment. Pin sketches are the sketches that patternmakers often pin to the neck of the mannequin when they are drafting patterns or draping, hence their name. The sketch is kept in constant view

for reference. Sketches used by the patternmaker are like an architect's blueprint. They are the visual plan for the garment. (See Figure 6.2.)

Pin sketches are also referred to as *flats*. The garment is not three-dimensional, it is not drawn on a body, and it appears to be a flat map of the seaming and construction of the garment. This is not the place for designers to showcase their artistic flair with fancy renderings. Such renderings are unnecessary and often confuse patternmakers. It is not necessary for the sketches to be drawn on a little girl or teenager. The simplest sketches work the best for this purpose. There is nothing to be gained by sketching faces or feet. It only wastes valuable time that the designer could be spending on other garments.

FIG. 6.2. THE DESIGNER'S PIN SKETCHES ARE READY FOR THE PATTERNMAKER. ALL THE NECESSARY INFO IS GIVEN EITHER IN THE SKETCH OR WITH THE NOTES AND ARROW INDICATORS.

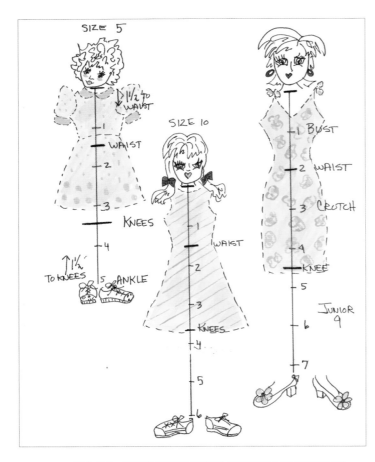

FIG. 6.3a. THESE THREE FORMS SHOW THE PORTIONS OF
EACH OF THE DIFFERENT SIZE RANGES. THE DESIGNER
GIVES A PIN SKETCH TO A PATTERNMAKER AS THE FIRST
STEP IN DEVELOPING A NEW GARMENT. THE PIN SKETCH
MUST ANSWER ALL THE QUESTIONS OF APPEARANCE,
PROPORTION, AND FIT.

Pin Sketch Shorthand

There are many details that must be conveyed
in a sketch for the first patternmaker that show
the proportion, seam lines, and accompanying
detail. To help communicate all those items, a
shorthand of sketching for patternmaking acts
like a universal language in a design room. (See
Figures 6.3a and b.) On the pin sketch chart, it
is evident that drawing straight lines for pleats
and curved lines for gathers immediately answers the question of what the fabric will do as
it drapes over the body or reacts to darts, seams,
or other design and fit features. Generally, the
cleaner the lines of the sketch and the more care
given to detail, the easier the sketched garment
is for the patternmaker to understand.

When sketching, the designer must show re-
alistically how the fabric drapes on the different

parts of the body. Two things alter the drape of
fabric. The first is the body and the second is the
designer's application of a feature to the material, like a dart, pleat, shirring, or ease. The flat
sketch given to the patternmaker must show
how the body and the design have influenced
the natural drape of the fabric in order for the
new pattern to achieve the designer's vision and
the proper fit.

Sketch Indicators

If there are specific measurements that the
designer wants on a garment that would not
be obvious from the flat sketch, the simplest
way to impart that information to the patternmaker is by drawing a **line indicator** or arrow
pointing to the specific place on the sketch and
putting the measurement clearly next to it. For
example, the width of a cuff on a sleeve would
normally be 2″ to 3″ wide, and the first patternmaker would use personal judgment to determine the width within that range. If the designer
wants a much narrower cuff for a 7–14 top, the
line indicator would point to the cuff and have
1 ¼″ written at the end of the arrow. These line
indicators eliminate the possibility of the patternmaker guessing or wasting time wondering
what the designer really wants and having to
track down the designer for clarification.

These little arrows are used for design
features to make sure the patternmaker gets a
particular feature exactly as the designer has
envisioned it. They are not usually used for fit
issues, only for style changes. The patternmaker
has the fit measurement standards to go by and
does not need that information on a sketch. The
line indicators or arrows are used to provide
clarity when the designer has an exact measurement in mind.

Some first patternmakers and designers
work so well after a season or two that the
designer will leave some measurements to the
patternmaker's discretion and only use line
indicators when absolutely essential. At the
beginning of a season, the patternmaker and
the designer may discuss particular hem lengths
and pick a measurement that will be the stan-

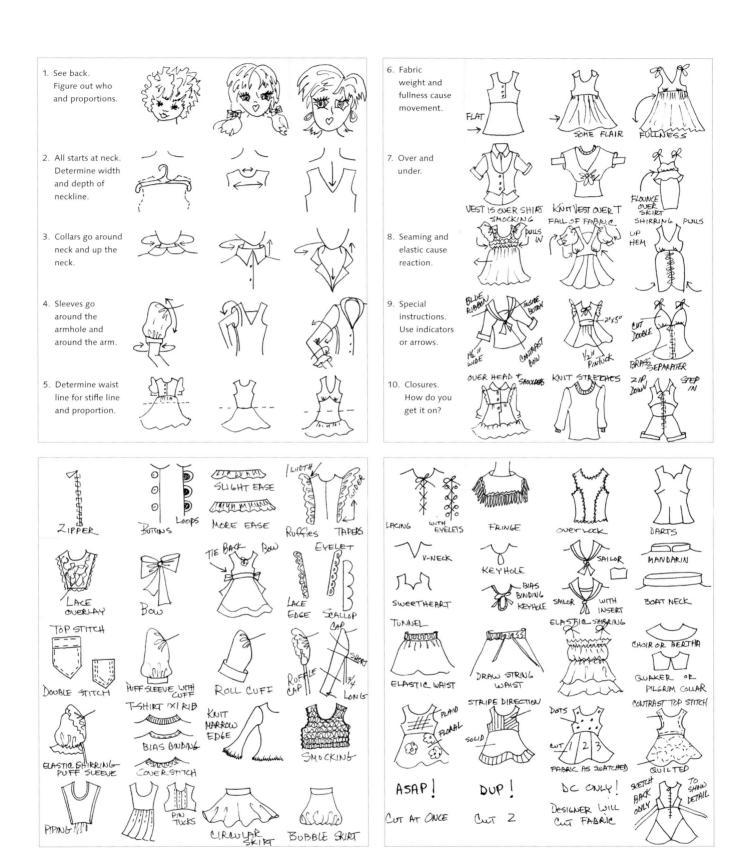

1. See back. Figure out who and proportions.

2. All starts at neck. Determine width and depth of neckline.

3. Collars go around neck and up the neck.

4. Sleeves go around the armhole and around the arm.

5. Determine waist line for stifle line and proportion.

6. Fabric weight and fullness cause movement.

FLAT · SOME FLAIR · FULLNESS

7. Over and under.

VEST IS OVER SHIRT SMOCKING · KNIT VEST OVER T FALL OF FABRIC · FLOUNCE OVER SKIRT

8. Seaming and elastic cause reaction.

PULLS IN · SHIRRING PULLS UP HEM

9. Special instructions. Use indicators or arrows.

BLUE RIBBON · INSIDE BUTTON · 1¼" WIDE · CONTRAST BOW · OVER HEAD + SHOULDERS · 2"X5" · ½" PINTUCK · KNIT STRETCHES · CUT DOUBLE · BRASS SEPARATER · ZIP DOWN · STEP IN

10. Closures. How do you get it on?

ZIPPER · BUTTONS · LOOPS · SLIGHT EASE · MORE EASE · WIDTH WIDER · Ruffles · TAPERS · LACE OVERLAY · Bow · TIE BACK BOW · EYELET · LACE EDGE · SCALLOP CAP · TOP STITCH · PUFF SLEEVE WITH CUFF · ROLL CUFF · RUFFLE CAP · SHORT ¾ LONG · DOUBLE STITCH · T-SHIRT 1X1 RIB · KNIT NARROW EDGE · BIAS BINDING · SMOCKING · ELASTIC SHIRRING PUFF SLEEVE · COVER STITCH · PIPING · PIN TUCKS · CIRCULAR SKIRT · BUBBLE SKIRT

LACING · WITH EYELETS · FRINGE · OVERLOCK · DARTS · V-NECK · KEYHOLE · SAILOR · MANDARIN · SWEETHEART · BIAS BINDING KEYHOLE · SAILOR WITH INSERT · BOAT NECK · TUNNEL · DRAW STRING WAIST · ELASTIC SHIRRING · CHOIR OR BERTHA · ELASTIC WAIST · QUAKER OR PILGRIM COLLAR · PLAID FLORAL · STRIPE DIRECTION SOLID · DOTS CUT 1 2 3 · CONTRAST TOP STITCH · QUILTED · FABRIC AS SWATCHED · SKETCH BACK ONLY · TO SHOW DETAIL · ASAP! CUT AT ONCE · DUP! CUT 2 · DC ONLY! DESIGNER WILL CUT FABRIC

FIG. 6.3b. THESE SMALL PIN SKETCHES ARE USED AS THE SHORTHAND OF PIN SKETCHING. THIS SHORTHAND FOR DIFFERENT TREATMENTS IS EASILY RECOGNIZED BY THE FIRST PATTERNMAKERS. USE THESE EXAMPLES TO HAVE THE PIN SKETCHES EXPLAIN THE GARMENT DETAILS.

Pin Sketch to Pattern   115

FIG. 6.4. THE BASIC BLOCKS IN THE DESIGN ROOM ENABLE THE PATTERNMAKER TO QUICKLY DRAFT THE NEW STYLES.

dard for all that season's garments, which will cut down on specific information the designer would usually include with the sketch. If the fit of garments for a season is unusual, like baggy pants, or extra-long layered T-shirts, there might be a discussion to generalize the fit of all those seasonal changes.

Basic Blocks

All manufacturers have **basic pattern blocks** in the design room that fit their sample size **mannequins**. The first patternmakers use the blocks to draft new styles. These blocks, sometimes referred to as *slopers,* or *master patterns,* can be stored in the computer or be drafted onto durable, thick pattern paper or plastic plexisheets. Generally, these slopers have no seam allowance so that the first patternmaker will add seam allowance. The patternmaker will also add in ease to allow for movement and comfort as appropriate to each new style. Using these blocks as a beginning reference simplifies the work of the first patternmaker and keeps the line uniform in size. These blocks ensure that the samples

fit the mannequins and that the first pattern will be accurate enough to get a proper fabric yardage estimate when the style is adopted and priced for the line. (See Figure 6.4.)

Some manufacturers tweak their slopers according to the current designer's personal flair for fit. Other manufacturers have a house fit and will not alter their blocks as various design room staff come and go. All first patterns must fit both the form in the design room and the average measurements of the company's range of retail buyers' specifications. Samples sent to stores to obtain orders made from first samples need to fit on the retailer's mannequins or face the possibility of being discarded.

The basic patterns are for the first sample drafting only, and they eliminate the extra work that a patternmaker would have to do if each garment was draped or drafted from scratch. These basic blocks evolve from year to year as body specifications change over time.

Currently, all large retailers have their own particular measurements in the girls' and junior departments, making the manufacturing sector create the fit of garments specific to those megacorporations. Design room sloper measurements usually match the mannequins used for fit in the design room, but the expectation is that they will be altered, corrected, and refined for production. Production patterns will then be altered as necessary to fit the measurements of individual retailers.

The sizing on basic blocks is size 5 for the 4–6x range, size 10 for the 7–14 range, and size 7 or size 9 is used for the junior 5–15 range.

Pattern Files

In addition to the slopers, the first patternmaker has access to all the patterns for styles that have been produced in prior lines. The production patterns are numbered and catalogued. The patternmaker has a filing system of both production patterns and first patterns that can be used to make new styles with minor adjustments in order to save time. The designer can pick a particular pattern that comes closest to the new style or leave it to the patternmaker to find a very similar, previously drafted pattern.

First patterns that were drafted prior to the current season but did not sell or go into production are catalogued separately from the production patterns. They are kept on file because the silhouette may be viable, but for some reason it didn't sell well in the last season. The fabrication might not have been desirable, the timing might have been wrong, or there may have been some other problem. Flat sketches of these styles are filed, and the designer or patternmaker may choose to reintroduce these patterns in order to achieve one of the new designs.

Filing systems differ from one company to the next. Some patterns are kept on file in a computer software program, and others may be hung on hooks in a closet. A pattern library can be invaluable to a company, so patterns are rarely discarded. Sometimes a production patternmaker will clean house and discard the graded sets if there are space issues, but he or she will keep the basic size original. (See Figure 6.5.)

FIG. 6.5. WHEN THE FIRST PATTERN IS COMPLETE IT GOES TO THE SAMPLE CUTTER WITH A SKETCH AND SWATCHES.

Each set of patterns that can be used over and over again represents a substantial savings to the company. Because the pattern exists, there is no additional cost in patternmaking salary, no time delay in fitting the garment, and the grading costs have already been paid. Depending upon the similarity of fabric width, and use of **contrast**, it is possible that **markers** also exist that can be pulled from the files, and no marker cost will be involved in the recuts. With this accumulated savings, it is easy to understand why checkout garments are so profitable for manufacturing companies and why they are essential to the bottom line. (See Figure 6.6.)

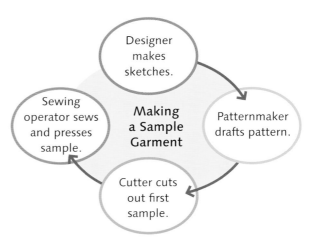

FIG. 6.6. THE PROCESS OF MAKING A SAMPLE FOLLOWS A SIMPLE SEQUENCE.

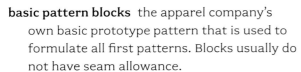

Designer's Diary

Dear Diary,

I filled a binder with sketches last night while watching TV. I just let my subconscious take over, and the artsy part of my brain ran free. My fingers were almost numb by the time I took a break. Tomorrow is the big day. I start my own line. Not fill-ins or add-ons . . . my own line. This is even bigger than designing that group we took up to Dallas. Carmen called earlier and told me not to stress because she has my back. She is the best patternmaker. I can't believe we got off on the wrong foot! My life in school would have been so much easier if I had had her patternmaking speed! Her trick with collars alone could have saved me hours on my senior presentation.

It's amazing how many of the outfits I saw on *Gossip Girl* last night were the same as those I noticed in the files of the company best sellers! I wore that stuff when I was in high school. It really goes to show that watching hit shows can help me stay abreast of trends. The *Ugly Betty* show has some quirky styles, too. Watching the *Golden Globe Awards* ceremony on Sunday will be so cool.

I have to get the line pulled together ASAP. I'd love to ask for a day off to have a three-day weekend. Just thinking about all the coming work makes me tired. Oh, and I didn't know there was so much fabric in the world, let alone that I had to review it all to find what I needed for the line.

Designer's Dictionary

basic pattern blocks the apparel company's own basic prototype pattern that is used to formulate all first patterns. Blocks usually do not have seam allowance.

bread and butter expression for garments that sell season after season that are as dependable as eating bread and butter.

contrast the term for a secondary fabric that is trim to the primary fabric. There can be several "contrasting" fabrics to one garment.

knockoff as an verb, this means to copy. The noun form, knockoff, is a copy of another designer's garment. Copying is called "knock-ing off" and it can be simply copying some part of a style, like an unusual sleeve or fabric. A knockoff is usually as close to an exact copy as possible. Exact copies are illegal and greatly discouraged!

line indicator small arrow pointing to specific parts of a pin sketch to give extra or exact information to conform to the designer's vision of the new style.

mannequins dress forms in a design room that are made to the specific measurements of the sample size.

marker a plan for cutting the pattern pieces for a specific garment style (Calasibetta, Tortora, Abling 2002, p. 322). Also the long paper that has the graded pattern pieces outlined so cutters can follow the lines to cut garments. The marker is laid out on top of the plies of fabric.

swatching cutting swatches (small snips of fabric) and attaching to pin sketches or pattern cards, or any other fact sheet for selling or design purposes.

Activities

1. Designing in a box. Samples in the line have certain criteria that must be met in order to fit into the line and sell.

The criteria: A—Season, B—Price Point, C—Occasion, and D—Size Range

The A choices under Season are: Spring, Summer, Fall, Winter, or Holiday

The B choices under Price Point: Department Store, Mass Merchant, or Specialty Shop

The C choices under Occasion: Play Clothes, School Clothes, or Special Occasion

The D choices under Size: 4/6x girls, 7–16 girls, or junior

Draw 2 boxes on a page. Label each side with A, B, C, and D. Now pick from the above choices and label each side according to a random selection. For example: a box could be a spring, party dress, mass-merchant price point, for a 4–6x girl. Another box could be fall, school clothes, department store, and junior.

Now sketch two different garments. Each separate piece should fit the criteria on all four sides of the box. Start all over with new criteria and do four more. This is a great way to design for specific requirements.

This exercise can be done individually as above, or the teacher can print all the criteria out on small slips of paper and students can draw out their criteria as the slips go around the room. This exercise closely resembles the creative process that a designer might employ.

2. Find a fashion magazine. Tear out or copy four garments that have distinct treatments or design details. Draw two boxes on an 8 × 10 page using different criteria on each box. Now knockoff the inspirational detail according to the box criteria. The result will be beneficial practice in sketching, and great creative practice to use garment details on the different size ranges and for different occasions.

3. Practice sketching for first patternmaking by doing several pages of pin sketches. Make sure to include several sketch indicators with measurements. The sketches can be made of existing garments from magazines or student designs.

The objectives for Chapter 6 are to help students pull their research together into four organized groups for a line. Using the basic sketch ideas given in the pin sketch shorthand, and the girls' figures (See Figures 2.4, 2.5, and 2.8) with tracing paper if necessary, students should be able to start sketching the groups for their mini-lines. They have already selected fabric that can be used for swatches in the groups.

1. Read Chapter 6.
2. Do activities for Chapter 6.
3. Review Designer's Dictionary.
4. Get all your files, reference sketches, and swatches assembled in one place.
5. Organize an outline of main fashion trends.
6. Do an inspiration board explaining your vision.
7. Narrow down the trends to four most important and present the board, with preliminary group names and outline to the class and instructor.
8. Taking one group at a time, start sketching designs making sure to incorporate checkout bodies.
9. Redraw each style as a flat or pin sketch for the patternmaker (in this case you!).
10. Start the necessary first patterns as directed by the instructor.

Box 6.2 They Rule the School

CALENDAR DESK

Fall Sneaks / On the Set

The stakes are higher as the "High School Musical" franchise moves to the big screen. But the cast members still act like kids.

By Mary McNamara, *Times* Staff Writer

You MIGHT expect the set of *High School Musical 3: Senior Year* to be a bit like summer camp, with a bunch of young actors running around in shorts and T-shirts. And to a certain extent, it is. During a recent visit to a night-shoot set in a junkyard here, the preternaturally familiar cast members are surrounded by the colorful rusted-out carcasses of cinematically groomed classic cars and are killing time between shots doing what any group of high school or college kids might do between classes.

Zac Efron, 20, who plays alpha dog and basketball star Troy in the series, nuzzled the neck of his on-stage and off-stage girlfriend, Vanessa Hudgens, 20, who plays the lovely brainiac Gabriella. She then bumped shoulders and banged fake swords with Corbin Bleu, 19, who plays Troy's best friend, Chad. At one point between takes, Efron and Bleu threw themselves into the canvas chairs recently vacated by director Kenny Ortega and cinematographer Daniel Aranyo and requested a playback, watching the scene they just shot the way any other guys might review their *Grand Theft Auto IV* scores.

"Did you think about asking the director if it was OK to sit in his chair?" Ortega said, looming suddenly over the two for all the world like a high school principal. Efron grinned sheepishly and leapt from his chair, but everyone, including Ortega, laughed.

After five years of working with this cast, Ortega is clearly a director who rules through love, not fear—and it's hard not to love a man who walks around orchestrating an extremely complicated dance number with his teacup terrier Manly (yes, the same one owned by the scheming Sharpay in the movies) carelessly cradled in his arm.

But don't be fooled. The minute the cameras and lights are ready, everyone is all business, and if something—a light, a car, a line—is not the way he wants it, Ortega's displeasure is expressed in clarion tones.

For all the playfulness, high spirits, and collective chorus of "we really are one big happy family" that infuses the set of Disney's bullet train of a film franchise, the folks involved in the third *HSM* are focused. Because there's a lot at stake. The little movie Peter Barsocchini wrote as a simple paean to his own high school experience, that Ortega took as a way to get back into films after spending years choreographing dance numbers at mega-events like the Super Bowl, that was cast with kids previously known only to Disney Channel devotees, has become an international multibillion-dollar industry.

All over the world teens and tweens jam to the soundtrack and scarf up the merchandise. It has become one of the most popular plays staged by real high school drama departments; there's a traveling show, an ice show and a new reality series called *High School Musical: Get in the Picture.* But even with its built-in audience, *Senior Year* is a very big deal. This one isn't being shown free on TV; this one will be headed Oct. 24 for the multiplex, where families must shell out roughly $9 each to see the cast sing and dance. And as Efron, Hudgens, Bleu and the rest of the cast continually mention, it's the last film that this particular group will do together.

So although no one seems nervous exactly, the terms "high energy" and "110%" are used a lot. Even Efron, who expressed impatience with his Disney fetters during the filming of *HSM2,* has, as one insider puts it, put his game face on.

"Let's do it again, just better," he says at one point after Ortega has pointed out a few ways in which he could improve a scene.

Gracious and friendly, Efron, who stretched his wings last year in *Hairspray,* seemed clearly in his element here. Yes, there were problems with the paparazzi earlier on, but now it's all about the work. And as with many young men, home always seems sweeter after you've been away for a bit.

"You definitely appreciate it more," he says between takes. "I feel lucky to come back. With other projects it was just scene work. Here it's more like fun and music."

"Everyone came egos checked at the door," Bleu says. "We were all ready to work, even more so than on the other films. We know this is it, so we have to enjoy the moment."

"I really do love these guys," Hudgens adds.

The scene being shot on this night is a much-anticipated dance number featuring Efron, Bleu and a coterie of male dancers tricked out in junkyard chic. By the time the sun goes down and the lights go up, a crowd of nonparticipatory cast and crew are huddled together in jackets and sweaters.

As artistically ambitious as the previous two films were, the transition from television to feature film has meant many changes—a larger budget, for example, that no one will discuss in detail, though Ortega says it is half that of most musical features.

Laying the groundwork for at least the possibility of a *High School Musical 4,* new and younger characters will be introduced, including a Sharpay protege named Tiara (Jemma McKenzie-Brown) and two Chad devotees: Jimmie "the Rocket" Zara (Matt Prokop) and Donny (Justin Martin), while some established characters, like composer Kelsi (Olesya Rulin) and uber-thespian Ryan (Lucas Grabeel) will be given new chances to shine.

But the most noticeable and most remarked-upon difference is the dancing. There's more of it, 17 numbers compared with 10 in the first *HSM,* and it's much more complicated. So complicated the cast had a five-week rehearsal just for the choreography.

"The numbers are harder and more intricate," Hudgens says. "We've definitely had to step it up. In a way, it feels like the other two movies were all a run-up to this one."

The junkyard scene is a perfect example and will probably be one of the most talked-about. "Look at us," says Ortega, motioning to the stacks of cars, some smashed, some almost drivable. Across from the set, a machine steadily grinds cars into mulch (the sound drives Ortega crazy, but there's nothing to be done). Behind runs a railroad track; it is the cinematographer's dream to get a take in which a train rumbles by.

"We're in the middle of a real live junkyard. The boys are dancing on cars. It's challenging— there are rough edges, hard cement, and we want everyone to be safe. But we wanted a backlot feel in an actual location, and we got it. It's beautiful, isn't it?" he says, taking a moment to step back from the upbeat professionalism that fuels the production and looking around like a kid who took a wrong turn and wound up in the middle of a movie set.

"It's going to be so great on the big screen," he says, back in director mode. "The best one yet."

Source: *Los Angeles Times,* Sunday, September 7, 2008. Home Edition; Part E, pg. 12, Calendar Desk.

Chapter 7

From Sample Cutting to Construction

Most of the newly ordered sample fabric that was painstakingly chosen by the designer has arrived. The designer has planned several line groups, designed individual garments in innovative silhouettes, and then sketched those new bodies for the first patternmaker to begin the process of making the patterns. The new season is going from vision to reality, and the sample cutting is the next step in the formation of the sample line. There is usually a sample cutter or assistant designer who assists the first patternmaker by cutting the samples after the pattern is completed. In some cases the patternmaker will cut samples in addition to making the patterns, and in a pinch, the designer may have to pitch in and cut out some of the new designs. In order to gain momentum toward completion of the line the entire design staff will have to work as a team.

SAMPLE GARMENT IMPORTANCE

Each garment that is designed, cut, sewn, trimmed, and hung on a fancy hanger is a prototype that has to qualify at every level before it can be priced and presented for sale. The sample is a test of the designer's creativity in combining fabric, silhouette, and trim. The designer must be satisfied that the new garment is as good as or better than originally envisioned. The newly sewn garment is a test of the new fabric sample cut's appearance, drape, hanger appeal, and coordination with other fabrications in the line. The sample is also a test of both the patternmaker's skill in capturing the fit and proportions of the original sketch, and the difficulty or ease of construction by the sample maker. A new sample represents the possibility of future sales and income for the company, so sample perfection is a goal, but the investment in employee time and talent, along with the cost of materials put great stress on the design staff.

Design room samples are expensive. The cost is between $100 and $200 for each original sample created in a girls' wear or junior line. The initial cost would include design room salaries, fabric, and trim costs, but not overhead costs like rent and utilities. The true cost could even be somewhat higher in the upstairs market but this amount will work as an illustration of the importance of each sample. Visualizing a $100 bill hanging on pants hangers instead of little size 5 dresses, or 7–14 skirts, or a junior knit top, puts this in real perspective. For every sample that is sewn but discarded because it is not up to the standards of the designer, the sales team, or the company, the design staff needs to think in terms of having just wasted a $100 bill.

Recognizing the importance of the new line, which is made up of all the costly individual samples, a designer can feel the weight of enormous responsibility, knowing that the jobs of the entire company rest on the salability of the new season's sample line. In a nutshell, the samples are very expensive and need to be planned carefully. Lines can be designed on computers and sent to buyers before making the samples. If the buyer is interested, samples can be sewn. This is not the usual circumstance, however. It takes a buyer who has a good imagination to visualize a style without seeing the drape of the fabric, the vibrancy of the material, or the finished product hanging with the complete line. A sample shown on the computer will enable a buyer to say what he or she doesn't like more than it will convince the buyer to purchase the garment.

A new line must be created, and the cost of the sample making process is one of the risks in the garment manufacturing business. The designer who is aware of the stakes is armed with the insight to keep sample mistakes to a minimum.

WORKFLOW

One of the responsibilities the designer has is to have a sufficient workflow in the design room to keep every staff member busy with a backlog of work. To do this there have to be enough new sketches to occupy the patternmaker, enough first patterns drafted to keep the sample cutter cutting, and a backlog of cut sample garments to employ all the sample makers at full pace.

If there are three sample makers sewing a line, and they can sew five garments a day, the backlog of cut and ready to sew garments needs to be greater than 15 in. order to occupy the sewing staff. Store samples, duplicate line samples, and even stock repairs are often used to fill in when design room staff is not ahead of the new sample workload, but this method of filling in does not move the designer's new line toward completion. Most designers react to each completed sample by adding to the group, adjusting some portion of the sample for a better result, or recutting the new silhouette in a different fabric. Since the new samples that are created can inspire additional styles and treatments, the design staff must work at a pace that allows for constant improvisation by the designer.

Maintaining a full-speed design room on a new line is not always an easy task. If the fabric for the new line comes in late, it can throw the entire room into gridlock. If the designer has not given the patternmaker ample new design sketches with adequate information for the pattern process, then the room slows to a standstill again. Any breakdown in the flow results in employees not having sufficient work to keep them busy, and both time and money are wasted. The pace in the design room needs to be steady in order to get the new line sewn in time to be ready for the sales force's **market dates**.

Sample makers sew at the rate necessary to finish the work set before them. If garments are not cut at a rate to keep workers assured of a full day's employment, they slow their pace subconsciously. Getting the sample cutting done and putting the bundled cut pieces in line to be sewn by the sample makers is an important part of this chain.

SAMPLE CUTTING BASICS

It is the job of the sample cutter to use the first pattern to cut the correct fabric on the proper grainline, using the fabric's print or pattern according to the designer's sketch. If these requirements are met, the sample cutter only needs to make sure that the cutting pace is fast enough to stay ahead of the sample sewing crew. (See Figure 7.1.)

Check the Pattern

The very first thing the cutter needs to do is to check the pattern against the **pattern card** and the sketch to make sure the pattern is complete. The pattern card lists each pattern piece that should be included in the set. A missing pattern piece, if overlooked, could result in the sample being cut incompletely. This could result in a waste of time and fabric. (See Figure 7.2.)

Check the Fabric

The next step is to visually inspect the sample yardage for defects. Common defects are runs or snags on knitted goods and misprints on printed patterned goods. Also troublesome are fabrics that are skewed. This happens when a yarn is not woven or knit at the proper 90-degree angle required to keep the fabric from twisting off grain. Garments sewn up with skewed knits never hang correctly and look distorted. If there is a problem with the fabric, if, for example, the pattern is faded in spots, or the stripes are not straight with the grainline, the sample cutter must alert the designer. If there are flaws or irregularities of any kind, the designer may want to stop use of the fabric before continuing to cut in order to make a substitution of goods. No designer wants to cut into a fabric that may come with potential production headaches later on.

The sample goods' **tag information** has to be checked against the sample cut order form in order to make sure it is the correct pattern. The fabric needs to be cut in the right color as ordered, and it needs to match the swatch on the sketch or pattern card.

The width of the fabric needs to be measured and compared to the order form as well. Fabrics are sold with two width measurements. For example, some woven goods come 43/44. That means the narrowest the stock goods will be is 43 inches wide. The widest will be 44 inches wide. The rolls shipped against the stock order, if the style is sold and goes into production, might vary up to 1 inch so the marker will be made to the narrowest width so that all the goods can be cut at once, if necessary. Yardage estimates

FIG. 7.1. IT IS IMPORTANT FOR THE SAMPLE CUTTER TO MAKE SURE THE PATTERN IS COMPLETE BEFORE IT IS LAID OUT OR CUT.

will be figured on the narrow width also. Knitted goods are often ordered 58/60 inches wide. Those markers are made 58 inches wide and the phrase "58 cut-able" would be assigned to the fabric. If fabric is shipped that does not meet the minimum width tolerance, that shortage can affect the production cycle, because the markers may have to be completely revised. Yardage estimates would go up, and the cost of each garment might increase as well. The first step in checking for this potential problem is in the sample cutter's preliminary appraisal of the sample goods.

Layout of Pattern on Fabric

Next, the fabric should be laid out either upside down open to cut in a single layer, or folded in half with the wrong side facing up in order to cut on the fold. The pattern should then be placed on the fabric in its entirety so the cutter can figure out the very best placement of the pieces. This is done to conserve as much of the remaining fabric as possible, in case additional samples in the group are required. At this point, the sample cutter should be able to recognize any problem with the layout of the pattern. If the pattern cannot be laid out without wasting an unacceptable amount of fabric, the sample cutter has to alert the patternmaker. (See Figure 7.2a.) The patternmaker will then see if adjustments can be made

FIG. 7.2a, b. (a) Top. SAMPLE CUTTER HAS PATTERN LAID OUT TERRIBLY WITH BIG HOLES WASTING GOODS. (b) Bottom. THE PATTERN IS LAID OUT PERFECTLY.

that is easy to handle can be folded in half with the good side on the inside. Next, the pattern pieces should be placed in a tight layout and secured with small cutting weights. Pins may be used to hold the fabric still, if the cutter feels the fabric shifting while cutting, but many fabrics don't need that assist unless they are slinky knits or slippery, woven fabric.

Very slippery or sheer fabrics that may be used for dressy dresses should be cut with tissue paper on top with pins to hold all the layers securely. The scissor cuts should be smooth and continuous, not jagged. The scissors should remain on the table, sliding beneath the fabric with the support of the cutter's other hand held across from the scissor hand out of harm's way. Notches for woven fabric should be snipped not to exceed 1/8 inch and triangular tab notches on knits should be carefully centered then cut to insure proper seam matching. Triangular notches are used because the common snipped 1/8 inch notch used on woven fabrics might cause runs when snipped into the edge of the knit fabric. The small triangular tab is cut off during the sewing process, but it is an easy gauge for the seamstress to align notches. If there is a problem with a knit sample cut, for instance, if the pattern is **skewed** or the stripes are not straight with the grainline, the sample cutter must alert the designer.

to the pattern that will enable a better marker. (See Figure 7.2b.) If the garment is sold and goes into production, these preliminary precautions are time saving and economical. Most often, the adjustment would be minor, like putting in a back seam on a skirt or bodice. Sometimes the designer will be consulted at this point, but often the patternmaker alone will make a minor pattern alteration.

Marking the Pattern

For the cleanest cutting, it is best for the sample cutter to mark the lines around the first pattern with a soft crayon, chalk, or pencil of contrasting color on the wrong side of the fabric. Fabric

Conserving Fabric

When the sample fabric is ordered, the designer usually has the intention to cut an entire group out of the goods. It is necessary for the sample cutter to place the first pattern carefully so that there is enough fabric remaining to cut the other garments that will be designed for the fabric. The designer may not give the first patternmaker the sketches for the completion of the group until the first sample in that fabric is sewn, and the resulting sample is adopted into the line. For this reason, the sample cutter may have no idea how many or what type of garments might be cut in addition to the initial garment. Marking a tight layout is essential. Reordering sample cuts can cause a delay in

FIG. 7.3. Left. THE SAMPLE CUTTER CAREFULLY FOLLOWS THE PENCIL MARKINGS.

FIG. 7.4. Below. THIS SKETCH IS LABELED WITH THE GRAIN LINE, THE SELVAGE, AND THE TRUE BIAS.

time and a financial cost that could have been avoided with both careful pattern layout and conservative cutting of the fabric by the sample cutter. (See Figure 7.3.)

SPECIFIC FABRIC CONSIDERATIONS FOR CUTTING

The fabric industry has broadened its selection of fabrics to offer an amazing array of different types of fabric with interesting textures, unusual surface finishes, expansive elasticity, and other unique properties. Each unique fabric needs to be carefully examined before cutting to make sure the cutting technique is suitable for the fabric. Some fabrics snag, so staples need to be removed from pattern pieces before laying them out on the fabric. Some fabrics stretch out when the fabric is laid out flat, and the fabric needs to sit for a period of time in order to recover its shape before cutting. Whatever the individual traits of a fabric are, the sample cutter must cut accordingly. Some specific information about grainlines, bias cutting, ruffles, plaids, and stripes can make that process run smoothly.

Grainlines

The grainline of fabric runs the length of the fabric parallel to the *selvage* edge. Unless there are instructions to the contrary, garments are always cut with the grain. All patterns should have the grainline marked. The sample cutter can measure the selvage edge to the pattern

grainline at two parallel spots to ensure that the alignment is on grain.

The *cross grain* is perpendicular to the selvage. (See Figure 7.4.) Many fabrics used in girls' woven apparel are considered to be grain perfect or of equal strength, so cutting cross grain will not change the durability of the fabric, but color shading is a possibility. Sample cutters must pay attention and make sure to note if any pattern piece was intentionally placed cross grain in order to save yardage and note it on the sketch. **Cutting off grain** should be avoided un-

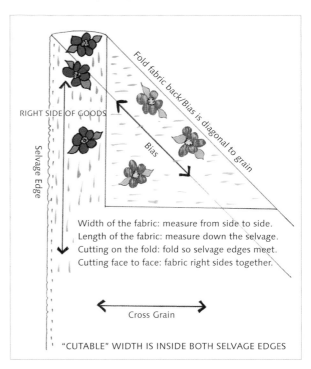

RIGHT SIDE OF GOODS

Selvage Edge

Fold fabric back/Bias is diagonal to grain

Bias

Width of the fabric: measure from side to side.
Length of the fabric: measure down the selvage.
Cutting on the fold: fold so selvage edges meet.
Cutting face to face: fabric right sides together.

Cross Grain

"CUTABLE" WIDTH IS INSIDE BOTH SELVAGE EDGES

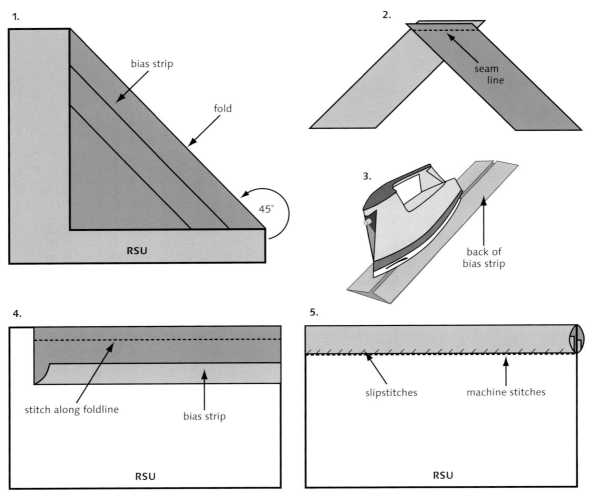

FIG. 7.5. WHEN THE TRUE BIAS IS FOLDED BACK THE SAMPLE CUTTER CAN CUT STRIPS FOR BIAS BINDING OR FOR MAKING SPAGHETTI STRAPPING.

less the designer has clearly instructed that the garment be cut that way. There is a difference between cutting off grain for a planned design result and cutting sloppily so that the grainline is not true. When a sample is cut sloppily, with grainlines not true, it is possible for the garment to take less fabric than it will when it goes into production. This will cause a costing issue.

Bias Cutting

The bias of fabric is the true diagonal to the grain. To find the bias, fold the fabric in half lengthwise. Take the top corner of the fabric and fold it back until it forms a 90° angle with the selvage edge. The true bias is the diagonal edge on that fold. An entire garment cut on the bias hangs differently than a garment cut on grain. It will cling and create a gentle ripple when the body moves. Bias garments are also harder to

sew than are garments cut on grain because the seams automatically stretch with the machine thread tension if the sample makers are not careful. The junior knit top and dress categories use bias cut garments more than girls' apparel. Bias cutting in girls clothing is usually done for **mitering stripes** or for breaking up the monotony of a plaid garment. (See Figure 7.5.)

To cut bias strips of fabric for samples that require binding or spaghetti trim, the cutter needs to mark the true diagonal on the wrong side and then mark parallel lines of the proper width over and over until the necessary number of strips is cut for the sample. The normal width for bias edging is 1 ¼ inch for spaghetti and bias trim, but the patternmaker may ask for a different specific width. Cutting bias strips on one layer of fabric, not on the fold, helps to conserve sample yardage.

seaming and fewer pattern pieces, novelty knits can be a challenge to cut. The goal is to keep the fabric from moving on the table as the scissors cut. This can be accomplished by using weights and straight pins. The first patternmaker will have already ascertained the exact stretch of the fabric and will have adjusted the knit pattern to fit properly. For stock orders, in ideal situations, difficult knits laid out and allowed to sit overnight to recover before cutting. However, many sample cutters do not have this luxury.

A few tricks can be used to calm disorderly knit fabrics. If commercial stiffener is not available, clear nail polish can be painted on the edge of a knit that is rolling after cutting. Clear tape and masking tape can be applied to edges that are unraveling. A square construction woven, like muslin, can be placed between the layers of knit, pinned together, and after the sample is cut, the woven lining is discarded. For stock goods, the production department may choose to treat the rolled edges with a heat treatment in order to minimize the roll of the fabric after it is cut.

DESIGNER PREROGATIVE

It is nice to have a guide to the methods of using fabrics in the design of girls' and junior apparel. However, it is important to note that creativity should not be held to any set of rules. Sometimes ignoring the normal expectation of how something should look is exactly the way to create excitement and originality in a line of clothing. For example, using huge floral prints that are way out of scale for a small garment can make a wonderful statement. Using several unrelated prints scrambled into a garment can create a fun sportswear grouping. Plaids that are cut on the bias in conjunction with stripes that are mitered might just make a boring shirt saleable. Fabric should be used inside out, upside down, and any other way a designer wants, in order to achieve a distinctive style. The one thing the designer must always remember is that it is his or her job to design garments that the stores are willing to purchase and that the consumers are willing to wear.

It is also the designer's prerogative to avoid using fabrications that increase the possibility of quality control issues. Designers may simply shun the use of unbalanced stripes and plaids because the marketplace has a wide variety of those fabrications in similar colors that are balanced and easier to deal with. Some designers are adept at using border prints and will lay out those pattern pieces themselves in order to make sure the borders are cut in the best way possible. Other designers might hate the predictable look that coordinated print groups tend to generate. There are no set rules for designers to follow while structuring their lines. There are only prior experience lessons passed from one design room to another.

FIRST GARMENT SAMPLES

The sample-making stage is critical to success in a new line's development. The designer is dependent at this point on the backup crew in the design room. The patternmaker has to make the first pattern in the correct proportions, and the sample cutter has to cut the garment so that the fabric is on grain and cut into the proper print, texture, and color. Now the sample maker needs to sew the garment up using the correct construction methods that are appropriate for the fabric and the price point of the company.

Sample Bundles

Once the sample cutter cuts out the garment, it has to be given to the sample maker. It is normal for the cut garment to be bundled into a collection of all the cut pieces, including linings and a sketch of the proposed garment. The bundle is then secured with a tie that is often a scrap from the cutter. If special thread color is needed for topstitching, it needs to be either taped to the sketch paper or placed alongside the bundle. Some designers will choose buttons, lace, and other notions before the sample is sewn. When that is the case, then the sample cutter will also provide those items, or swatch them onto the sketch, so that the sample maker can construct the garment with everything he or she needs. The bundled garment should contain all the

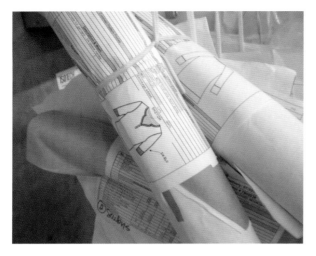

FIG. 7.8. EACH SAMPLE BUNDLE HAS A SKETCH SO THE SAMPLE MAKER HAS AN IDEA OF THE GARMENT THAT IS EXPECTED.

Sample Maker Input

Sample makers sometimes have difficulty sewing *prototypes,* or first samples, for new styles that are created by new first patterns. It is very helpful for the sample maker to address each problem with the first patternmaker as it arises. Since samples are sewn in a systematic process, it is easier to correct a problem before the next sewing stage begins. If the pattern needs adjusting, if notches don't line up, or if a process is simply too difficult to maneuver, the sample maker tells the first patternmaker so that corrections can be made and alternatives can be implemented. (See Figure 7.9.)

If there are no problems with the pattern, and sample sews together well, the sample maker simply keeps sewing as quickly as possible. A good sample maker will figure out the best way to construct the garment and then give that feedback to the first patternmaker. The garment, when sewn properly for the intended price category, will price out appropriately. When the design staff is working as a team, designing, making patterns, cutting, and sewing, the line comes together easily. (See Figure 7.10.)

information the seamstress needs in order to complete the construction of the garment without any delay. (See Figure 7.8.)

Some designers do not want to select trimmings until the garment is sewn up. The designer will then fuss with the garment and see what buttons look best, or which trimmings are necessary. Once trimmings are chosen, the sample maker will finish the garment.

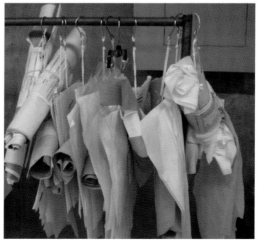

FIG. 7.9a, b. (a) Left. THE BUNDLES OF UNSEWN GARMENTS KEEP THE SAMPLE MAKERS WORKING AT A STEADY PACE. (b) Below. THE SAMPLE MAKER HAS A SKETCH AND SEWING INSTRUCTION INCLUDED IN EACH BUNDLE.

Sample Requirements

First samples that are sewn in the design room are meant to be showroom samples that the sales staff can show to buyers for the purpose of writing purchase orders. They are not necessarily fit samples, although designers make every effort to get the sample to fit the form correctly. They are not necessarily production quality samples, although every effort is made to have the samples look, inside and out, like the stock garments that will be shipped for purchase orders. These samples are usually sewn up quickly without the benefit of careful evaluation of the best construction methods. Most design rooms are equipped with very specific machinery that makes this process mimic the eventual perfected prototype.

After the sample is sewn and the designer is happy with the new garment's appearance, it will be priced. If the sample is sewn in a manner that is too expensive for the intended market, the production department will make suggestions to alter the garment. In most cases the changes will be unseen by the store buyer and consumer. If the changes are noticeable, then a new corrected sample will have to be sewn for the sales staff to show to the buyers.

Machinery

There are many variations of machinery from one design room to another. There is usually, however, a basic assortment of sewing equipment that the sample makers use to turn out the sample line.

The seam construction on woven samples is normally performed on a five-thread overlock machine, while the more detailed work, such as collars and plackets, are performed on a powerful commercial single-needle sewing machine. Each sample maker uses his or her single-needle machine as a home base and moves to the specialty machines as necessary. Folder attachments make the single-needle machine easy to convert for sewing baby hems. Knits are sewn on sergers or three- and four-thread overlock machines. Hems are done with either a three-thread or five-thread coverstitch, or a

FIG. 7.10. THIS GROUP IS WORKING WELL AS A DESIGN, MERCHANDISING, AND PATTERN TEAM.

single-needle stitch, or blind stitch. One of the machines in the design room is often set just to do the hemming, and clear thread is kept on the blind-stitch machine so time is not wasted changing thread colors. A coverstitch machine can be used for knit and woven fabrics, for both decorative and structural finishes on the samples. This machine finish shows threads on both the topside and the underside of the seam or edge. This finish makes contrast thread color on a girl's T-shirt look more interesting. A marrow-edge machine is commonly found in junior and girls' wear design rooms. The edging of tightly wound thread that is performed on the marrow machine can be used as a simple finish on a sheer collar. With tension applied to a knit edge, the marrow machine can ruffle the edge and create a very frilly finish. A buttonhole machine is also included in the most basic setups. If a specialty machine is not available to the sample makers, then outside sewing contractors will be utilized to give the designer any detail or design feature that is desired.

Sewing Techniques

The most common seam finish is simple serging on the edges of the stitched seam. Serging can be done on the fabric edge, with both sides of the seam caught within the chain stitch or single edges serged, in which case the seam is pressed open so that it lies flat. This is the cheapest method of finishing a seam that is acceptable to most retail quality control departments.

Most jeans are sewn with a finish that is called a flat-fell seam. This double-stitched seaming is done in one step. This finish is very durable because the fabric is folded under as it is caught with stitches on top. Welt seams look similar but are actually done in two operations and are considered to be a fake flat-fell seam. Welt seams are popular on girls' and junior garments.

French seams are done in two operations that involve stitching once, then turning, clipping, and restitching. French seams may be used on sheer fabrics and collars. This type of seaming is good on very thin, but easy to unravel fabrics, because the seam is actually encased within the next stitches. This is not the seam-finish choice for popular priced clothing except when used sparingly.

Bound seams go in and out of popularity in girls' and junior sportswear. Binding can be used as decoration. It is used in infant and toddler clothing to such an extent as to alienate the older girls because they don't like to look like babies. Contrast or matching color bias tape or bias-cut fabric is attached in a double-fold encasement around armholes, necks, and pocket trims to keep the garment from unraveling. This method of cleaning the edges allows knits to stretch where necessary, like over the head, but still look finished. Using contrast color in this method also provides an interesting design element.

Seam finishing and all other garment tailoring techniques are varied according to the price range of the line of clothing. Due to the trend of **deconstructed** garments, a movement that used unraveling edges and lack of tailoring as a design element, each manufacturer has to conform their garments to fit into the quality control requirements for each individual retailer. For a period of time, Barneys New York had exquisite gowns with frayed layers of chiffon selling at high retail prices that five years earlier would not have passed a JCPenney quality control inspection. Fashion is so fluent that the rules of construction need to be amended as the designs change from season to season. There is always an unstated requirement however, that the category of girls' garments, both 4–6x, and 7–14, should last until they are outgrown. Juniors are more flexible in their demands. They just want to be dressed appropriately for their peer groups. If that means torn jeans and frayed sweatshirts, that is what designers need to give them.

Pressing

Every design room should be equipped with commercial steam irons. Sample makers use the steam irons throughout the sample sewing process. When the sample is sewn up the sample maker gives the new garment a good pressing and puts it on a hanger for the designer to admire and approve for costing. At this juncture the designer may also chose to alter or add buttons and trims. (See Figure 7.11.)

Sample Garment Expectations

Experienced sample makers become adept at sewing samples up to appear very similar to how their company stock garments will be sewn if the new design goes into production. The buyers must be shown a fair representation of what they are purchasing for the specific price range. In girls' and junior clothing there are several expectations regarding the quality.

The garment should be sewn well enough to last the entire season. The garment will retain its original shape. Knitted garments should not stretch out without recovering, and woven fabrics should not become limp. Finally, the garment should look close to new if the proper washing instructions are followed. Color-fastness is important to consumers. With these

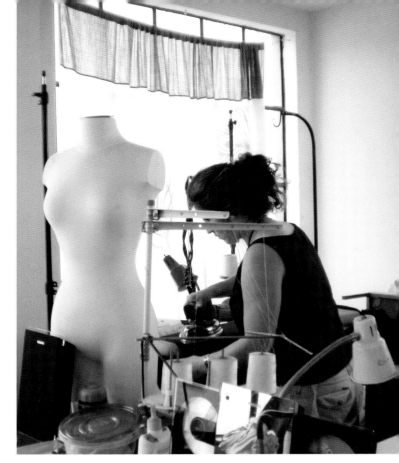

FIG. 7.11. PRESSING OF THE GARMENT SEAMS OCCURS IN THE SAMPLE SEWING PROCESS, BUT THE GARMENT IS COMPLETELY PRESSED BEFORE IT CAN BE SHOWN TO BUYERS.

criteria in mind, the designers must factor in the durability of the fabric with the construction strength of the seaming. Retailers from the low end, like Wal-Mart, to the high end, like Neiman-Marcus, expect the garments they offer for sale to have finished seams inside and out. Their price points will dictate how much labor is put into the garment. How well the individual garments are finished is left to the manufacturer as long as the construction passes the quality control examination by the store. There is certainly a greater emphasis on good tailoring at the higher price points, but the standards of quality for girls' wear and junior clothing are as stringent as they are for ladies' apparel.

Designer's Diary

Dear Diary,

I think I have aged five years in two months. In this business, you take two steps forward and three back every day. The line is being sewn, but production problems keep arising and interrupting my day. The slinky knit that the previous designer picked for those little hoodies for the holiday ad came in skewed. I spent all day today looking for a substitute. The fabric sales reps must hate me because they are expecting a big order, and I just cannot find the right texture.

My new sample maker is so fast that it has created a contest of sorts in the design room. Each sample maker is trying to outshine the next. Poor Henry has been cutting at warp speed just to keep them all occupied. He showed me a neat trick today. He lined up all six of the basic denim pants that go with the different tops and cut the pants with a round knife. Then he went back and cut the tops separately. It was like an assembly line in the design room.

I saw a great movie called *The Duchess.* The costuming was amazing. My friend Erika from school worked on the film and helped catalogue some of the period hats. If I decide to do a retro line, I know whom to consult. I see that networking outside of my company could be valuable now and in the future.

baby hem a method of finishing the edge of fabric by turning the edge of the fabric by rolling it over and then topstitching. This is primarily used on sleeves, collars, hems, and ruffles.

cutting off grain anytime the pattern is marked and the fabric is cut with the grainlines of the pattern *not* parallel to the selvage edge. Cutting cross grain and bias cutting may be at the designer's discretion. Putting the pattern down at an angle without noticing the actual correct grainline method of cutting is "cutting off grain" and not acceptable.

deconstructed garments that are designed to look unfinished from the outside. Some garments may be finished beautifully on the inside but have unfinished seams, raveling, or a seam finish that normally appears on the interior appearing on the right side of the garment instead.

market dates apparel manufacturers show new lines for different seasons on particular dates throughout the year. For instance, for mass merchants, Back to School in girls' wear is shown for a June delivery. Fall 1 is shipped in August. The September/October Holiday line is shown for a November 30 to December 30 shipping period. These dates vary according to the retail market. Catalogue sales are shown months earlier than the regular market is. Designers are given target dates, by which time the line should be completed and ready for market.

mitering stripes engineering the stripes to meet at a perfect angle. The angle can be 90º or less at the designer's determination.

pattern card the card attached to the front of a set of patterns. Written on the card are the pattern pieces and any other pertinent information as directed by the manufacturer. Normal information includes a style number, date, number of pattern pieces, and how many of each pattern piece to cut.

skewed when a knit is skewed it is knitted out of line so it will hang unevenly when it is sewn and look off kilter. The word askew means awry or uneven.

stock goods the fabric that is purchased to be cut into garments to fill orders from retailers. When samples are cut out of stock goods it means the garments will appear the same as the garments that the retailers will receive when their purchase orders are shipped.

tag information each sample cut is shipped with identifying information attached by some sort of tag. Some tags are stapled to the sample cut, and others are attached by being swift tagged. The tag information has the fabric company, phone number, style number of the fabric, and usually the color. Additional information, like fabric content and the number of yards, might be included. Sometimes it is the job of an assistant designer to make sure the fabric tag is removed from the sample cut and placed in a file, with a swatch, so the information is available when the sample garment is priced.

Activities

1. Take a measuring tape and affix it with clear adhesive tape on the edge of the cutting table in the classroom. Perpendicular to that tape, put masking tape across the width of the cutting table surface. Measure and mark off 43 inches. Now take existing patterns, either store bought, or student made, and take turns laying out the patterns in the space allowed to get the hang of putting pattern pieces down on fabric in the tightest layout with the grainlines correct. Now measure and mark off 58 inches, and repeat the same process. Students can have a competition to see who gets the tightest layout, thereby conserving the most fabric.

2. Using grid marked pattern paper, measure out two yards. Measure and mark the paper to simulate a 58-inch-wide fabric. Now draw a border print pattern with the repeat running a yard. Using finished patterns for a girls' 4–6x dress, a 7–14 skirt, and a junior top, lay out the patterns one by one, making sure to use the fabric in a tight layout. Now sketch what the garments would look like with the fabric border pattern placement reflected in the sketches.

3. Sketch a 4–6x short set with solid-colored fabric. Now redraw the same style lines but as the garment would appear as if it were cut in a plaid. Sketch a 7–14 skirt set. Now redraw the skirt with two coordinated prints. Sketch a junior top. Now redraw the same garment with bias stripes.

Weekly Planner

Chapter 7 acquaints students with the process of taking a design from the sketch phase through the first pattern, cutting, and sample construction. You can see the relationships between people in action, and you can avoid some of the garment construction and fabric selection pitfalls that experienced designers know about.

1. Read Chapter 7.
2. Do Activities for Chapter 7.
3. Review Designer's Dictionary.
4. Complete the first patterns that were started in the Chapter 6 Weekly Planner.
5. Make pattern cards for the completed patterns.
6. Cut the samples out.
7. Have the samples for the line sewn up, pressed, and quality checked.

Box 7.1

FEATURES DESK

Avatars That Play Dress-up

Players unleash creativity in new fashion games that let them
shop, tailor and design—competitively, of course.

By Emili Vesilind, *Times* Staff Writer

Next month, shoppers will be able to walk into H&M and buy a nautical-inspired minidress designed by 21-year-old Beau Fornillos, who created the sporty frock using a computer video game.

Fornillos isn't a professional fashion designer. He built the dress on the Sims 2 video game and uploaded it to an online runway, where it was judged by a panel of H&M designers in Stockholm. Coming in first meant having his outfit actually manufactured and sold by the chain store. Sort of like a *Project Runway* challenge in cyberspace.

The dress is bricks-and-mortar evidence of just how pervasive fashion has become in the shoot-'em-up world of gaming. What began as a few product placements in sports games has morphed into a category of its own.

Along with *Sims 2,* there are a slew of fashion games that allow players to shop, tailor and design—competitively, of course. The newest of the games is based on Japanese street style. Even Karl Lagerfeld has a cameo in the latest *Grand Theft Auto.*

Game-makers say style is helping them snare more female gamers, a demographic that hadn't been specifically targeted by the starships-and-shotguns industry. Today, 55% of *Sims 2* players are female.

"The female audience is the next step for video games to grow," said Jarik Sikat, U.S. sales and marketing manager for KOEI Corp., which will debut *Pop Cutie! Street Fashion Simulation* for the Nintendo DS in September.

The game, the first to tackle street fashion in the U.S., is based on a Japanese game called "That's QT." It's a homage to the audacious street style of Tokyo and Harajuku—the costumey Japanese maid and Goth Lolita looks that are popping up more and more. Players start the game as small-time designers with a tiny shop at a flea market. As they excel at running their shop, they move on to bigger boutiques, where they buy and design their own clothes and do battle against other shop owners. This is no Barbie fashion show—battles are judged on who's styled the coolest, most out-there Gothic Lolita, emo or glam style ensemble.

"You can create more conventional fashions in the game," said Sikat, "but the entertainment really gets punched up when you can create a pink cat costume." A little more this-world, Ubisoft Entertainment recently introduced two fashion games for the DS system. In *Fashion Designer,* players design clothes, choosing swatches of fabric and sample silhouettes. And in the newer *My Fashion Studio,* gamers are judged on tailoring time, fashion choices and accuracy as they create their own clothing collection, then customize models for the runway or a photo shoot.

In Sims 2, players can take their avatars shopping at a virtual H&M, plucking looks from the current season that are also available in the stores (dress like your character!), and stage runway shows where they pick the models, clothes and music.

In this virtual fashion show, models strut down the runway wearing cool half-smiles and, say, a floor-length H&M floral maxi dress with a plunging neckline. The avatar's stride is inhumanly fluid, long arms and legs swishing past each other with Rolex precision. At the end of the catwalk, she thrusts out a single hip, then swirls around and cheekily blows the audience a kiss. The turn could rival Kate Moss or Agyness Deyn for sheer sass.

Fornillos, the winner of last year's contest, managed to dress his avatar in something that walked straight into the real world.

"Judges were looking for a balance between creative design and commerciality," says Steve Lubomski, U.S. advertising director for H&M. "We wanted to be certain the garment would fit into our collection and would be something our customers would embrace and want to wear."

But forget H&M. What about Proenza Schouler? So far, most big-name designers have ignored gaming. The exception (and isn't he always?) is Lagerfeld, a 74-year-old early adopter who is so tech-happy he has several iPods and a designated assistant to carry them. The Chanel designer appears as a radio DJ in *Grand Theft Auto IV,* Rockstar Games' latest frenetic car chase game.

Still, the industry is showing signs of developing good taste. Nintendo, which offers the popular DS and Wii platforms, just debuted a style-y metallic rose-colored DS model, which tweens are blinging out with glued-on rhinestones and tassels. And new commercials for the DS feature Nicole Kidman playing Rock, Paper, Scissors, Liv Tyler tapping on virtual piano keys, and America Ferrera engrossed in the New Super Mario Bros.

In tech years, it's been a long time coming. Fashion's flirtation with virtual worlds started when gaming was still a boys' club: ballers in the basketball game *NBA 2K6* wore Nikes, Reebok branded on billboards and soccer balls in *Pro Evolution Soccer 6* and Tony Hawk is still clad in the latest Quiksilver looks in his Activision skateboarding games.

Then came *Second Life* in 2003, an online universe where users shopped at big-name stores such as American Apparel, Reebok, and Adidas as part of a virtual life they created. Less a game than a trippy pastime, and shopping is one of the major activities.

Fine. But they're selling T-shirts and sneakers, not Marchesa and Missoni.

And how thrilling would it be to dress in all that expensive stuff and not have to pay for it? There's a game we might really give up shopping for.

Source: *Los Angeles Times,* Sunday, June 29, 2008. Home Edition; Image, Part P, pg. 4, Features Desk.

Chapter 8

Trimmings and Finishing Touches

A designer can turn a plain 4–6x dress into a princess's ball gown by using some pretty trimming. A sweatshirt can be transformed by a hip designer into a must-have fall accessory for most teen girls in America. Both garments just needed an inspired choice of trimmings to take the basic and make it outstanding. Trims give garments personality. A garment can be made more feminine with the addition of lace. It can be made more tailored with **saddle stitching**. The choice of trim can run the gamut from glamorous to whimsical and all the designer has to do is pick according to the mood she is trying to achieve.

There are two ways a designer can approach using trim elements on garments. The first is to design with the trim in mind and have the body of the garment act as the display for a special embellishment that will catch the shopper's eye. When this strategy is used, the fabric and silhouette are underplayed, and the trim competes against other garments that are similarly decorated. In the junior and girls' markets, trimmings go in and out of style as quickly as silhouettes and hot fabrics do, so timing is crucial.

The second strategy is for designers to use the trim as decoration once the fabric and silhouette are determined. This is one of the most creative steps in designing garments for girls and juniors. Selecting the trim that finishes the new sample garment is a challenging task. Special trimmings on little girls' dresses or junior tops are like the icing on the cake. The garment is good, but like the cake, it is even better with the perfect frosting. Sometimes a garment comes out of the sample room, and the designer can see that it has potential but is just missing a little something. Often that little something is the perfect button or an exceptional appliqué. The designer who can identify the need for that extra something and can then pick a perfect accent trim is an asset to any manufacturing company.

The endless supply of trimmings and treatments need to be researched the same way a designer would investigate the fabric market. There is an abundant selection of trims, closures, and specialty treatments. Shopping

FIG. 8.1. KAY HERZ DEVELOPS TRIMS AND IMPORTS THEM FROM CHINA TO SELL TO CALIFORNIA DESIGNERS. HERE SHE IS SHOWING THE LINE TO CREATIVE DIRECTOR KATIE DELAHANTY. NOTICE THE VARIED CHOICES AVAILABLE.

the trim market frequently is essential when designing for the girls' and junior market. (See Figure 8.1.)

When a specific trim is the "hook" on checkout garments, it is important for designers in girls' and junior clothing to know where to shop for the trim, how to apply it, how much to pay for it, and when they can get it in house. By knowing what trims are popular and available, designers can have an edge over the competition especially when prices and delivery issues on popular trims create production problems. Some large companies have sourcing personnel who can assist the design staff when necessary. It is ultimately the designer who needs to stay up on trends. Looking at all the trim possibilities can inspire new ideas, too. (See Figure 8.2.)

TRIM REQUIREMENTS

Whenever trim is added to garments, several things have to be considered beyond the question of whether or not the trim is attractive. The trim must be safe, comfortable, durable as necessary, compatible with the design and fabric, and easily available or scheduled for production. Cost must always be considered.

Safety

First and foremost in little girls' wear, the trim must be age appropriate and safe. Small detachable items should never be used in the 4–6x range. A large three-year-old girl wearing a size 5 may not know that it is not a good idea to chew on her sleeve, especially when the buttons on it are shaped like ice cream cones. In little girls' wear, trims, such as bows or artificial flowers, should never be secured with safety pins. Drawstrings around hoods need to be attached in such a way that the child is unable to choke on the rope ends. The rule of thumb for safety issues is this: don't take any chances. Young children can manage to do some very creative things that can be harmful.

Apparel made for children is monitored to make sure some safety standards are upheld. Flammability issues are more of a concern for sleepwear than they are for regular apparel, although Halloween costumes also come under scrutiny. With so much of the apparel being imported, the task of policing has become enormous. The Consumer Product Safety Commission (CPSC), a division of the Federal Trade Commission (FTC), is the government agency that establishes and enforces safety regulations for children's apparel.

Comfort Issues

Whether a trim is comfortable or not is just common sense. Bulky, protruding buttons on the back closing of a top or dress would be uncomfortable to lean back against. Flat buttons make more sense. Lace that stands up around a neckline shouldn't be scratchy against the skin. Trim placement needs to be considered and adjustments made in order to rectify any discom-

fort caused by the trim and its attachment. Just as labels sewn into the neckline can scratch, so can the appliqués, artificial flowers, and bows when they are stitched on carelessly.

Compatible Care Issues

After safety, which is not typically a hindrance in the 7–14 or junior ranges, trim compatibility with the fabric and the garment use is the big issue. Whatever the wash instructions are for the garment, the trim should conform to that standard. It would not be prudent to put leather buttons on a girls' sweatshirt that will be thrown into the laundry after each use. Silk lace that needs dry-cleaning would not be the best choice for washable T-shirts. Sometimes the trim is the selling feature for the garment, for example **glitter screen printing**, where the glitter is only guaranteed for 12 washings. In this case, the trim sets the standard for the washability of the garment, and the fabric should be able to support more than the proposed trim tolerance.

Compatible Design Issues

Anytime design preferences are discussed, there is a certainty for legitimate creative disagreement. Since rules are simply guidelines to be stretched by the designer for creative license, the starting point for applying trims to garments has to be very general. A few things to consider are: scale of the trim both in size and actual weight; the affect the trim application has on the fabric; and the personality of the trim versus the character of the garment.

The easiest way to understand the scale of the trim is by visualization. If the pocket that needs an **appliqué** is 4 inches by 6 inches then a ½-inch flower appliqué will seem lost. A 3-inch-by-3-inch appliqué might seem overpowering on the same pocket. The question the designer needs to ask is if the flower should have that much impact. Does it look out of scale or make too strong a statement? If the answer is yes, it is overpowering, use a smaller appliqué. Two inches by two inches might be perfect. The choice of trim needs to stay within the designer's range of impact on the garment, or it could create a distraction from other assets. For example, a size 5 girl's woolen dress could have wonderful princess lines that turn into inverted pleats at the hips. Putting a small rosette at that junction could call attention to the seaming. Putting a large artificial rose in the same spot would ruin the clean lines. Another alternative for the designer could be to put the artificial rose at the neck, calling attention to a Peter Pan collar. In this case, the seaming and pleats would show themselves off, and the rose would accent the neck. The designer must decide if the trim is only a contributing factor to the overall design of the garment or if the garment is simply a stage for showing off the trim.

The same considerations can be discussed with buttons that are too large, too small, or unremarkable. Trims have actual weight, so their size can be an additional problem. If a designer has chosen a very large button for the closure on a jacket, the fabric must be able to support the weight of the button. A thin jersey will droop under the weight of a big button. So the size and weight of the trim must be considered when evaluating how it will interact with the fabric of the garment.

Putting a trim technique on the wrong fabric can cause production problems, too. If a designer has selected quilting as the perfect treatment for a group of knits and the multineedle-work causes runs in the knit, the group will have to be scratched. In this case, the fabric is not compatible with the technique being applied to it. If a garment is designed to have pleating and the designer chooses cotton, the pleats will be temporary. Paying for permanent pleating that doesn't last will be a waste of money. Had the designer chosen a polyester/cotton blend it would have been a more appropriate fabric selection. These are the types of complications that designers need to address before selecting a trim.

Trim should also mimic the mood of the group that the designer is creating. If a designer is working on a dressy dress group in pastels for Easter and needs a trim to edge the bottom of the skirts, then SpongeBob faces on grosgrain is not the best choice. Conversational trims should be used with good judgment. Trends can be overplayed, or they can be played for the wrong target audience on the wrong occasion. A pretty eyelet or fancy brocade ribbon would be a better choice for this garment.

Trim can be used as a nice surprise when it is the opposite of what one might expect to see on the garment. If a designer is working on a group of sporty plaid jackets, jumpers, and skirts, the white blouses to coordinate into the group need some sort of trim in the princess seaming to make them stand out. Two choices present themselves. By applying cording in a color that coordinates with the plaid in the princess seams,

the designer would be making an expected choice. Using a fancy eyelet edging shirred into the seam would be a surprising choice. The eyelet edging is feminine, and the group is sporty. The season is fall and the eyelet screams spring. The contrast between the expected and the chosen trim can be just the right touch to soften the group and make it unusual enough to please the buyers and ultimately the consumer.

Production Issues with Trimmed Garments

Adding trim to a garment can add several steps to the production cycle. A designer must be aware of what additional work and expense are created and whether the chosen trim merits that investment. There are two different approaches to trim for the production of clothes. There is a trim that is simply added or attached as the garment is being constructed. The easiest form of this would be a fancy button that is attached by machine, or if it is very unique, sewn on by hand. The production department only has to worry about whether they can get the unique buttons quickly enough to fit into the production schedule. Another example of this type of trim adornment would be setting eyelet edging into a seam. There is the investment of time to order and receive the eyelet yardage, the expense of adding the eyelet to the garment, and the cost of the labor for inserting the eyelet into the seam correctly. Trims that are added into the production cycle without outside contracting steps are easy to incorporate into a line.

The other method of trimming a garment is much more complicated. When an embellishment is a process, like **screen printing** a pant leg, the production of the garment is divided into several stages. First the garment has to be cut. Then, instead of being bundled with all the pieces together as would normally happen, the portions of the garment that are treated must be separated. Usually the separated pieces go to an outside contracting specialist (for this example the screen printer), for that application to be added. Once the screen print is dried, the garment is bundled once again and put through the rest of the construction process. This entire trim process is called a **send out** stage because the garment must be sent out for some part of its production cycle. Unless a manufacturer is using its own factory, that is well stocked with incredible multineedle equipment and screen printing facilities, specialty treatments must be handled as send outs to contractors who specialize in apparel embellishment.

Send out processes can also be handled by sending out rolls of fabric, with the embellishment or treatment done to the entire roll. An example of this would be quilting. The fabric is quilted and then returned to the cutting room. The pattern pieces that are supposed to be quilted are made into a separate marker and cut from the quilted goods. The rest of the garment is cut regularly, and the two fabrics are bundled together. This method can be used on pleating, quilting, **tucking**, **trapunto**, and any other treatments that cover the entire surface of the fabric.

It is easy to see why the extra send out stage can cause problems with a production schedule. Bundles can be lost or mixed up. Delays, unfortunately, are routine. Some of the strain on the production department with send out trimmings is made easier by working with offshore facilities that are trying to incorporate many embellishment treatments and machinery into their state-of-the-art factories.

Send out processes may include screen printing, pleating, beading, quilting, tucking, embroidery, and denim treatments like **distressing**, and **stonewashing**. If it is difficult to do an embellishment process in the normal assembly line sewing, the production manager will find the most cost-effective method to achieve the designer's intent. Designers, however, must be aware of the monetary affect their chosen trim has on the bottom line.

TRIM PURPOSE

All trimming added to a garment has a purpose. The most obvious and frequent purpose is to decorate. Adding some adornment can improve a plain garment and give it some pizzazz. Some trim, however, is useful, like closures on a blouse. Buttons, zippers, or snaps enable the garment to fit and stay secured to the body. Designers can also use trim to call attention to some part of the garment, for example an appliqué on a pocket. Contrast double-stitching will accent side seams on a pant. Trims can make a garment warmer, like quilting, or sturdier, like binding around an armhole. A certain trim can set a garment apart and enhance its salability. If the designer analyzes the job the trim is meant to perform, it becomes easier to make the right selection. (See Figure 8.3a.)

TRIM CATEGORIES

The trimmings used in girls' and junior clothing can be divided into five categories for our design purposes. The first category includes closures. This group encompasses buttons, snaps, zippers, and lacing. The second category includes trims that are set into seams or applied to seams. The third group includes general assorted trims that simply adorn a garment like bows, appliqués, and artificial flowers. The fourth category includes specific treatments that are used on denim, primarily for jeans. The final category includes specialty treatments that are applied to parts, or a finished garment, by an outside contractor. These trims include such design features as quilting, screen printing, **airbrushing**, **embroidery**, and pleating.

Closures

Unless a garment is a stretch knit that is just pulled over the head, or a poncho that is merely thrown on, some type of opening to comfortably access the garment is needed. Buttons, snaps, Velcro, hooks with eyes, **frogs**, and zippers are the most commonly used closures. All of these methods to secure garments can be insignificant to the garment's design. Many times the designer chooses one over another because it is the least noticeable. An invisible zipper in the back or side of a dress can nearly disappear from view and blend with the design of the dress without interfering with the structure or drape of the material. Sometimes, however, interesting closures can steal the attention from other garment features. (See Figure 8.3b.)

FIG. 8.3a, b. (a) Top. EYELETS AND LACING SHOWN AS A TREND MAY START WITH ACCESSORIES AND THEN SPREAD FROM DESIGNER CLOTHING TO JUNIORS AND GIRLS' APPAREL. (b) Right. MANY VARIED CLOSURES CAN BE INCORPORATED INTO DESIGN DETAILS THAT ARE FUNCTIONAL BUT CAN ALSO DECORATE A GARMENT.

Buttons come in vast assortments of shapes, sizes, colors, and materials. Unusual buttons, like **toggles**, or oversized shell buttons, can turn a plain jacket into something unique. Self-fabric covered buttons are another nice design detail that gives flair to a garment. Buttons can be dyed to match any color, but they often have the biggest effect when they are in contrasting color to the fabric used in a garment. Using different colored buttons down the front of a blouse is a creative way to make a basic item seem more interesting. It is the norm for a design room to have a large selection of buttons on hand. Designers can invite button venders to bring their samples to review periodically in order to stay abreast of the new choices each season. For the 4–6x girls' size range, novelty buttons are often used. Little flowers, bows, and other fun buttons can add a whimsical touch to a top or dress. Manufacturers purchase buttons by the gross, 144 pieces, and the costs can be minimal, from less than one cent, to extravagant. Most buttons come in a range of sizes and they are priced accordingly.

Zippers can be used as design elements. The teeth and ribbon of zippers can be made to contrast or match fabrics. The attachment can be done inside out so that the ribbon of the zipper becomes a stripe feature. Zippers can be used as decoration when placed on the top of seams or on the top of pockets. Out-of-scale zippers can also be used effectively. Contrasting color separator zippers are a popular sportswear trim.

Snaps come in an array of bright colors and shapes including feminine, dainty, **pearlized** snaps and big, industrial snaps. Using an industrial snap can give a garment a tailored influence. Snaps are often included in button vendor's lines, but they can also be a contractor's send out phase of construction. Production issues with snaps need to be discussed with the production department because snaps require more time to attach than buttons and buttonholes.

Velcro is useful as a decorative closure on sportswear. The fabric needs to have a fairly substantial weight in order to be compatible with the tugging necessary to separate the two sides.

Hooks and eyes are normally used when a hidden closure is desired. Sometimes, however, hooks and eyes are a trim feature in junior tops. When corseting looks are hot, hooks and eyes sold on tape that was sewn in strips into the garment can make a garment look authentic. The tapes that hooks and eyes are attached to can also be dyed to match any fabric color.

Lacing with either cord or spaghetti made from fabric is another closure technique to consider using for an interesting design element. Periodically, lacing is used for neckline openings in junior tops. When peasant tops or dresses are in style, lacing is used at necklines, at the waist, and even on sleeve treatments. In the girls' market lacing is utilized as a treatment in the front of dresses for Tyrolean and peasant dresses and tops but it is usually a decorative feature not a functional one because the garment is too difficult to get into and out of.

Whenever an Asian influence is strong in the marketplace, frogs made from shiny cordage or purchased as appliqués create an instant Oriental imprint. The knots that accompany frogs are difficult to work, so this trim must be used sparingly in the 4–6x range. However, if juniors are wearing them, 7–14 girls will copy the look.

Seam Decorations

Sometimes a seam needs emphasis. For example, a junior princess line dress in a pale shade of gray looks dowdy on the hanger. The wool is brushed just enough to obscure the definition of the seam. If the designer has cording sewn into that seam, even in the same shade of gray, the seam will be defined and stand out, giving the garment a more structured appearance. If the designer uses deep red and trims the neck or pockets in that same red, a totally new personality pops from the dress. In this case, the trim is just making the seam lines come alive.

The choices for this type of enhancement are endless. (See Figure 8.4.) Cording and piping, where bias fabric in self or contrasting fabric, or satin rope cord, is inserted into the seam, are

FIG. 8.4. THERE ARE
MANY CREATIVE
WAYS TO EMBELLISH
GIRLS' APPAREL WITH
TRIMMINGS.

used with regularity on girls' and junior sports-wear lines. Edging laces can be used on top or set into seams. Cording in several sizes is available. Soutache, although difficult to apply when narrow, can have an interesting effect. Rickrack can be inserted by half into the seam or attached on top. Embroidered ribbons and bands, hemp edgings, and braids can also be used in this same fashion. **Fagoting**, a trim with slots to insert ribbon, can be sewn between the seams or atop the seam with or without the inserted ribbon.

Seam finishes can be used to add emphasis to the seam lines. Double stitching in self-color or contrast, often seen on jeans, can be enough trim to make a plain garment sell. Other fancier stitching, like zigzags, can also be done. Seam binding is a way to call attention to the lines of a garment. French seams, flat-fell seams, and raveling the seams are other ways to make an interesting finish on a garment. Contrast color saddle stitching (coarser thread in big stitches), used as decoration along an edge like a lapel, can make a plain blazer look expensive and sophisticated.

Fringe can be set on top of seams or into the seams. Types of fringe vary. Flapper satin fringe comes and goes out of style in the junior market, as does cowboy fringe. When either fringe is in style in the junior market garments trimmed in fringe will also sell well in the girls' 4–6x and 7–14 ranges. Western-styled clothing is cyclical in these markets, but fringe is a mainstay when the cowgirl look is hot.

Ruffles, made from fabric, eyelet, or lace and set into seams, are common in the girls' market. Juniors use this design technique also, but only when it is a stylish influence in the marketplace. The girls' dress market employs ruffles of some sort constantly. This softens silhouettes and makes a more feminine appearance than just a plain seam. Eyelets, particularly in spring and summer lines, and lace for holiday, can often be seen as a trim for 4–6x garments. The older girls will have lace trim on fancy dresses but not on their school clothes, unless trims are popular in the junior market. Circular flounces, those made from fabric cut in circular shapes, appear in the junior market around necks and hemlines, or cascading down a seam on the bodice. Sleeve

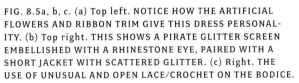

FIG. 8.5a, b, c. (a) Top left. NOTICE HOW THE ARTIFICIAL FLOWERS AND RIBBON TRIM GIVE THIS DRESS PERSONALITY. (b) Top right. THIS SHOWS A PIRATE GLITTER SCREEN EMBELLISHED WITH A RHINESTONE EYE, PAIRED WITH A SHORT JACKET WITH SCATTERED GLITTER. (c) Right. THE USE OF UNUSUAL AND OPEN LACE/CROCHET ON THE BODICE.

treatments with circular flounces are also common.

Simple Adornments

The trimmings vendors have such an array of appliqués that looking through the sample books can take hours. (See Figures 8.5a, 8.5b, and 8.5c.)

An appliqué is material that is cut out and sewn with a backing so it can be attached as an ornament on apparel. Most of the time appliqués are embroidered into some sort of object like a flower and backed with a synthetic facing. There are pretty flowers, funny lions, and silly faces among an assortment of fabulous, horrible, and odd machine-made appliqués that are sewn or ironed on to fabric. There are appliqués that are small and dainty like a tiny butterfly,

FIG. 8.6. THE LITTLE ALLIGATOR LOGO GIVES THIS LACOSTE PLEATED SKIRT A BIT OF CLASS AND IDENTIFIES THE BRAND NAME.

FIG. 8.7 THIS LITTLE GIRL MODELS A SIMPLE DRESS WITH PIPING TRIM. ALL THE OTHER DRESSES ARE MADE FROM THAT SAME PATTERN WITH VERY SMALL ALTERATIONS BUT THEY LOOK LIKE ENTIRELY DIFFERENT STYLES BECAUSE OF CLEVER USE OF ASSORTED TRIMS. TRIMMINGS ARE LIKE THE ICING ON A CAKE.

and large ones like the numbers on a letterman's jacket. When appliqués are popular in juniors, they sell exceptionally well in the girls' market. The little girls' 4–6x range uses cutesy appliqués sparingly because they are used frequently in the toddler area, unless a trend for **licensee** appliqués is currently popular with a particular cartoon character. When a special character, like Ariel, or Dora the Explorer, is popular with girls, those appliqués are reliable sellers.

Artificial flowers go in and out of style, but they have a niche on girls' fancy dresses either on the waist or at the neck. Juniors tend to use self-fabric flowers and artificial flowers only on prom dresses until these hit the market as a fad.

Bows, made from fabric or from ribbon, fall into the same use as artificial flowers. Girls' fancy dresses are often styled with tie-back bows. Tie-back bows used on dresses are not usually considered trim unless they are made from wide ribbons. Trim salespersons carry an assortment of small bows that can be sampled in satin, grosgrain, and embroidered braids. Interesting design elements can be fashioned from multistrands of narrow ribbon and bows.

Labels and **logos** are used as trims. The obvious example of this is the Ralph Lauren polo horse that has been an American icon for many years. Recently, that little polo horse has greatly enlarged on the front of polo shirts. Using labels and logos in creative ways to advertise brand lines, invoke brand demand, and embellish tailored clothing can be seen all across the apparel market from men's to infant clothing. Screen printing of neck labels for comfort has also inspired the inside-out screen printing of logos as decoration. (See Figure 8.6.)

Pockets and collars are not normally considered to be trim but are simply part of the design of the garment. However, there are so many trim choices that can be applied as both collars and pockets, they deserve mentioning. In the resource trim books showing lace and appliqués, there are many selections of lace collars and lace pockets that are finished around all the edges and need only to be stitched on the garment to embellish a basic pant or T-shirt.

Knit pockets and collars can be found in trim books also. These can be ordered in any number of stripes, knitted patterns, and sizes. The knit trim companies also offer braiding that will coordinate to have matching waistbands and cuffs. Lace, eyelet, and novelty ribbons can also be used as collars, cuffs, and pockets. (See Figure 8.7.)

JEAN TREATMENTS

Junior departments rely on the strength of denim, especially jeans, but also skirts and jackets, for a large percentage of their sales. When there is a hot treatment on junior denim, it is likely that something similar will be tried in the girls' market as well. Jeans have been embellished in some way ever since hippies hand-painted, fringed, bejeweled, appliquéd, and **tie-dyed** their bell-bottom jeans in the late 1960s and early 1970s. Even when jeans are in a cycle

of basic appearance, designers add flair with their line's special label or pocket stitching. The different creative ways to give jeans alternative design details is an innovative category of garment design. (See Figures 8.8a, 8.8b, and 8.8c.)

FIG. 8.8a, b, c. (a) Above. DENIM EMBELLISHMENTS INCLUDE FANCY EMBROIDERIES OF WORDING AND SYMBOLS. (b) Right. THE DESIGNER HERE IS PUTTING GLITTER ON DENIM APPLIQUES. (c) Far right. SOMETIMES THE EMBELLISHMENT IS REPEATED FROM THE TOP TO THE JEAN FOR A COMPLETE OUTFIT.

There are sophisticated contracting companies that have an assortment of methods for distressing denim fabric. Stonewash, where the denim is tumbled with actual rocks, was the first major successful commercial treatment of denim. Since that time, denim has been bleached, torn, raveled, wrinkled, crimped, and acid-washed. High-end designer jeans companies and junior jean companies find creative ways to make their jeans either look differently or fit differently than the competition every season. Stretch denim is now engineered in jeans to hold some parts of the body in and up for individual body enhancement, but in girls' wear and junior denim, the stretch denim goes in and out of favor seasonally, and the stretch is used in the pants uniformly rather than for enhancement. Designer denim jeans have been specifically dyed in deeper colors in strategically located spots in order to give the appearance of slimmer thighs and give the illusion that the leg is longer, or the hips are slimmer. This effect has been emulated in junior jeans. Chemical treatments used with heat can give jeans a variety of different appearances. Girls' jeans follow in the footsteps of the junior market, and they especially follow when a particular fad is hot. Just as juniors can purchase any number of dark blue jeans or pale blue distressed jeans, the girls market will offer similar choices.

In addition to changing the color of denim and the hand of the fabric through various different processes, jeans are often embellished with trim components. Screen printing is used for decoration both in plain paint and in glitter. Character licensee companies often screen print characters down the leg of a girl's 4–6x denim pant or on the pockets. If juniors are decorating with screen printing successfully, the 7–14 market will follow.

Airbrushing denim goes in and out of favor in the same way that other forms of decoration like nail heads, rhinestones, and appliqués do. Embroidery is a popular trim in denim in all size ranges. Quilting, especially pockets, comes in and out of style cyclically.

Seam stitching on denim is usually the sturdy, flat-felled finish with the traditional golden orange contrast thread topstitching, but on occasion eyelet or lace will be inserted into the seams for girls' 4–6x pants. Cording is also used as a seam enhancement. Seams are also raveled, saddle stitched, and fringed.

SPECIALTY EMBELLISHMENT TREATMENTS

Designers who create the designs for apparel in the girls' and junior markets have the luxury of using an endless assortment of special treatments on their garments. In the junior market, a designer who stays abreast of the entire fashion scene can anticipate teenagers' tastes and use trim to offer individuality on basic garments. All teens wear jeans, hoodies, T-shirts, and sweats. Taking these basic bodies and having them reflect the mood of the consumer with specialty treatments is one of the most successful approaches to designing for juniors and girls. The 7–14 girls' market will want to copy the junior hot decorative trims, and those designers who work in this range just need to make sure the trim is age appropriate and priced correctly for the target market.

Any time special embellishments are going to be used when designing a line, the designer must plan ahead to allow for the time it takes to send the sample fabric out and get it back with the new treatment. Contractors will return samples with pricing so that the design staff can make sure to get the proper information onto the cost sheet. Designers must allow for the garment to be cut out. The parts that are to be embellished need to be separated from the bundles and sent out to the contractor. The remaining bundles are usually set aside, and all the construction takes place once the trimming process is complete. Garments that have embellishment that is done by the yard, like quilting, are cut after the quilting is completed.

The embellishments that are most commonly used in girls' and junior apparel are embroidery, screen printing, pleating, quilting, pin tucking, scallop edges, smocking, and adorn-

FIG. 8.9. Left. THESE THREE TWEENS WEAR CLOTHING EMBELLISHED WITH DIFFERENT TRIMS. ALL HAVE A MOCK VEST SEWN INTO THE GARMENTS. NOTICE THE PLEATED SKIRT, CHAINS, APPLIQUÉS, BUTTONS, AND BOWS.

FIG. 8.10. Above. THIS TWEEN WEARS A BRAND NAME SCREEN-PRINTED T-SHIRT WITH A PLEATED SKIRT. TWO SIMPLE GARMENTS THAT MAKE A FASHION STATEMENT TOGETHER.

ments like sequins, beads, rhinestones, and nail heads. (See Figure 8.9.)

Screen Printing and Airbrushing

Screen printing is a printing process where each color to be applied in a design has a screen cut with particular shapes to allow the paint to show just where that color is designated on the image. Each color requires a separate screen, and the process is priced according to how many colored screens are cut and applied. The application of screen printing is commonly used on all types of casual garments, but particularly on basic knit shirts in logos, wording, and pictures. With use of different paints, the look can be shiny, matte, or rubbery. This process should not be confused with another type of painting on garments called airbrushing, where paint is misted out of an air hose by an artist who paints a picture with various colors of paint in separate applications. Screen printing is a more exacting production process that is faster and easier to control. Screen printing can be done rapidly. Airbrushing requires each garment to be done one at a time. Girls' boutique clothing shops often carry airbrushed decorated garments for little girls and infants. (See Figure 8.10.)

Licensee screen printing is a large category of the girls' apparel business. Apparel companies pay from 8 to 14 percent for the rights to use cartoon characters, movie scenes, or current pop stars' images on their clothing. There are corporations like Jerry Leigh of California, that are so proficient in screen printing for licensee properties, and have been for so many years, that companies like Disney prefer they handle movie, television, and cartoon characters. Jerry Leigh of California is ideal for major quantities of screened garments because it has its own factories and quality engineers from the licensing firms strictly audit all production facilities to make sure there are no labor abuses.

Designing for licensee merchandise requires the normal apparel design talents and strong computer skills, graphic art talent, and attention to detail. For example, the design work for some licensee characters is carefully worked out between the designers at Jerry Leigh and the Disney graphic department designers. All design work is done on computers. The colors are painstakingly matched to Disney standards, and are rigidly controlled. For instance, Cinderella is still a fantastic character that sells well, and only one blue hue is ever used for her dress. Among the many other licensee rights at Jerry Leigh of California are the Jonas Brothers, *High School Musical,* major league football teams, Hannah Montana, Miley Cyrus, and Avril Lavigne's new line Abbey Dawn, among others.

Designers who work with celebrities who style their own lines have to deal with celebrity oversight just as they have to deal with character oversight issues when they put a line together. They have the usual design challenges of finding the perfect style, fabric, and price, and they deal with the celebrity's strong personal taste preferences and style involvement. Jerry Leigh of California handles the Gwen Stefani upstairs line, Harajuku Lovers, and the Abbey Dawn line by Avril Lavigne. Both celebrities have strong opinions about their clothing and are closely involved in all designs. Gwen Stefani and her designers shop in Paris, Tokyo, and other fashion-forward cities to make sure the Gwen Stefani line is avant-garde. Avril Lavigne's trendy personal fashion knack for combining interesting colors and styles from her own wardrobe are emulated exactly in her young junior line. Both lines have been successful in different markets, and both lines combine some screen printing with current fashion trends.

Designers who work on lines where licensee properties are the selling feature have some specific guidelines. There are color restrictions, theme restrictions, and size issues to maintain the integrity of the property. The contracts may be written by size range, and entirely different screens could be cut for the different ages. All designs must be approved by the licensing art department before the line is shown and again before it is shipped. All aspects of the garment must be approved including color, sewing quality, character pose, and wording. This is an exacting design challenge, and attention to detail is essential from design all the way through production.

Licensee designing is such big business that usually only specialty apparel companies even attempt to break into this slice of the fashion pie. When licensee screens, for example Mickey Mouse, are selling well in girls' apparel, screened garments that do not have the hot character will sell well, too. Other cartoon screens will sell because of competitive pricing. This selling boost may be because simple cartoon graphics, for example a cute pink flamingo instead of Tweety, are at least 10 percent cheaper than licensee characters are.

The garment industry knocks off garments from different inspirations, but a word of caution: don't ever knock off a licensee screen print. Apparel companies that pay dearly for the right to use a character, name, or image prosecute all copyright infringements. If Tinker Bell is selling well and a designer wants to put a fairy on the front of a T-shirt, that fairy must look entirely different.

Pleating and Tucking
Pleating is simply folding the fabric. Notches can indicate to a seamstress where to fold and the pleating can be done as the garment is sewn in regular step-by-step fashion. This method of pleating is generally just soft pleating, and it is not expected to stay crisp after the garment is worn. Soft pleating needs to be repressed after each laundering. This simple pleating is done in the regular assembly of the garment, and it is figured into the labor cost rather than as a special send out operation.

Pleating as a specialty treatment is done with the application of heat and sometimes stitching to hold the pleats permanently. The pleats for garments in the junior and girls' markets are usually done on synthetic fabrics and set with heat so that they are permanent. School uniform skirts are a perfect example of this process.

Fabric can be pleated by the yard and then cut according to pattern pieces or done per skirt panel or other cut section. There are many different kinds and sizes of pleats. The biggest difference between them is the angle of the pleat. Some pleats are the same measurement at the top as on the bottom. By contrast, an accordion pleat is narrow at the top and flared out at the bottom. This flare causes the fabric to stand away from the body if done in a skirt. A box pleat or an inverted pleat would cause the fabric to fall straight from the waist. Generally, uniform skirts for girls are done with simple inverted pleats. Stitched-down pleats are simply pleats that are stitched at the edge of the folds to hold each pleat flat. (See Figure 8.11.)

Tucking is also folding the fabric, into small rows, then pressing firmly to hold them in place. The size of the folds is left to the designer to choose. Pin tucks are the really small tucks that have very narrow rows of stitching. Often tucking is done with row after row of stitching of various lengths. In this case, when the tucking stops, the fabric is freed to be full again. This type of tucking must be done from cut fabric pieces. Most tucking is done from an entire roll of fabric and then cut into the individual pattern pieces as designated by the garment design.

Embroidery and Embossing

Embroidery is fancy needlework that makes images in thread on the surface of fabric for decoration. Schiffli-machinery stitching offers a vast range of color, texture, and virtually any image that a designer can imagine. Embroidery used on girls' and junior clothing can range from small floral touches on a collar to a flying horse spanning the leg of a jean. Logos are often embroidered. Garment line names are sometimes

FIG. 8.11. THESE THREE TEENS WEAR PLEATED SKIRTS, BUT EACH SKIRT HAS A DIFFERENT APPEAL. ONE HAS RAVELED SHORTENED PLEATS, ANOTHER AN INVERTED PLEAT, AND THE LAST CHECK SKIRT IS MUCH MORE TAILORED.

embroidered on pockets. Computerized Schiffli embroidery machines have brought the prices down on this embellishment method, so that it is no longer an expensive or tedious process. Hand embroidery is rarely done in the girls' and junior markets.

Embossing is a process of using heat to create a motif that rises up from the surface of the fabric. If this process is used on a pile surface, the opposite happens, and the motif is imprinted by heat into that fabric. This treatment is used particularly well on fleece.

Quilting

Quilting is a technique that sandwiches a few layers of fabric together, and stitches the layers

FIG. 8.12. Above. THE QUILTING NEEDLE IS PROGRAMMED WITH A PATTERN, AND THEN IT STITCHES THROUGH THE TOP FABRIC, THE BATTING UNDERNEATH, AND THE LINING.

together in an allover pattern. The most common kind of quilting is one that has batting stuck between the garment fabric and lining, and it is stitched in a chicken wire, or square pattern across the goods. Quilting is done across the entire roll of fabric, and the individual pattern pieces that require the quilted surface are cut. Pockets, lapels, and yokes are the usual pieces that are quilted as trim in the junior area. In girls' wear, quilting is also used as a treatment on the bodice of fancy dresses for holiday lines. (See Figure 8.12.)

Trapunto is a special type of quilting that is done with straight-line stitching. When padding is sandwiched between, as in regular quilting, the parallel lines form attractive ridges. This is used more often in the junior market when Asian influences are popular.

Smocking

Smocking is fancy needlework that pulls fabric together, sometimes with elastic threads, and secures it with stitching. The stitching shows in a crisscross pattern, which can be in vivid thread colors that contrast with the fabric color. Multicolored thread is also fun to use. (See Figure 8.13.) Anytime baby doll looks are in style in

the junior market, smocking treatments will be used. Smocking is overused in the toddler and infant market, so 4–6x and 7–14 range girls shy away from this look, unless it is on fire in the junior area. When peasant looks are in style, particularly those from Central and South America, smocking treatments have done especially well in the junior and 7–14 range.

Scalloped Edges

Fabric edges can be cut into scalloped, or pointed, edges and finished with an embroidery stitch edging. The most common use of this application of a specialty trim process is on the hem of a girls' dressy dress, or a lapel on a junior blazer. Scalloped edges soften a tailored garment and make it more feminine. Although scalloped edges are a staple in the bridal mar-

FIG. 8.13. Below. SMOCKING WITH ELASTIC THREAD IS USED HERE IN A SUNDRESS FOR A COMFORTABLE AND ADJUSTABLE FIT THAT EXPANDS WITH SIZE AND MOVEMENT.

ket for flower girl frocks, it is not a treatment that is overused in the regular girls' and junior markets. This finish also works well on neckline fronts in the junior T-shirt market.

Sequins, Beads, Rhinestones, and Nail Heads

When holiday seasons are glitzy, and gold and silver touches are in style, beads, sequins, rhinestones, and even nail heads seem to come into play. All of these embellishments have decorated T-shirts, jeans, jackets, tops, and dresses in the junior and girls' markets. Sometimes these embellishments are added on top of glitter and screen printing. The method of adhering the beads and sequins may vary from embroidery stitching to glue processes. Nail heads and rhinestones are generally set with metal prongs. (See Figure 8.14.)

TRIMMINGS AS DESIGNER SIGNATURE

The sketching and fabricating of a design to be made into a garment is only the preliminary stage of that garment's journey to becoming part of the new season's line. It is the trimming of that garment that is the finishing touch that will enable that garment to stand on its own merit. Good designers always give the trimming process as much attention as they do any other step in producing the garments that reflect their vision for the upcoming season. Trimmings and embellishments added to garments are as much a signature of the designer as are the original concept or the choice of fabric. Once accepted into the line, a well designed, executed, and trimmed garment will command the exposure and sales it deserves. The next step is to get that garment priced.

FIG. 8.14. THIS DESIGNER IS ADDING NAILHEADS ON ALREADY SEWN AND PRINTED T-SHIRTS TO GIVE A UNIQUE CREATIVE TOUCH TO HER DESIGNS.

Designer's Diary

Dear Diary,

What were the odds that I would go to college to learn how to decorate Christmas trees? That is what I feel like I am doing on the knit tops for the 4–6x girls' line. You need an angel, a butterfly, a funny cat, and a partridge in a pear tree. Just kidding, but that is how it seems. I do love drawing the predesign rough artwork and then having the screen printer's artist turn it into a darling picture. When I think about being in school and daydreaming that I was going to be designing in Paris when I graduated. . . I pictured myself draped in fabulous black wool with a red beret. LOL! I'm sitting in the design room with glitter all over my face, lint on my pants, and nails chipped and broken from helping my staff sew on wooden toggle buttons. Not the image I used to dream about. I wouldn't trade it for anything. I'm enjoying seeing the line come together.

I know I need to get some sleep tonight, but I'm afraid when I go to bed I'll have that recurring nightmare that the notches disappear, and my garments never get sewn up in production. The production manager is paging me over and over and the clothes just keep piling up, and I can't climb over them. Hey, that's a neat idea for another screen. It could be a huge mountain in the background with pretty snowflakes and a sled coming down with a girl and some polar bears. Everything could be white and silver but glittery. I need to go sketch. Another couple of weeks and my first complete line goes to New York. Wow!

Designer's Dictionary

airbrushing paint treatment where paint is blown out an air hose in a feathering effect.

appliqué an embroidered shape that is placed on top of a fabric for decoration. Or, a surface pattern made by cutting out fabric or lace designs and attaching them to another fabric or lace by means of embroidery or stitching (Calasibetta, Tortora, Abling 2002, p. 14).

distressing process done to fabric or sewn up jeans that beats it up and makes it look and feel used.

embroidery fancy needlework or trimming using colored yarn, embroidery floss, soft cotton, silk, or metallic thread (Calasibetta, Tortora, Abling 2002, p.136).

fagoting stitch, similar to single featherstitch, used to join two edges of fabric together in decorative openwork effect (Calasibetta, Tortora, Abling 2002, p. 140). Rolls of fagoting strips may be purchased to sew between seams.

frog ornamental fastener using cording or braid through which a soft ball made of cording or a button is pulled. Used for closing garments, especially military uniforms and some Chinese clothes (Calasibetta, Tortora, Abling 2002, p. 76).

glitter screen printing see screen printing. Glitter is put directly into the paint mixture and applied in the same manner.

licensee company, corporation, or person that has paid for the rights and has contracted to use a certain image. The image can be a person, movie, cartoon character, or even a phrase that is copyrighted.

logo a compact symbol, drawing, or name for a designer, manufacturer, or other organization that is easily recognized by a target audience or market (Calasibetta, Tortora, Abling 2002, 317).

pearlized objects that have a finish applied that emulates the iridescence of pearls. Buttons, belt buckles, and paint can be pearlized.

saddle stitching running stitch made in contrasting or heavy thread. Frequently used for trim on coats, sport dresses, and gloves.

screen printing printing process in which a design for each color is etched on separate pieces of pure dye silk or manufactured fiber enclosed in wooden frames. Fabric to be printed is stretched on a long table: each screen is placed individually over the fabric; and paint, applied with a squeegee, is pushed through the etched sections. Process produces especially vibrant colors and unusual designs. When made, using silk fabric, called silk-screen printing (Calasibetta, Tortora, Abling 2002, p. 380). Modern screen printing is also done by automated machinery that revolves, stopping at individual stations and imprinting one color at a time on garments or pieces of garments at each port.

send out the processes performed on parts of garments or full garments that have to be "sent out" to another contractor for completion. If a yoke of a top is embroidered the yoke alone might be the sent out piece to be joined to the body of the garment after it is decorated.

smocking decorative needlework used to hold gathered cloth together. The stitches catch alternate folds in elaborate honeycombed designs. Used especially on infants' and children's yokes and on waists and sleeves of dresses in late 19th and early 20th centuries, revived in early 1970s (Calasibetta, Tortora, Abling 2002, p. 144). Smocking is used on girls' and junior tops and bodices.

stonewashing a process in which garments or fabric, usually denim, are tumbled in large washers with stones to soften and alter the appearance of the fabric.

tie-dyeing hand method of coloring a fabric by tying strings tightly around puffs of fabric and dipping the fabric into a dye bath to get a two-color design, Repeating the process by covering other areas and using different dye colors can add still more colors. Designs are usually circular with feathered or blended edges. A technique originating in Indonesia and popular in the 1920s mainly for scarves. Revived in 1960s and after for blue jeans, T-shirts, dresses, and furs (Calasibetta, Tortora, Abling 2002).

Activities

1. Go into the junior department of a major department store. Count and sketch as many trims and embellishments as you can find. Do the same research in the girls' 7–14 department, then the 4–6x department. Discuss in class the similarity of trims between the departments and the differences you see coming from the little girls' area. This activity is designed to make students aware of current trim trends.

2. Bring to class five different trim swatches or samples. These can be unusual buttons, laces, appliqués, or any other trims. Place all the trims in one container mixed together. Student by student, draw out five trims without looking to see what you are picking. Each student sketches five different garments in any of the three size ranges, 4–6x, 7–14, or junior, which best showcase each individual trim. One area to discuss, when the sketches are presented, is the age-appropriateness of the student's choice of trim for the size range they select for each garment. This particular activity is to inspire students

to design around trim trends that they may not necessarily like, but that could be trendy and that, someday, they may need to incorporate into a line.

3. Sketch a basic top for juniors with no trim on it. Pass the sketch to the student to your left. Each student now decorates that new sketch with some sort of embellishment. Repeat this with a 7–14 basic jeans and a 4–6x basic dress. Discuss in class how well each embellishment works for each style.

4. Each student brings three swatches of interesting fabrics to class. The swatches are gathered into a container and students draw out three swatches without seeing what they are getting. Each student now sketches three different garments in any size range using the fabrication treated with a send out type of embellishment. These embellishment treatments can include pleating, quilting, embroidery, screen printing, or any other special treatment appropriate to the age and fabrication. If time permits, redo the exercise changing swatches or size ranges for the sketches. This activity helps inspire students to be creative designers.

Weekly Planner

The objectives for Chapter 8 are to acquaint students with the varied trim and finishing options available in the trimmings resource market, and to provide insight into the creative but utilitarian selection of trims for girls' and junior garments.

1. Read Chapter 8.
2. Do the activities for Chapter 8.
3. Review Designer's Dictionary.
4. Continue sewing samples for the line.

5. Review current fashion magazines, Internet sites, and forecasting materials and carefully examine which trimmings are either in style or will be coming in style.
6. Shop and pick notions for the samples.
7. Schedule an appointment to show the progress on the samples to the instructor and get all closures and trimmings approved.
8. Finish trimming and pressing garment. Put the garment on a hanger so it is presentable for the merchandising meeting.

Box 8.1

Lavigne pins name to clothes line—
her own Abbey Dawn, for Kohl's

By Olivia Barker, USA TODAY

Avril Lavigne, the rock star known for her kohl-rimmed eyes, is teaming up with retailer Kohl's and launching her own rocker-chick clothing line in July.

Dubbed Abbey Dawn (Lavigne's childhood nickname), the back-to-school juniors' collection will draw on the eclectic contents of Lavigne's own closet: 'a lot of hot pinks and blacks and stars and purple and zebra,' she says. 'Basically, everything I wear.' (But nope, there's nary a necktie.)

"I have a very particular style," says Lavigne, 23—one that's often replicated by her fans and one that's not readily available at the local mall. "I want it to be available to a lot of girls, and I want it to be affordable." Apparel prices will range from $24 to $48. "I walked through (a Los Angeles) Kohl's the other day and said, 'Oh, when my line is here it's totally going to stand out.'"

. . . it's going to be a sexy fit, not just, 'Oh, T-shirts and hoodies.'

Mixing skulls and plaids with checks and stripes, it's "a rock collection with a feminine edge," says Don Brennan of Kohl's. "I think it will broaden who we bring into our junior department," which is dominated by the Candie's brand (last month, Hayden Panettiere was named the new spokeswoman).

Unlike other celebrity-endorsed collections, Lavigne stresses she's not just entering into a licensing deal. "I

actually am the designer. What's really important to me is that everything fits well and is well-made, so I try everything on and approve it all."

And she says she'll actually wear it, including on stage during her Best Damn Tour, which launches today in her native Canada, in Victoria, British Columbia. The second she can get herself into an Abbey Dawn hoodie and pair of jeans (her most-anticipated pieces), she will. "I can't wait," she says. And "juniors" label notwithstanding, "I'm making sure that I think people in their 20s are going to wear it because it's going to be a sexy fit, not just, 'Oh, T-shirts and hoodies.' The hoodies are slimming. It's not a thick, bulky material."

Having conquered the music industry (her third album, 2007's *The Best Damn Thing*, made its debut at No. 1), Lavigne says she's thrilled to be tapping into a "new creative energy" through fashion. "I'm very visual. It's time for me to do something new."

There's another visual medium she's looking to put her stamp on. "I want to—it's just going to sound crazy, but I'm going to make it happen—I want a film career," says Lavigne, who acted in 2006's *Fast Food Nation* and voiced a role in the animated *Over the Hedge*. "So I go on auditions, I read scripts. It's not going to be one of those things, 'Oh, a singer doing a movie.'" Come fall, after her tour, "I'm really going to focus on that."

Her husband of two years, Sum 41's Deryck Whibley, is "excited for me because he knows, especially with the clothing, I've wanted to do this for a while. He's really supportive. He likes anything I like pretty much."

Source: *USA TODAY,* Wednesday, March 5, 2008.

Chapter 9

Garment Costing

The new line has come together beautifully. The line includes some refabrications of checkout bodies, lots of new innovative styling, and a few offbeat garments that are a tad too trendy for the retailers in the target market. However, those garments add a little zest to the mix. The designer is sure that the new season's collection is ready to wow the buyers, but not so fast. It needs costing.

Costing each individual garment that makes up the entirety of the new line's presentation is an enormous job and one that has no room for "guesstimates." Making sure the cost sheets are accurate usually falls to the assistant designer, who is helped by the sample cutter or a marker assistant for the fabric estimates. There are strict methods of costing within each company that must be adhered to before the garments are ever shown to retailers.

The *wholesale* price of the garment is determined by a careful analysis of the cost of fabric, trimmings, and labor, in addition to the **markup** necessary to cover the cost of doing business plus make a **profit**. The apparel business is just that—a business that exists to make money. As much fun as it is to put together a line of girls' or junior clothing, it is not done only for artistic entertainment, or as a creative outlet for designers. It is done in order to make a profit.

THE IMPORTANCE OF COSTING CORRECTLY

The easiest way to understand the importance of making sure cost sheets are a true reflection of the exact costs that go into the garment is to envision a cost sheet with errors. For example, consider a 4–6x promotional summer dress that is being sold by the sales staff for $9.00. The design room has filled out the cost sheet showing $6.00 worth of trimmings, fabric, and labor. The additional $3.00 is to cover overhead expenses and profit. After selling 6,000 dozen dresses in assorted cotton prints, the garment is put into production. The first problem discovered is that the **spaghetti** straps were never mentioned on the cost sheet. Fabric was not measured for additional goods, nor was the cost of making the spaghetti figured in. That compound error was a problem, but it only got worse. The initial yardage estimate was also incorrect, because of fitting issues. Each dress needed three more inches of goods than the original yardage estimate. Lastly, the bodice design called for four novelty buttons but the count was three on the cost sheet. If we figure the cotton prints used in the garment at $2.00 per yard and we need three inches more per dress, plus two inches more per missing spaghetti. These numbers add up to five inches of missing fabric under our material portion of the cost sheet. This adds up to $0.28. The cost of making the spaghetti for the straps

is three cents per garment. The additional button is three cents, making our erroneous cost sheet $0.34 short. The sales staff sold 72,000 dresses that should have been priced much higher. The mistake cost the company $24,480. That amount of money could pay the wages of an hourly worker at the rate of $11.00 per hour for an entire year!

Accountants can figure out the percentage loss, the diminished profit margins, and many other computations. However, every employee involved in creating the line must know that minor errors can become very expensive, indeed.

Cost sheets establish the initial pricing for garments in the line. Filling in the information correctly is essential to the companies' bottom line. Designers must oversee their staff to make sure that the cost sheets for the garments they design reflect the most accurate information possible.

THE FORMS USED FOR COST SHEETS

Most companies develop their own cost sheet forms, but all cost sheets reflect the same basic information when completed. The cost sheets that are prepared may be filled in manually or done on the computer with special software geared to the company's particular requirements. Each cost sheet, whatever the method used, needs a flat sketch of the garment, fabric swatches, and a style number. A style number is assigned per garment for the preliminary costing. Other specific information like season, garment category, and range, and a brief description are usually required. (See Figure 9.1.)

Cost sheet information is divided into three main areas. The first is the materials cost. The second area is the trimmings cost. Lastly, the labor for the garment is accounted for.

At the bottom of the cost sheet is the computation area where the selling price is figured out by combining the three sections together and including the company's formula for figuring out the markup. The selling price is reflected as the wholesale price of the garment, or the target price the manufacturer would like to be paid by the retailer.

FIG. 9.1. THIS IS A TYPICAL COST SHEET USED IN MANUFACTURING. IT CAN BE USED AS A TEMPLATE FOR CLASS REQUIRED COSTING.

DATE _____ SEASON _____ STYLE# _____

DESCRIPTION: _____

FABRIC

	WIDTH	RESOURCE	STYLE#	CONTENT	COST	YD. AMT.	FREIGHT
#1							
#2							
#3							
#4							
S.O.						TOTAL	___

TRIMMINGS

	RESOURCE	TYPE	STYLE#	CONTENT	COST	YD. AMT.	FREIGHT
#1							
#2							
#3							
						TOTAL	___

LABOR COST _____

CUTTING/MARKETING _____

INSIDE COST _____

FABRIC TOTAL _____

TRIMMINGS TOTAL _____

TOTAL COST _____

MARK UP % _____

SELLING PRICE _____

SWATCHES   TRIMS   SKETCH/PHOTO

Common Mistakes to Avoid

By avoiding the list of what not to do wrong on cost sheets, the task of filling them in correctly becomes more manageable. Mistakes of omission are the most common errors on cost sheets. In the rush to get the line ready for **market week**, mistakes are easily made. To avoid making errors the cost sheet sketch should reflect every trim. If the strap is ribbon, it should be drawn with some shading in order to indicate an appearance difference from the fabric. If there are four buttons in front and two in the back, all of them need to be easily seen in the sketch. The inside of the garment should be examined to make sure that all inside bias or notions are indicated on the cost sheet. One trick to help remember all the treatments is to visually count all the items on the garment that need to be accounted for on the cost sheet and then double check that count against what is written on the form. For example, a junior top has six buttons, one rope tie, one back zipper, and one grosgrain around the neck. The count on the cost sheet should reflect nine treatments.

Omission errors are also frequently made on send-out operations. If fabric is sent out to a contractor for a process (for instance the fabric needs quilting), there are two separate prices that need to be reflected in the cost of the garment. The first price is the cost of the fabric that is being used for the process. Cuffs and yokes that are quilted may take 12 inches of fabric, and the cost sheet needs to reflect this measurement. The additional cost is the amount of money paid for the labor of actually quilting the fabric. If the quilting cost is $3.60 per yard, it will cost another $1.20 for the garment to be quilted. This part is either reflected under the trimmings cost or in the labor section as directed by the production department. Not all companies conform in their methods of costing send-out operations. Some may simply add the $3.60 to the regular fabric cost, and show it in the fabric estimate. The important thing is that the quilting price is somewhere on the cost sheet and is not overlooked. Recording the

FIG. 9.2. THIS ASSISTANT DESIGNER IS FILLING OUT THE COST SHEET.

name and the contact number of the quilting contractor is also helpful.

Another common error made on cost sheets is an incorrect yardage estimate. This problem can be eliminated if the garment is tried on the form in order to check the fit, paying special attention to the length of the hem. Checking to make sure the pattern used for the estimate is complete is also important. Taking a measurement of the cut-able width of the goods is essential in order to avoid yardage errors. Sometimes fabric has large selvage edges that prevent the use of the entire width, and this will cause the marker to be made narrower, thus increasing the length of the marker.

Incorrect information leading to the wrong price of trims and material is another issue commonly found on cost sheets. Making a follow-up call to vendors to double check prices can be helpful before filling in the information on the cost sheet. From the time a fabric is sampled until the time it is sewn up in a new sample, price changes can occur in the marketplace. This is especially true if the fabric or trim is trendy. When items become hot, the prices tend to increase, and deliveries tend to get tighter. It never hurts to check price and delivery a second time before submitting a cost sheet. (See Figure 9.2.)

FIG. 9.3. THIS ASSISTANT DESIGNER IS LAYING OUT THE PATTERN TO FIGURE OUT THE YARDAGE ESTIMATE.

Material Costing

Fabric can be the biggest cost for a garment. The average portion allotted for fabric is 40 percent of the garment's total cost. In the girls' and junior markets, designers tend to put less trim on trendy fabric that is expensive so that they do not have to compromise the quality of the goods. Getting exact yardage costs is especially important when the fabric is the selling feature of the garment.

Several steps are involved in figuring out the cost of the fabric. First, the fabric information is recorded on the cost sheet. The style number and a description of the fabric need to be provided. The pattern number for the exact print has to be written down, as does the width of the goods. Under the column, "price," the negotiated price of the fabric is recorded if the fabric company is willing to work out a special price when purchased. If not, the sample price is sufficient. If the fabric has already been purchased, the price is what the manufacturer actually paid, and the design staff needs to check to make sure they have recorded the correct purchase price. Some cost sheets also have room for fabric content information. The more information that is clearly stated on the cost sheet, the

easier it is to keep track of all the costs involved in making the garment. (See Figure 9.3.)

In order to figure out how much fabric is used, the pattern must be laid out and measured. To facilitate making **yardage estimates**, it is helpful to measure out the different fabric widths and mark them in masking tape on the cutting tables. By taping down a measuring tape parallel to the length of the table, and marking off several commonly used fabric widths, like 58 inch and 44 inch, it is easy to see the amount of inches each garment requires when the pattern is arranged within the width demarcations. The pattern should be configured into the tightest marker possible that leaves adequate ease between the pattern pieces. Because this estimate is made with the sample size pattern, which is usually midway from the smallest to largest size in the range, it works as an average. Because of grading up on the larger sizes, the yardage estimate has to include a couple of inches extra for expansion of those bigger pattern sizes.

In the girls' 7–14 size range, 10 is the sample size. This size was chosen when the normal range had size 7, 8, 10, 12, and 14. Size 10 was the middle size, and it gave the average amount of fabric for the style when a yardage estimated was taken. Since some garments are now graded up to size 16 to accommodate the overweight epidemic in America, size 10 is smaller than the average of size of the range. This increased sizing is making it necessary to make the original estimate generous enough to cover the added use of material.

A similar situation exists in the junior market, where the sample size is usually size 9. If the clothing is sized 5, 7, 9, 11, and 13, size 9 is the average. When larger sizes are added, like a 15 or, in tops a size XL, the same situation arises with the larger sizes throwing the average off. Again, extra fabric must be averaged into the estimate in order for the cost sheet to reflect the larger amount of fabric that is needed. Larger sizes can throw off the average measurement to a greater extent when the pattern pieces themselves are large, as opposed to lots of tiny components pieces, because the middle size pattern will fit across the goods but when graded larger the pattern pieces may not. Smaller component pieces can be maneuvered more easily into a reasonable yardage estimate. In the junior market, there is a balance in the sizing that does not exist in the girls' wear market. Sizing in this market is affected by social pressures and the influence of very thin teen idols. There are consumers who are so petite that the junior lines are grading down to size 0, 1, and 3. Manufactures of those very small sizes encourage girls who wear 7–14 size range clothing to purchase their clothes in the junior department. At the other end of the size range are consumers who are grossly overweight. Manufacturers are forced to offer many size choices that increase the expense to the production costs because of added grading, marking, and bundling required.

Yardage estimates take time to do correctly, and special attention must be paid to the width of the goods, grainlines, and one-way fabrics that may be napped, have pile, or are printed in a one-way directional pattern. All first samples should be tried on the appropriate mannequins in order to make sure the fit is close enough to use the pattern for an estimate. If the garment is too small, the estimator needs to consider those and allow extra space as needed when laying out the pattern pieces. At this point notations should also be written on the pattern card indicating that the pattern needs alteration.

When figuring out yardage estimates the pattern card should be consulted in order to ensure that all the pieces of the pattern are included in the **minimarker**. The garment should be right in front of the estimator so that it can be carefully compared to the pattern card. If sashes, belts, or biases made from fabric are shown on the garment, there must be a pattern piece for each of them, or a measurement of fabric that will be cut for a send-out operation. It is the duty of the estimator to make certain everything is reflected on the cost sheet under the fabric or materials section.

The perfect layout in a fabric estimate ends with a *squaring off* at the end measurement so that all the width of the goods is used evenly. If there is a pattern piece that does not fit into this rectangular configuration, that piece must be figured on its own measurement. If the left long sleeve pattern piece was not fitting into the marker, the estimator would lay out that sleeve pattern, by itself, to see how many sleeves can fit across the width of the goods. If the sleeve is 24 inches long, and fits four times across the 58-inch-wide fabric, each sleeve would use 6 inches of goods. The 6-inch measurement for the sleeve is added to the number of inches the rest of the pattern took when it was laid out. The important thing is to make sure the estimate reflects all the fabric necessary to make the style. Each fabric, whether it is self or contrasting fabric, needs to be measured and recorded separately on the cost sheet. That includes all linings and interfacings.

MATH FOR FIGURING FABRIC COSTS

Figuring out the cost of the fabric is easily done on a calculator. In order to grasp the concept it is helpful to think of fabric in terms of inches. Fabric is purchased and priced by the yard. Each yard has 36 inches. To calculate how much an inch of the fabric cost, the yard price is divided by 36. When the estimate is taken, the estimator can record the yardage in inches. For example, 100-percent-cotton sheeting is $2.50 per yard. If the $2.50 is divided by 36 inches, to tell us the price per inch, the amount is $0.0694444. That would be rounded off to $.07, or 7 cents per inch. $.07 × 36 = $2.52. If a garment takes 27 inches at $.07 cents, the price for this fabric would be $1.89. Some computer software actually does the math, but it is important that designers know the basic concept so that they can design with an instinct toward value.

Different companies do cost sheet math using various mathematical computations. Some large corporations price their garments by the dozen. Some use tenths of yards instead of inches for their cost sheets. There is no one right way or one wrong way. The exact garment costing method is set up by the production department, and the design department follows their instruction in this area.

Freight Considerations

Freight costs are what the manufacturer has to pay in order to get the materials into the plant. This is cost is different from the shipping costs, which cover sending the finished garments out of the plant and into to the stores. Freight costs affect the cost of the finished garment, and they must be included on the cost sheet.

There are many ways to include fabric freight costs on the cost sheet. Some companies figure out the average annual freight charge per yard that it costs to ship the bolts of fabric to their cutting facilities. Those companies add that average freight amount per yard to the purchase price of the fabric per yard, and do all the computations based on the total cost of the fabric and freight. Other companies use a sliding scale figuring bottom weights at one rate and lighter bolts of fabric at a lower rate. Other cost sheets have the line for freight cost blank at the bottom of the materials category. In this instance, the fabric company's standard freight "guesstimate" per yard should be multiplied by the yardage amount of yardage used for the garment. For example, if two yards of denim

are used for a junior overall, the cost for shipping the bolt of denim is approximately $.10 per yard. 2 × $.10 = $.20 cents, and that amount is shown in the materials section of the cost sheet.

It doesn't matter where on the cost sheet the freight charges are listed, but this information should be recorded uniformly on all the cost sheets. It is important to note that the freight for the fabric to be shipped is not to be confused with the shipping cost listed under the labor section of the cost sheet because that shipping cost is the cost of shipping the finished garment to the retailer that purchased the apparel.

Trimmings Costing

Trimmings on apparel are considered to be anything but the material. This includes all decorative treatments and functional treatments like closures. They must be identified, counted or measured, and priced. In the middle section of the cost sheet under the subtitle ***findings*** and *trimmings,* or just *trims,* there are several types of trims listed. Each item of trim on a garment should be listed in the appropriate spot on the cost sheet.

The math calculations for trims follow the same basic formula for figuring out the cost of fabric. Many trims, like ribbon, cordage, eyelet edging, or lace edging, are sold by the yard. The price of the trim per yard is divided by 36 inches to figure out the price per inch. The price per inch of trim is multiplied by the measurement in inches of trim used on the garment. It is important to always add a little extra into the measurement to cover both the grading up of the garment and any possible increases due to fit issues or waste. If a garment takes 11 inches of trim then putting 12 inches on the cost sheet would be the standard procedure. Ten percent **shrinkage** due to loss is customary so adding in just a little bit over on the cost sheet is necessary.

The count is important when pricing buttons. Buttons are sold in quantities counted by the gross. There are 144 pieces in a gross. If a garment has six buttons on it, the price of a gross of the buttons is divided by 144 and multiplied by six. For example, a 4–6x dress has

FIG. 9.4. THIS PRODUCTION COST ANALYST IS FIGURING OUT THE WHOLESALE COST OF THE GARMENTS. NOTICE THE COMPUTER INPUT AND THE CALCULATOR.

four buttons on the bodice and two buttons on the pockets. The buttons are all identical. The buttons cost $5.00 a gross. $5.00 divided by 144 = $.0347 cents per button or $.21 for all the buttons on the garment. In this example, the buttons were alike. If they had been of two separate sizes or styles, the calculation of cost would have had to be done for each type of button. The size of the buttons, the style number, and color should also be identified on the cost sheet.

Some trims, like belts, are sold by the dozen or by the piece. It is important to put the resource contact name and the price per item on the cost sheet. The price should be written indicating the way the item is purchased for orders. The purchasing agent or production staff member looking at the cost sheet should be able to order stock buttons and trims from the accurate information detailed on the cost sheet.

Send-out treatments, like screen printing on T-shirts, are considered trim by some companies and are reflected in the trim section of the cost sheet. Other companies, particularly those that have the garment sewn and printed at one

contractor, put this cost in the labor section. This decision is left to the production department. The design staff creating the cost sheet has to conform to the company's methods. The important point is that all costs are reflected in some place on the cost sheet.

Labor Costing

The labor section of the cost sheet is the easiest for the design staff to fill in because they generally don't have anything to do with determining the labor prices for garments. This is left to production managers or production assistants to estimate what the labor will cost per style. A **labor estimate** is simply an educated guess based on past style history. The production department makes price adjustments from one season to the next for the current market cost of labor. (See Figure 9.4.)

In many design rooms, the first sample is completed and the cost sheet is filled in completely except for the section on labor. The production department takes over and fills in the labor estimate and all the other costs like cutting, marking, grading, and shipping. Since some companies ship garments on hangers, and other companies ship garments in flat packaging, those various expenses are also estimated under the labor category.

Determining the amount of money that must be paid in order to produce a garment is not as cut and dried as simply counting the different sewing operations involved and adding up the cost for each step in the process. Supply and demand issues come into play and alter the equation because labor is cheaper when contracting shops need work. Labor costs are more expensive when contractors are busy, and they can pick and choose what garments they can make more profitably. Production managers will complain about being unable to place *dogs*. Dogs are those styles that had the labor cost under estimated, and the production department can't find any shop that is willing to sew the garments for the labor that the company wants to pay as reflected on the preliminary costing. This can happen because the garment is more difficult to sew than was realized or other garments are easier and the contractors have enough business and don't want to take less-profitable work.

Many factors that determine the labor cost of a garment must be examined by experts before the costing can be completed. Production managers have to be able to assess the difficulty of the garment by the number of operations necessary for completing the garment. They also have to assess how easy or difficult it is to handle the garment. For example, it is more difficult to sew velveteen or satin than it is to sew sheeting. It is more difficult to handle a junior's full-length prom dress than it is to handle a sweatshirt. The types of operations that make a garment unusual may limit the number of factories that have the capabilities to take that garment's completion and this will also affect the price. An example of this situation would be a garment that has marrow-edge ruffling in several places on a 7–14 girl's angel top. Not all factories will have enough marrow machines to process a large quantity of tops. The production manager may have to factor in some extra money for the labor estimate just to ensure a factory will produce the top in the timeframe needed to make the delivery dates.

Short delivery dates can also affect the cost of the labor needed to sew up production apparel. If a manufacturer contracts the sewing labor out and needs a particular style to be made quickly, the sewing contractor may ask for more money as an incentive to insert the style into the production schedule.

Components in the Labor Section
The listing of different costs in the labor section varies on cost sheets according to how the manufacturer operates. A manufacturer that uses all contracting shops for all the needlework performed on its garments has certain specific labor costs that may differ from a company that owns its own factories. Importers also have specific costs that may differ from garments made in the United States. There are, however, some basic labor steps that all companies need to price in this section. Those blanks that must be filled in are: cutting, marking, grading, construction labor (including pressing and inspection), packaging/hangers, and shipping.

The production department estimates the cutting, marking, and grading costs using company data accumulated from past seasons. The labor costs for each garment are determined by the production department and depend on the availability of factories and how easy or difficult it is to construct the garment. Whether a garment is packaged or shipped hanging depends on the garment and the retailer. Companies usually have a set amount that is used for this estimate. The shipping cost is also determined by the garment's weight and average shipping rates.

Garments that are developed offshore by an independent contractor can be priced to include all the components of a regular cost sheet plus the shipping and tariff costs. Different deals can be made to extend the shipping to the consolidator or to the port. It is not usually within the scope of the designer's information to participate in the details of these transactions. The quotas and duty arrangements are also outside the scope of the design room.

A company that owns its own factories may operate those factories as independent entities. If so, it has to markup the garment labor in order to show a profit in those shops. Other companies list the labor cost as exactly what it costs to make the garment. With global garment manufacturing as diversified as it is, there are infinite possible methods of figuring out labor on cost sheets. Fortunately, the design department does not have to oversee this process. (See Figure 9.5.)

FIGURING MARKUP

After the cost sheet is filled out to include the materials, the trimmings, and the direct labor making up the garment, those costs are then tallied up. This sum is the "cost of goods" figure, which is the basis for the wholesale price of the garment. Additional costs need to be added to this amount. They include the company's operating expenses and an amount for profit.

The operating costs can include the rent, utilities, showroom fees, travel expenses, taxes, insurance, wages for indirect labor like shippers and administrative assistants, and so forth, and any number of other costs that make it possible to design and ship a garment without actually using a needle and thread. The owner or chief financial officer of the company determines exactly what the formula is for its specific overhead costs plus the extra percentage to add in to arrive at the wholesale price.

There are various ways an apparel company can be managed. Some small and medium companies try to keep very low overheads and focus on good wages for their employees and large profits for the owners. Other companies have different management styles and spend a larger portion of their profits on their facilities while paying lower wages. The variables in management priorities are unlimited. Figuring out the markups is part and parcel of the management philosophy of the particular company that employs a designer. The markups on garments may

| DATE | 9-7-09 | | SEASON | SPRING | | STYLE# | #2475 |

DESCRIPTION: Puffed sleeve dress w/ flounce & shoulder ties
Customer if special cut: Susie's Sweet Shop
Cost Sheet prepared by:

FABRIC

	WIDTH	RESOURCE	STYLE#	CONTENT	COST	YD. AMT.	FREIGHT	
#1	58"	Marcus Bros.	182-floral	100% cotton	2.25	28"	.06	1.75
#2	44"	Fabyads	22-solid	100% cotton	3.10	13"	.03	1.20
#3	58"	Meadows	Tex-103	50P/50C	2.00	30"	.06	1.67
#4								

S.O. No Send out   TOTAL $4.62

TRIMMINGS

	RESOURCE	TYPE	STYLE#	CONTENT	COST	YD.AMT.	FREIGHT	
#1	Talon	14" Zipper	001	Nylon	.30	1 pc.	.01	.31
#2	Herz	Eyelet edge	#A-37	100% cotton	.60 yd	40"	.03	.63
#3	Decor	4 Bud Applique	3489	100% cotton	.12 ea.	4 pcs.	.01	.49

                                                 TOTAL $1.43

LABOR COST	$2.50
CUTTING/MARKETING	.40
INSIDE COST	1.50
FABRIC TOTAL	4.62
TRIMMINGS TOTAL	1.43
TOTAL COST	$10.45
MARK UP %	33 1/3%
	15.67

SELLING PRICE $15.75

| SWATCHES | TRIMS | SKETCH/PHOTO |

FIG. 9.5. THIS IS AN EXAMPLE OF A COST SHEET DONE FOR A FICTICIOUS GARMENT MADE IN FICTICIOUS FABRIC. IT SHOWS THE ATTENTION TO DETAIL THAT IS DEMANDED IN THE INDUSTRY.

or may not be something the design department is privy to.

In budget, volume, or mass merchant levels, this markup is quite tight. As apparel increases in price, the markup gets substantially higher. A 33 percent markup is terrific in the girls' and junior mass-marketing manufacturing fields. The markup rises from 40 percent to 60 percent for department store and specialty shop manufacturers. Many moderate manufacturers use a

1. Determine most important features.
2. Change least important parts.
3. Conserve fabric and labor cost.

FIG. 9.6a, b. THIS PARTY DRESS HAS BEEN PRICED OUT VERY HIGH AND ALTHOUGH IT WILL BE OFFERED IN THE LINE THE SALESPERSON REQUESTED SEVERAL LESS-COSTLY VERSIONS. VERSION A CHANGES THE AMOUNT OF THE YARDAGE OF THE MOST EXPENSIVE FEATURE, THE DOTTED LACE. VERSION B USES A MUCH LESS-COSTLY LACE BUT KEEPS THE SILHOUETTE INTACT. VERSION C TAKES FULLNESS OUT OF THE SILHOUETTE TO SAVE YARDAGE BUT KEEPS THE SWEETHEART NECKLINE.

keystone markup method and double the cost of the garment in order to arrive at the selling price for retailers. Some manufacturing companies share their markup formulas with the design staff and others do not. By reviewing the cost sheets at the end of the costing cycle, designers can learn to understand how the wholesale prices are established.

Garment Pricing Orders

A stunning reality in the girls' wear and junior markets is that the actual wholesale price of the garment can be thrown out the window when the largest retailers dangle a big order of thousands of dozens of garments under a manufacturer's nose. Vast quantities of apparel are sold for considerably less than the price that the cost sheet indicates as the wholesale price. It is for management to decide when the selling price is acceptable given the quantity purchased and the *net markup* on the garment. This is an area where the designer has little or no input. There is a trickle-down financial impact, however, that the purchase power of the largest retailers has on the marketplace, and this is something that designers must be aware of.

As soon as an order is taken for **tight margins** the production manager starts figuring out how to cut the various costs that were computed on the cost sheet. Fabric companies often partner with the manufacturer to cut their fabric price, as do the trim companies. It is when the labor cost needs to be trimmed that the result can be damaging to people. Substandard labor conditions are the result of factories taking in work that should not be sewn at the prices negotiated, or because the factory owners are just exploiters of a poor labor force. The owners and managers of factories that exploit the weakest group in the labor chain are the cause of industry-wide shame and embarrassment. This component of the apparel industry gives all apparel manufacturers a bad name. Great strides are being made to improve the lot of the factory workers all over the world with strict oversight, but many steps that are more comprehensive must be taken in order to protect the lowest rung in the labor pool.

When a Garment Is Too Expensive for the Line

Just when the designer thinks the garments in the line are perfect, reality strikes. The first garments being priced are coming back too expensive for the price points the merchandisers are aiming for. What to do? Four little words will take care of this problem: *conserve, compromise, camouflage, or convert.* (See Figure 9.6.)

First, figure out the important issues with the garment and *conserve* all those design details that are impossible to do without. *Compromise* and change what can be changed to bring the price down without messing up the garment's integrity. Next, *camouflage* what you took away or altered so that someone seeing the garment for the first time will not feel like the garment is missing something. Lastly, if the garment is perfect and there is nothing that should be done to change any part of it, *convert* the sales staff or merchandiser to appreciate the garment's intrinsic value and ask them to try to sell the garment at a higher price point as is. This is a hard sell because it is very difficult to coax sellers to ask their buyers to pay higher prices.

If garments are pricing high because of the cost of material, the obvious fix is to use less fabric. Sweep can be removed from skirts, sleeves shortened, and contrast fabrics that cost less can be introduced to cut back on the yardage of the expensive goods. Substitute fabric is another, less favored option.

If trimmings are too expensive, cutting back on the amount of trim is the first option. The substitution of less-expensive buttons or trims is the second choice. Inside buttons can be different from the expensive novelty buttons that show on the front of the garment. In girls' clothing, trimming can be used on the front of a garment and not on the back. It is important to note that when trim is the selling feature it is better to use the checkout trim, and use less of it, than it is to use a similar trim whether it is the girls' market or the junior market. Sometimes this substitution kills the sale.

Fewer seams and fewer sewing operations on a garment will reduce the labor price. A six-gore skirt can be made with five gores, each with a little more flair. A collar with a separate stand can be converted into a collar with a stand in one piece. Pockets can be removed in some cases. Careful inspection of the garment may reveal simple changes that won't kill the design and that will bring the garment into the desired price point. Designers have an entire staff of sewing experts in their sample department to advise them of ways to cut back on the difficulty of sewing up a garment.

Changing a wonderful style can be heart-breaking to the designer who is caught up in the creative whirlwind of putting together a line. The one important factor that must be remembered is that the clothes are being designed to sell to a particular market, and that market has price restrictions. It is the job of the designer to offer the most wonderful garments for the amount of money the target consumer can afford to spend. Any designer can design a gown in gorgeous fabric with an unlimited budget and no deadline. It takes a talented designer to pinpoint the perfect garment, at the exact timing, at an affordable price, to catch a rising trend for a picky girl or a junior princess.

Designer's Diary

Dear Diary,

This day is one I won't forget anytime soon. The production department got a panic attack call from the cutting service. The fabric came in for the Easter dress ad and it was wrong. The production manager asked if it was the wrong print. No. Wrong color? No. Losing patience he screamed, "What the hell is wrong with it?" Did I mention that the intercom was on? The entire company was silent. The cutter replied, "It stinks." They sent me over to see why the cutter was hysterical. The fabric came in stinky. It smelled awful. The formaldehyde that is used to finish the textiles hadn't had time to dissipate or cure. When things go wrong, it is really a domino effect. Now they have to send the goods to a finishing facility in town to fix the problem. It will have to be split among several contractors instead of one shop. Quality control will be working overtime to stay on top of this mess. If they were going to use my "nose" I would have preferred testing perfumes. This was like rotten eggs.

Anyway, on the way back to the office I stopped for a sandwich. I ran into Gina. She was at school with me. She is working as a buyer. Her title on the card is Professional Purchasing Agent for Extraordinary Clothing. She started a Web company with a friend, and they are selling expensive but funky clothes from all over the world on the Internet. She said I could have all the photos as she finishes with them. It will give me a great opportunity to see her unusual stuff and maybe give me insights to new trends that my competitors haven't seen yet. I'll take any edge I can get. Coming up with new ideas day after day is exhausting.

I had 23 garments in for costing yesterday, and six of them didn't hit the right price range. Tomorrow I'll have to see how I can keep from butchering two of my favorite styles. The other four garments I'll be able to figure out. Just once, I'd like a salesperson to say "oh, I can get more money for that!"

Designer's Dictionary

findings in the garment industry or in sewing, all the smaller items and trimmings that complete a garment (e.g., buttons, hooks, bindings, laces) (Calasibetta, Tortora, Abling 2002, p. 159).

labor estimate the price that the production staff thinks the garment can be produced to the level of quality demanded for the customer.

market week any of the weeks of the year in which apparel companies show their fashion lines (Calasibetta, Tortora, Abling 2002, p. 322).

markup the amount of money added to the garment's cost to determine the selling price the manufacturer needs to get from the retailers. Or, the amount of money added to the manufacturer's cost in order to determine the final retail sales price. The traditional markup on the apparel doubles the cost of the merchandise and is called a keystone markup. (Calasibetta, Tortora, Abling 2002, pp. 322–323).

minimarker when the pattern is laid out to determine how much yardage is used for each sample the assistant designer or staff des-

Chapter 10

Merchandising the Line

The sales staff is getting antsy because the big market week is quickly approaching. Appointments with buyers are slotted into busy schedules in the coming days, and they will be for many weeks ahead. Airline and hotel accommodations are lined up. The only thing keeping the sales staff from having a successful market trip is a cohesive new line of clothing. The line still needs to be pressed, tagged with prices, and hung in the showroom on display hangers. The line seems to be coming together well, but it is strewn around the facility in bits and pieces. Some samples are being sewn up at the last minute, some are priced, and others are awaiting the production department's labor and costing input. The merchandising phase of the line's development is at hand and the entire line needs to be gathered together and presented as a cohesive unit to the sales staff for final approval. The merchandising meeting is scheduled.

There are typically several viewpoints brought to the initial merchandising meeting. Most importantly there is the designer exhibiting the new line. Depending on the size of the manufacturer, there might be owners, CEOs, stylists, merchandisers, sales managers, and sales staff sitting in to preview the new season's line debut. The designer's purpose is to show and tell what the trends are and how they were interpreted for the target market. All others present at the meeting are there to critique, question, and hopefully admire. (See Figure 10.1.)

Sometimes the production manager will sit in on the meeting in order to get a feel for the types of special machinery that will be required to manufacture the garments. Seeing all the garments together will also enable the production department to get a general feel for how easy or difficult manufacturing the garments will be.

The end of each season is both exciting and stressful for the designer. It is a daunting task to unite the various groups of garments for the initial presentation to the sales staff. There is a strong personal investment of creative ego that binds the designer to each of the garments like a mother hen to her chicks. The designer must show, and defend if necessary, each fabric selection, each trim choice, and the line as a whole to professional

181

FIG. 10.1. THIS MEETING WAS CALLED TO THE LINE PRESENTATION TO FIRM UP THE GROUPS BEFORE MARKET WEEK.

sellers whose livelihoods rest on the success of the designer's decisions. If there is a trick to doing this successfully, it is to be confident and to believe in one's own intuitive fashion sense and artistic creativity. Sellers are only smitten with a particular garment when it sells. They like to see the purchase orders, and the money. When they do, all the best-selling garments become their favorites. The designer comes to the meeting with his or her personal favorites, but he or she must also be open to constructive criticism. The designer must learn to compromise on design changes when the management deems it necessary. The secret here is to hold fast to important design features and make concessions when the changes don't ruin the designer's original vision for the garment.

It is the job of the designer to communicate the importance of various trends to the sales force so that the sales force can excite the retail buyers. The more excitement the designer shows when presenting each group to the sales representatives, the more confidence the sellers will display to their buyers. The designer can bring original concept and inspiration boards that show how the inspiration and innovation are embodied in the different garments. The new line should exhibit all the trend research, competitive shopping, and original ideas that influenced the creation of the line. The design-

er's job is to sell the line to the sales staff with enthusiasm and charm them into falling in love with their new product line.

SALES FOCUS

As a general rule, successful sales personnel in the fashion business know, from their years of experience, which garments in a new line look like winners. Fortunately, they are also smart enough to expose all the garments to the buyers. Sellers are primarily experts in reading the buyers and selling themselves as trustworthy and in selling their company as reliable. Sellers will present the line and pass on the information regarding the designer's trend research and design inspiration. After that, they let the buyers select the garments that the buyers deem best for their stores. Once the most important buyers, those with a **big pencil** (those who can purchase large quantities), begin selecting garments to order, the sellers then start touting those garments as the "hot" booking numbers, as though they were already shipped and retailing nicely in the stores. A good seller, who is also able to merchandise a line and offer constructive input to improve garments, is an invaluable asset for the company.

Sales personnel who have moved up from selling to owning or managing a girls' or junior company usually have great talent for merchandising, and they will often act as the major merchandiser for the new lines. The purpose of merchandising the line is to maximize the strengths of the line's new trends, to insure existing successful garments are restyled in the best fabrications, and to make each garment as saleable as possible. A line that is merchandised well will have no weak groups. It will be a collection of different groups that appeal to different tastes and personalities.

When a salesperson shows a line, each group should flow into the next, and as a whole, the line tells the story of the season. Each sales professional will organize a finished line and sell the groups in an order they thought of before the presentation. Most sellers like to start the line showing with a strong statement group and close the same way, but their choice for which groups are the strongest may differ from the designer's perspective. After a few showings the order may change depending upon the buyers' receptiveness to particular garments. Designers have to remember that every seller's favorite design is the one that is ordered in the largest quantities and performs well at retail.

PROCESSING THE LINE FOR PRESENTATION

There are five steps involved in completing the line for presentation after the cost sheets have been finished. These final steps are necessary in order to inform the sales staff of all the information regarding colors, delivery, and price. Garments will have information regarding fabric content and care instructions attached.

The first step is to gather all the garment groups together and make sure the groups are complete and competitively priced. The second step is for the designer to communicate the assets, or selling points, of the groups to the selling staff. Designers often explain the sources of their inspiration for different styles so that the sales force can handle questions from buyers. Style tags, pricing information, and other data, like delivery dates, will then be discussed, finalized, and attached. The color choices and assortments need to be clarified with the sales staff's input. Finally, all the necessary art

FIG. 10.2. THIS SAILOR-INSPIRED GROUP FOR THE GWEN STEFANI LINE FROM JERRY LEIGH OF CALIFORNIA SHOWS GREAT AS A GROUP.

boards, sketches, brochures, and fliers must be organized and presented as selling aids for the line. When this process is complete the line will be ready to be shown.

Unifying the Groups into a Saleable Line

All the garments for the line, at whatever stage in finishing they are in, must be collected in the showroom. At this point, the groups could be further organized on a rack in order of the importance of each group, from the designer's point of view. By ranking them in order, the designer makes a statement about the trends that are most significant. At this point, the separate groups are put up on a **sales grid** one by one. A sales grid is a metal rack that is flush to the wall that enables garments to be hung together so that the entire line can be seen in one place. Most showrooms are equipped with grids, but individual wall hooks also work for this preview. (See Figure 10.2.)

Compatible Grouping

As an apparel group is reviewed, the garments are inspected to ensure that they all go together in a complementary way. If it is a coordinate group, the different components should be able to be mixed and matched. The sales staff

FIG. 10.3a, b. (a) Above. THE DESIGNERS MEET TO FILL IN GARMENTS TO COMPLETE GROUPS BEFORE THEIR PRESENTATION. (b) Left. THE DESIGNERS HAVE ISOLATED SOME OF THE NEW STYLES THAT NEED MORE EXCITING FABRICS. THEY WILL CAREFULLY SELECT SUBSTITUTIONS.

will want to make sure all the different pieces in the group can be shown in such a way as to look good together as outfits when each top is combined with each bottom. For example, a plaid group for 4–6x back to school may have a plaid skirt, a solid skirt, and a plaid pant. The tops to go with the bottoms may include two knit tops, a sweater vest, and a long-sleeve woven blouse. When looking at the group all together the sales manager might request a solid pant, in the hopes it will work better than the plaid pant with the knitted tops. If this is the case, the designer will make a note and add that piece to the collection.

Filling In Garments

After several seasons, a designer does pre-merchandising while groups are being planned in order to try to fill in all areas before the line review. (See Figure 10.3.) What constitutes a group within a line is defined differently from

one manufacturer to another. Some companies use a fabric as the unifying element for a group. Within the use of the fabric, the designer will do assorted garments that may coordinate together. Other companies may define groups as types of dresses, perhaps sundresses. In that scenario, the group of sundresses, in varied styles and fabrics, is shown together. Whatever the product line of the company, the designer needs to make the groupings of garments a cohesive collection that has variety of style, depth of color, and visual interest when viewed together. It is difficult to hold a buyer's attention if a line is too long, so part of the filling-in step also includes an elimination step. If a group has too many pieces, pieces that are considered irrelevant are eliminated.

When a seller finds a line excessively unwieldy, the tendency is to hold some of the garments in the bag, which means they don't take

offering. In the merchandising meeting, the designer will present the color assortment that the fabric company is offering. Then, the designer will usually choose two or three different colors that best fit into the original color story that the line was created around. At this point, a sales staff member may ask to include a basic color, one that is not necessarily touted for the season, in the assortment as well.

It is easy to pick three colors for a print dress but it is not so easy if the designer has combined several fabrics into one garment. If a red and navy plaid has been combined with a yellow cord edge, a red solid knit, and a red and yellow dot, there needs to be a discussion about what colors go with the green and navy plaid. The designer may have already tried to combine the green and navy plaid with the same contrast colors and it doesn't show as well as combination number one. Perhaps the designer wants the green and navy plaid to be shown with orange cordage, green solid knit, and a green and orange dot. The merchandise meeting solidifies the color choices.

Sometimes the resolution of color choices is to offer fewer choices instead of every color offered by the fabric company. In this case, the designer may have to re-cut a few samples that are sewn in a discarded color.

In the junior market, seasonally popular colors can be as important as styling. If hot pink is the "in" color, pale pink will sit on the racks in the stores. A designer must stick up for the color direction that is considered essential. However, since most garment orders are pre-planned and purchased in color assortments, there are usually enough color choices to satisfy all opinions. Eventually the buyers will determine which colors they want shipped to their stores. It is the job of the designer to point both sales staff and buyers in the right color path, but most large retailers have a color direction for the entire store that has to be considered and weighed against any contrary advice from a single designer.

In the 7–14 size range, the color direction will follow the junior area with a few exceptions. Dark, dusty, or muddy colors need to be cleaned up for this age group even when a dark junior pallet is successful. When natural colors like ecru, khaki, sage, and rust are in style in juniors, they sell best for the middle range girls if a clear pink and sky blue are somehow mixed into the prints or coordinated with the solid natural hues. An example of this would be if skin prints in their normal colors in junior tops, like leopard or zebra prints, are selling well, skin prints in pink and blue backgrounds will retail well for the girls' market. This particular phenomenon has occurred repeatedly in this market.

The little girls in the 4–6x size range enjoy many color choices, but pastel pink and sky blue retail as their favorites. If bright colors are the color of the season, one can still find pink and blue pastel, and often lilac, in any girls' department. When bright hues are the seasonal choice for junior and middle girl clothing, those colors will also be mixed into the little girls' color assortment with green as the weakest color, followed by orange and yellow. Bright blue and bright pink will be the best sellers. One of the enjoyable benefits of designing clothing for the 4–6x range is that they have their own opinion about what they want to wear, including what colors they like. They are not as pressured as the older girls are by their peers into conformity. Once the 4–6x girls start exerting their personal taste into dressing themselves for preschool or elementary school all manner of color combinations are shown in their wardrobes.

Some merchandisers in the girls' and junior markets like to offer several fashion colors, those colors touted to be the in colors for the season, and a staple color that would appeal to a less fashion-conscious buyer. An example of this type of color assorting would be to offer a top in three jewel tone colors, when jewel tones are the in colors, like rose, gold, and jade mixed with an ecru and navy choice. The jewel tones are to attract the fashion-conscious consumer's attention, and the ecru and navy, more basic colors, will appeal to a more practical consumer. Ecru goes well with denim and if it was the hot color last year for this particular season it will go with some of the consumers' existing clothing. The additional merchandising aim is to get the consumer to also think about purchasing an additional garment in a basic color.

Once the color choices for each group in the line are selected, the sales staff will present only those chosen colors to their buyers. At this point swatches are either attached to the garments to show the color choices or a swatch board is made and shown alongside the garments. The stock fabric, fabric ordered to produce the garments on order, will be purchased according to the amount of each color sold. The consumers purchasing the clothing in the stores will actually answer the question about which color is the strongest for the season. The stores will then pass that information back to the manufacturer for future reference.

FINAL POLISHING OF THE LINE

When the meeting is over, the designer will have to fill in, finish off, and complete the line. The amount of work required to get the line ready varies from insignificant to mind boggling, depending upon how well received the line was. The easiest way to deal with the workload is to attack it according to what needs to be done in each group and working group by group, to make sure all the adjustments, additions, and corrections are made to each garment. Doing the easiest fixes first helps get the momentum going, and the quick sense of accomplishment is a boon to the worn-out workers in the design room.

Filling in is perhaps the easiest of these assignments. If a group needs a pair of pants or a skirt in order to finish it, the designer has only to sketch an additional piece or two and give the sketches to the patternmaker. Most of the time, **fill-in garments** combine design features already prominent in the group. The fabric is already adopted, the trims are already chosen and the project is to design a garment that fits within already established criteria. An example of this would be a group of corduroy garments for a 7–14 range. The jacket, dress, and skirt all have princess seam lines. The merchandise meeting members suggested that a jumper be added to the group. The obvious additional

piece would be a jumper with princess lines. The jacket has large, gold military buttons and cordage. Putting the same buttons on the shoulder of the jumper and cordage down the princess lines would bring in two of the elements that are prominent in the group. The one area of concern would be to make sure the blouses included in the group could be worn under the jumper. The filling-in step is successful and complete.

Finishing off a group that has more pizzazz can be trickier. If the merchandise meeting members like a group, but it doesn't seem as strong as other groups and needs a design boost, then the designer has a bigger challenge ahead. First, the designer needs to determine exactly how many more garments need to be sketched and how many more samples need to be sewn. Sketching the entire group as it exists now, and then sketching new garments to complete the group will keep the assignment focused.

Time is of the essence at this point in the process of completing the line. Finding the new detail, trim, or selling asset for a half-finished group is not always easy, but with concentration, the perfect fix will present itself. An additional design detail may need to be introduced in order to add strength to the group. Sometimes changing to larger or more unusual buttons that contrast with the fabric is all that is necessary. Occasionally in the 4–6x range, the addition of a little bow or floral appliqué sewn on a collar can tie the entire group together. In the junior range, it may be the addition of a pocket flap. The adjustments don't have to be earth shattering; they just need to be attractive and unify the entire group. It is important to make sure the newly sketched garments are fresh and not just a rehash of other garments already in the line. Going back to research trends and seeing if something was missed may help in this process. Garments that are altered, enhanced, or added will need to go through the entire pricing procedure before joining the line.

The line is considered ready when all the different groups hang well together, and every garment contributes to the theme or vision of the designer. To be complete the line must be pressed, priced, tagged, and hung on showroom hangers. The cost sheets should be complete and filed in the appropriate storage units or computer files. The fabric swatches and color choices should be compiled in the manner the company demands.

SELLING PROPS AND VISUAL AIDS

The designer has an additional chore once the line is completed. That chore is to assist the sales staff with whatever visual aids they feel would help them show the line of clothing to its fullest advantage. Some sellers prefer that the designer put together art boards that describe the different groups. Other sellers are happy with just having swatch cards and the garments. Whatever the sales staff requires, the designer works along with them to ensure they feel confi-

dent they have all the components necessary to outshine the competition. The swatch card is a valuable aid because of the many varied fabric options. (See Figure 10.5.)

Art boards often include the flat sketches of a group in the line, with perhaps one single garment sketched larger with fabric swatches displayed to showcase the assets of particular garments. Sellers may put the boards up as they show the line to buyers, or present the group of boards first, then one by one, show the garments. The garment sketches can be done on the computer or manually. Flat sketches that show the seam lines may be particularly helpful to sellers. Boards that concentrate on one particular asset of a group are generally better selling aids than boards that try to be too flamboyant. The garment will show all the bells and whistles. The boards are used as gentle reminders and detail enhancers. (See Figure 10.6.)

Brochures that are printed to advertise the line are not usually the responsibility of the designer, but on occasion the designer may offer insight to the marketing department or graphic designer.

DESIGNER AND BUYER RELATIONSHIP BENEFITS

Sometimes a seller will ask the designer to accompany the line to early showings for buying offices and to buyers that have a strong relationship with the company. In those instances the designer will explain trends, her creative insights, and even the thought process of how the line direction came into being. An experienced buyer can be very helpful to a designer's development as a merchant's designer. This special type of designer learns not just to design cute or innovative clothing but also to have the rare ability to design garments that have exactly the right combination of style lines, trim, color, and fabric for a particular consumer that hits the market with perfect timing. A buyer who hits it off with a designer can give insights from a completely different experience and point of view that enables a designer to see past the aesthetics of clothing (whether a garment is simply

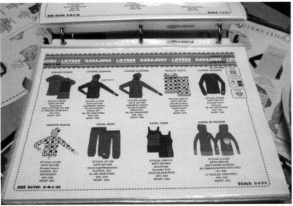

FIG. 10.5. Top. THIS IS A EXAMPLE OF A COLOR CARD USED BY SALESMEN WHEN THEY SHOW THE LINE.

FIG. 10.6. Bottom. THIS STYLE CARD IS COMPUTER GENERATED TO GIVE ALL THE INFORMATION NEEDED ABOUT EACH STYLE FOR SALES PRESENTATIONS.

FIG. 10.7. THE SALES ASSOCIATE PACKS THE LINE GARMENTS TO SHIP THEM TO NEW YORK FOR MARKET WEEK.

appealing to the eye), into the business of selling clothing in a very competitive field.

Designer and buyer relationships can be useful for both the retailer and the manufacturing company. Designers bring their innovative ideas and trend instincts to the table. Buyers bring their experience and market exposure to the table and help designers understand how the entire market is reacting to current trends. Buyers who help a designer put together a group or a garment also have a vested interest, partly due to their egos, for that group, or garment, to succeed. Often this leads to an order on the garments plus the buyer's inclination to put the collaborated garments in the best area of presentation and possibly even in special advertisements.

It is easy for a designer to think her line is the best and that she's captured the new trends in a very saleable and innovative manner. A designer needs to feel that confidence, but buyers see how every designer translates the trends. They see all the new color direction across the market. They also get to view all the new fabrications and the exciting silhouettes. It is hard

for a designer to imagine having the benefit of viewing all of the garments in a certain category, a certain trend, and in a particular season hung together for a mass comparison. It is then the buyer's job to judge which of the garments available are best suited for the consumer. Buyers will sample different styles from different vendors and hang them together to see which garment actually has the most flair and which garment is the best value for the price. It is important for every girls' and junior designer to remember that the competition has similar access to market research, the same access to new fabrics, and possibly the same exposure to cultural phenomenon. The competition is stiff, and the payoffs to having a successful selling season are lucrative. Each designer must try to put his or her own individual stamp on a line in order to make it stand out among the many similar, but hopefully, less-creative garments. Having a buyer as a sounding board is a wonderful asset.

Buyers have a limited amount of money they can spend on the new season's clothing. There is also a finite amount of retail space in each department. The responsibility of the buyer is to fill that space and budget that money in the best possible manner to make the largest profit for the retailer. Each manufacturer wants a portion of the money and a part of the selling floor space. Anything a designer can learn from the buyer to have an advantage over the competition is clearly a boon to the clothing manufacturer.

THE LINE GOES ON THE ROAD

The line is complete and ready to hit the road. The fill-ins are inserted, the alterations are complete, and latest trends are included. Art boards are packed, swatches are organized, buyer appointments are made, and order books are ready to be filled out. The sales representative is ready to take the line to New York for market week. (See Figure 10.7.) The next stage is the waiting game. Waiting to see which of the garments will be the first to start booking. Waiting to see which garment will get a national ad. And, waiting to see which styles will be ignored

Chapter 11

Pre-Production New Style Preparation

The sales staff's hard work is generating purchase orders on the new line. At long last, the designer can sigh with relief. The line is selling well. The stress of wondering if the new designs would be appreciated and, more importantly, worrying if the line will be purchased by the retailers, is diminishing. A different process that causes stress is heading toward the designer. The preparation of samples for production is at hand and getting all the newly booked garments translated into production prototypes is a huge undertaking. Designing new looks and trendy garments in the girls' and junior markets is only the preliminary stage of the designer's workload. Making sure the production garments fit properly and look as good as the original concept is part of the designer's pre-production responsibilities.

PRODUCTION PREPARATION SEQUENCE

Stock garments, the term for mass-produced garments that are shipped to retailers, are fit-corrected and refined by experts in several departments. There are five steps that must be completed before a sample is released for production. The first step is to process the purchase order and determine that the retailer is financially secure. This step demands the attention of the credit department. Next, orders will be placed to purchase the fabric and all the trimmings necessary to meet the order obligations. This computation of the quantities of fabric and trimmings, and then the issuing of the purchase orders to obtain those goods, must be completed by the production department's purchasing agent. Production patterns need to be **drafted**, and production samples must be sewn, tested, and approved. The patternmakers in the production patternmaking department oversee these tasks. The production pattern must be graded and, finally, the marker will be made. This last stage may be done manually, or with the aid of computerized programs. Some grading and marking is done in house, and other companies contract out for these services. Each of these five steps will command attention to detail, and each step is vital to the company's bottom line.

Handling the Purchase Orders

The purchase orders received from retailers go through several hands before the order is filled and garments are shipped. The purchase order must be credit checked and logged into a **cut and sold system**, which is a fancy name for keeping tabs on how many garments are ordered, when they will be cut, and when they will be delivered to the retailers. A purchase order is a legally binding agreement.

If the clothing manufacturer is **factored**, which means it sells its **receivables** to a bank, the order must be credit checked and approved by the bank before the production department can even start the pre-production process. If the manufacturer is not factored, the bookkeeping department will have to do the credit checking through other channels. One way or another, the clothing manufacturer will have to make sure that the purchase order is being written by a company that is capable of paying the bill when it comes due and that the company has had a reliable record of making its payments in full. Some retailers are notoriously late in paying invoices, and other retailers fabricate miscellaneous markdowns, which make clothing manufacturers hesitant to do further business with them. The entire financial picture regarding credit and terms has to be investigated by financial managers prior to the production department issuing their purchase orders for fabric yardage.

Before the age of computers, manufacturing companies received purchase orders by snail mail. The order quantities were recorded by hand, according to each style ordered, in a large ledger, which was called the *cut and sold ledger*. It was a time-consuming, but trusted method of keeping track of which purchase order had been received and which on-order garments had been cut. Sales representatives could look in the ledger and see if the production department was keeping up with its cancellation dates. The inventory of garments that were cut over the quantity needed to fill purchase orders already in hand was also indicated so that the sales

personnel could sell those extra garments to smaller stores.

If we fast-forward to current company practice, the purchase orders usually come through sophisticated computer programs. Retailers have the ability to consolidate the paper trail involved in purchasing garments through linkups with vendors. Conversely, the manufacturing sector can actually follow the sell through of the garments once they hit the selling floor via the same computer links. Even with the convenience of electronic data processing, the cut and sold system is still the basic method by which manufacturers keep track of the work in process for the company. The computer has simply cut down on the man-hours it takes to input and keep track of orders, inventory, and contracting facilities. Computers have made tracking the garment through every stage of production a much more manageable chore.

Every manufacturer has a *minimum cut*. This is the fewest number of garments of a particular style that can be cut, sewn, and shipped for a profit. This minimum varies from company to company according to its garment price points, overhead, and possible production issues. For example, a dress manufacturer that averages $195.00 per prom dress might need to only make 240 units to meet its minimum for a department store purchase, while a screen-print T-shirt manufacturer may need 10,000 units in the mass-market in order to break even because of expensive graphic art or licensing agreements. In another example, it may take 3,000 garments to meet the fabric company's minimum yardage requirement, so an order for 500 garments may have to be cancelled if the sales force cannot get other retailers to purchase additional quantities of that particular style. The investment in patterns, grading, and marking each style becomes less per unit as the volume increases.

The new purchase orders received from all the different retailers are logged in by style and number in order to see if the minimum cut is met. Once the minimum cut is satisfied,

FIG. 11.1. THE FABRIC SALESPERSON IS THRILLED TO RECEIVE A LARGE ORDER FOR FABRIC FROM HER LINE.

the style goes forward into the next stage of pre-production.

Pre-Production Style Scheduling

Once the production department has determined that a style has met the minimums and is going into work, they set the production sample process in motion. It is the production department that determines which style the production patternmaker is required to work on first. The production manager usually makes up a list of styles that need pattern work, and he or she lists those styles in the order in which they should be completed. That work order is determined by several criteria.

The first consideration is the delivery date by which the style must be shipped. However, if several styles or many styles have the same delivery date, the sequence can get complicated. The production department has to determine which fabric will be received first, which garment takes longer to sew, which style is being constructed offshore. Many other factors may contribute to production problems or delays as well. This juggling of many styles and issues makes production departments such a vital part of the success of the apparel industry.

Ordering Stock Piece Goods and Trimmings

Ordering the necessary piece goods is the next step in the production process. (See Figure 11.1.) Manufacturers can purchase fabric on *speculation* or per demand, as orders are taken for the new production. If the manufacturer purchases fabric on speculation, it means the company has strong opinions about the fabric's potential to sell garments, or the designer develops a fabrication and orders it presuming that a trend is going to sell well. This usually means the design and merchandising team think that the fabrication is so strong, they are certain that it will sell, and management is willing to go along with an initial investment with no paper or purchase orders to cut against the spec fabric. The only decision left after selecting the fabric in this scenario is determining how much to purchase, and when to have it delivered. This method of purchasing fabric gives the manufacturer the distinct advantage of being able to ship garments for earlier ship dates as the fabric was preordered before the line was shown and put into work prior to the rest of the market. This makes the production process easier because the fabric is in stock, waiting to be spread or cut as soon as the pattern process is completed. There is no *downtime,* which is the term for the span of time that cannot be utilized if the marker is ready to cut and there is no fabric available. Of course the downside of this is the possibility that the design team is incorrect and they cannot actually sell the fabric, or the company is left with a portion of the fabric unsold, thus tying up dollars in useless fabric inventory.

The alternative to purchasing fabric on spec, or speculation, is for the manufacturer to *chase* the piece goods. This means that the fabric is not purchased until the styles in the line sell enough to meet the minimum fabric yardage quantity. This method can create some obstacles for the production department. First, of course, is the problem of getting the fabric fast enough to make the delivery dates required on the retailers' purchase orders. The second problem is getting the fabric at the price that was originally quoted. Sometimes prices in the fabric market rise between the time the sample fabric is received and the time the style is sold. The price may increase due to an increase in the greige goods pricing or simply because supply and demand. Greige goods, or raw fabrics before they are processed in **finishing**, are subject to more price fluctuations than finished goods are. When fabrics get hot, the market price will go up. Other factors, like changes in the price of oil, or instability in a region that is producing either the fabric or the fiber for the fabric, will also affect the price of material.

Once a fabric has sold enough to go into production, it is not uncommon for the clothing manufacturer to *step out* and purchase more fabric than needed for existing orders in the belief that more orders on the same fabric will follow. One indication that a fabric or print might be hot is when the initial sales show several different retailers gravitating toward the same style. When this happens, the manufacturer has incentive to order more fabric than the company currently needs.

The method for determining how much fabric is actually needed for the stock goods is similar to determining the costs on cost sheets. If 2,400 garments sold in two colors, red and blue, and each garment takes 39 inches of fabric, the amount of fabric needed is $39 \times 2,400$ divided by 36 inches, which equals 2,600 yards of fabric or 1,300 yards of red and 1,300 yards in blue. The purchasing agent for the company, usually an assistant to the production manager, will figure in waste during cutting, percentages of possible damages during construction, pos-

sible increase in yardage from first sample to production sample, and then buy enough fabric to cover the orders on hand, with additional yardage for projected sales, if instructed by management. To control buying too little yardage, manufacturers can, over time, estimate the average fabric and garment damages, thereby enabling them to purchase a fixed percentage above their required amount.

The purchase of trimmings is done in the same manner as fabric. Purchasing trimmings however, is often more time consuming. Each garment may need several different trims. Besides the buttons, zippers, and other closures there can be decorative trims like lace edgings, appliqués, or many other trimmings. Each different notion must have the quantity needed projected onto a different purchase order, and all those items must be monitored in order to make sure they arrive in a timely manner. If the trims are not received prior to the stock garment being cut, then downtime can create backlogs in the production cycle. For a manufacturer that deals specifically in a particular product, for instance a jeans company, it is sometimes necessary to purchase huge quantities of its logo buttons or specific-length metal-teeth zippers in order to stay ahead of a production crunch.

Trims that are trendy for the season are seldom bought in bulk prior to a season because the volatile nature of fads can be too risky. There is nothing harder to use on the next season's line than old trims. Sometimes they have to sit in boxes for several years before they come back into style.

Some purchasing agents order trim quantities to match the exact quantity of garments that are cut for specific stores. The cut figure will include the expected loss or damage number. The trims are labeled to match that cut. This method of coordinating cuts with trimmings decreases surpluses at the end of the season. Trim quantities that are overestimated for stock and sent out to contractors have a way of disappearing and costing the manufacturers extra in the long run.

The purchasing agent also needs to coordinate the delivery of fabrics and trims so that no stage of the garment's production is held up due to late shipping. Sometimes this time coordination is more difficult. If buttons have to be sent out for dyeing, or fabric is treated with a process like pleating or quilting before it can be cut into garments, production time can be lost. All the different components of each garment, and all the different handling processes of each garment, have to be carefully analyzed and planned in order to keep the production flow moving in a timely manner toward the delivery date. The ideal is to have the fabric in house and ready to cut, with the trim received by the time the production pattern is made, and the testing done so that the garments can be cut as soon as the retailer approves the sample. Unfortunately, in manufacturing, having all components ready with ideal timing is a rare phenomenon and the very reason manufacturing can be such a risky but lucrative venture.

THE PRODUCTION PATTERN

A **production pattern** is a pattern that has been carefully fit to specific measurements. It is drafted in a manner that eliminates any production problems or issues. All the seams must match. All the notches must be aligned. Punch holes for pockets must be placed strategically so that pockets will align correctly. When cut, production garments are being sewn from a perfect production pattern, there is no question how the garment should be sewn up, because the patternmaker has laid out the matching of seams with notches in such a way that it is obvious to the seamstress how the pieces go together. When notched correctly, the seams will not match in any other direction, which keeps the mistakes in check and lets the assembly of the garments go smoothly through the sewing machines.

The sample makers who sew up the production sample will note any construction problems, and they make sure that factory workers will have no option but to sew the garment as the production patternmaker intended. A pro-

duction pattern is the foundation on which the entire garment's selling success is based. If the garment does not fit, it won't sell. If the garment is not sewn together well due to confusing or mismatched notches, it won't sell. If the pattern is wrong, perhaps a placket attached to the wrong side of a shirt front, the garment won't sell. The best analogy for the pattern is that it is the chicken for a pot of chicken soup. If the chicken is rotten, it will not matter that the soup was cooked for the right amount of time or that the carrots were the best offered. The soup is ruined with bad chicken. The garment is also ruined if the production pattern is faulty.

Accompanying the production pattern is a **production pattern card**. This card is like a preliminary pattern specification sheet. On the card is the style number of the garment with a technical flat sketch of the front and back of the garment. Some companies also have each pattern piece sketched on the card and labeled. Other companies simply list the specific number and description of the pattern pieces, along with the total number of pieces required for the garment. The pattern pieces for the garment are listed according to **self-goods**, or **contrast** fabrics, or linings and interlinings. Notions and their measurements are also listed. For example, the grading measurements for all the sizes are usually listed with both the cut elastic lengths per size and the finished waist measurement for the elastic tunnels per size.

Initial Line Sample Fittings

The production patternmaker's work schedule coincides with purchasing. There is no time delay while one department is doing the purchasing or another is working on the fit and the pattern correction. Both events happen simultaneously. Once the new style number is on the production patternmaker's list of priority styles needing to have patterns perfected, the production cycle is put into motion.

The first step for the production manager and the production patternmaker is to review the garment and decide if any changes to the construction will be necessary. If so, the

FIG. 11.2. THE PRODUCTION SAMPLE HAS TO FIT THE FORM, PLUS MEASURE TO FIT THE SPECIFICATIONS ORDERED BY THE STORE, AND FINALLY FIT COMFORTABLY ON A LIVE BODY. THE PATTERNMAKER HERE IS MEASURING THE LENGTH OF THE GARMENT ON THE LITTLE GIRL. NOTICE THE PROPORTION OF THE HEAD TO THE BODY OF THE SIZE 5 CHILD. NOTICE ALSO THE IMPATIENCE OF THE CHILD. FITTINGS ON LITTLE GIRLS ARE ALWAYS TRYING.

changes will be noted and changed on the production sample.

The second action required is for the production patternmaker to arrange a fitting time with the designer to go over what changes in fit need to be made. (See Figure 11.2.) The changes in construction will be discussed, but normally these will not be changes that would affect the outward appearance of the garment. The production patternmaker has to make the pattern conform to specific measurements that are given either by the purchasing retailer (the customer) or by the manufacturer's own in-house measurement standards.

Fittings are done on both live models and on mannequins. There are some obvious benefits to having a live model. She can complain if something is uncomfortable. She can move in order to give the patternmaker a feel for how much ease needs to be added or removed. Seeing the garment on a moving figure also helps the designer to finesse some flair and proportions that may give the garment more personality. Most importantly, the model can state her opinion about the overall look of the garment, which can be a great asset. The designer and patternmaker may listen to the opinion, but realize that it is simply a personal taste comment and not representative of all little girls or teens or, most importantly, the target consumer.

The actual fit of a garment often depends on the retailer's measurements, so it is not uncommon for manufacturers to have mannequins that are made to fit a retailer's standard. For example, if a company ships a lot of clothing to Wal-Mart, as well as a sizeable amount to JCPenney, there may be two separate dress forms in the production patternmaker's space labeled with the individual store's name. If both retailers buy the same style, the patterns will be labeled with the store's name in order to prevent any confusion when they are cut. Different style numbers will also be assigned to the garments. There are rigid acceptable tolerances in measurements once the garments are sewn, so conforming to the required standard is essential. If a dress is supposed to measure 30 inches from neck to hem, the acceptable tolerance may be ½ inch. A dress that is finished at 28 inches would not pass inspection and could result in a cancellation of the dress order.

The designer and the production patternmaker work together to keep the proportions of the designer's new style intact, while still allowing for adjustments in fit to conform to the required measurements. In addition to fitting the measurements, the pattern must include ease for movement. Both the designer and the production patternmaker must agree on how much ease is necessary and how the garment may need to be altered to fit correctly. First patterns are often made so quickly that proper fit is not sustained throughout the new season's line.

The original line samples are tried on for the first production fitting. This is when any projected alterations will be determined. Decisions regarding whether the garment needs specific changes in construction, fit, or proportion are addressed at this juncture. Sometimes garment changes involve an increase in the yardage estimated on the cost sheet. This is why prudent designers will have put all garments made for the new line on the mannequins in the design room prior to showing the line. If the garment was snug or short and that information was known prior to doing the yardage estimates for the costing process, the yardage estimate would have been adjusted to account for the increase and the garment's price would reflect that change even if the garment was not altered.

Designer Fit and Style Input

Turning over a new style to the production patternmaker to re-do according to different specifications is a difficult process for a designer. Designers normally think their original looks perfect and any alteration is detrimental to the garment. By the time new styles are selling, the designer has forged a bond with each garment and seeing them transition from design concept to assembly line is a real leap of faith. The designer must trust the experts in the production departments to do their best to keep the style from wilting under the strain of conforming to a product that can be profitably produced.

It is the designer's job to protect each new garment from alteration that affects the style, the trend, the proportions, or the flair of the garment that has been sold. If there is an area of contention between the designer and the production department, it is in the nuance of style change that can happen if a production patternmaker is not carefully monitored. It is the designer's job to make sure the style looks just as good after it is altered as it did in the original vision, and certainly as good as it did in the version that the store purchased.

Because the scale of girls' and junior garments are rather small, minor changes in length and width can affect the entire proportion of a garment. If the bodice on a 4–6x girls' dress is hitting just above the waist as it should, and the production patternmaker wants to bring it down toward the waist by 1½″ it can throw off the proportion and ruin the designer's style. If the seam line beneath the bust on a junior clingy knit top is lowered by a fraction of an inch it can make the top go from cute and perky to frumpy in a flash. If the cap sleeve ruffle is short and flirty on a 7–14 sundress, a patternmaker can ruin it by adding an inch in length. Designers must be ready to insist that the garment's integrity not change in the initial fitting. Letting a competent production patternmaker know which style lines are untouchable is a way to head off a possible impasse.

Sometimes a garment has to be drastically altered to fit properly. If this increases the yardage, it can have a negative impact on the profitability of the style. In this scenario, it may take more than the designer's okay or the production patternmaker's opinion on the correct fit to continue the production cycle. Executives may have to approve major expenditures.

For example, a 7–14 capri pant, that is so tight that the model is unable to sit down, needs alteration. The increase to each side seam of the pattern is ¾ inch. Added together, front and back, the increase in the layout of the patterns is 3 inches across the goods. Before the adjustment, two front patterns and two back pattern pieces fit across the goods. With the adjustment made, only three pattern pieces will fit. The increase to the marker is 8 inches. The additional 8 inches of fabric equates to a $.65 increase in direct cost. The retailer should pay at least a price point higher for the capri pant. The production manager will have to review the style to see if there is any room on the cost sheet to absorb the increase and still be profitable. If not, the sales department will have to go back to the buyer and ask for more money. Asking for additional money on a garment that has been purchased in good faith at a lower price is a difficult proposition for the sales staff. Many buyers are unwilling to be flexible in this situation and the purchase order for the pant may be cancelled.

The proper fit of a garment is slightly subjective. Generally in the girls' and junior markets the amount of ease, that extra allowance to make sure garments are comfortable and not skin tight, is determined by the expected activities for which the garment will be worn. Obviously, exercise clothing must stretch and give easily. Party dresses for little girls don't require any special allowance for stretch, but they may need a good pinch of ease under the armhole for potential growth room. Comfort is an important issue for young girls, so making sure there is enough ease for putting on and taking off clothing is essential. In most cases, the production patternmaker and the designer will agree on exactly how much ease is necessary. The amount of ease is normally ½ inch per seam on the bodice and slightly less on sleeves and cuffs. Prior to approving any pant fit, the designer and the production patternmaker should have a model sit and squat to make sure the ease is enough to make the pant comfortable.

Production patternmakers have to be detail oriented in order to do their jobs well. There are so many exact measurements to conform to, and so many detailed forms to fill out, that they bring a special set of abilities to the company. They also work under stressful time constraints. That being said, designers must find a way to work amicably with them because both designers and patternmakers are crucial to the success of the company. Designers may see the garments in a rainbow of colors, but production patternmakers work in black and white. There is no gray area in production patternmaking. The pattern is either right or wrong. The garment either fits perfectly or needs more alteration to meet the measurement specifications. The garment either sews together perfectly or it needs the pattern to be perfected. Excellent production patternmakers make the original design shine, and savvy designers appreciate their talents.

The designer is on the sidelines once the production sample has been approved. The real laborious duties of patternmaking, sewing up of samples, and filling out **specification sheets**, or *spec sheets,* are performed in the production

patternmaking department. The later pre-production duties of grading, marking, and testing fall to the production department staff.

Production Pattern Process
Production patternmakers may use the first pattern as the basis for the production pattern. In this case, they will make their changes to the first pattern, either manually or in the computer. Some production patternmakers prefer to draft their patterns from scratch using the appropriate sloper that uses the measurements of the retailer that is purchasing the goods or the measurements that the manufacturer prefers.

In the girls' and junior markets, the measurements used for fittings vary greatly. There are definite measurement variations from retailer to retailer. In the upstairs and specialty market, clothing tends to run larger, unless the current trend is to be snug, like the terry jogging suits made popular by Juicy Couture. Department stores will allow their manufacturers to produce their own fit standards, and as long as there are no complaints about the garments not fitting, the retailers will allow each manufacturing house to use their unique fit as a selling feature. When it comes to mass-market retailers, there is a rigid expectation that garments must adhere to each retailer's own specifications. Unfortunately, these measurements never match, so the manufacturers are forced to make different patterns, markers, and spec sheets for each purchase order. This added cost in production is justified by the larger volume quantities.

Once the pattern is made, it is cut in the correct fabric and sewn up. Expert sample makers will point out any notching issues or difficulty with the pattern so that it can be refined further. If the production sample is sewn, and it fits to the patternmaker's satisfaction, another fitting will take place. The production pattern is so important, that it might take several prototype samples just to get a sample that fits correctly and is sewn perfectly.

The production pattern should have a production pattern card attached that has a technical or flat sketch of the style, plus the style number, and the number of pieces cut in each fabric, including the linings and interlinings. (See Figure 11.3.) Depending upon the company, more detailed information can be also filled in. (See Figures 11.4a and 11.4b.)

Production Sample Fitting

The final fitting for a style's production sample is held immediately upon the sample's completion. It is imperative that the production department not be delayed by fit sample scheduling conflicts between the design and pattern departments. The designer must accommodate the production patternmaker and be available regularly to inspect and approve each sample, even if it repeatedly breaks up the designer's day. This fitting requires that both the designer and the production patternmaker approve the garment's fit, the construction finishing methods, the ease, and the overall appearance. If the designer is still unhappy with the fit, adjustments will have to be

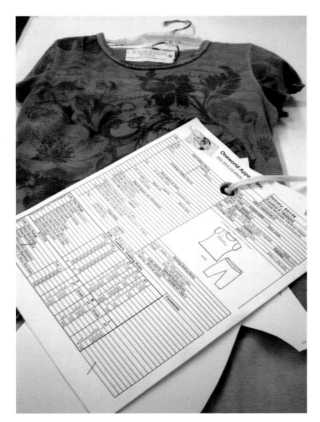

FIG. 11.3. THE PATTERN CARD, PATTERN ON HARD PAPER, AND SAMPLE ARE KEPT TOGETHER.

made on the pattern, and a new sample will be sewn. The process repeats itself until all parties agree that the production sample is satisfactory.

If a disagreement on the fit occurs, it may take intervention by either sales staff or the retailer for resolution. This is rare but it does occur. It is not uncommon for the retailer to approve the sample fit prior to production, and take the decision out of the hands of either the designer or the production patternmaker. Designers don't always have the last say, but they need to be strong enough in their opinions to project their views to all concerned.

Production Sample Requirements

A production sample by definition is a sample garment that is sewn as a perfect example of how replications of that sample will look when they are shipped to the customers. The sample must be finished inside and out exactly as instructed by the production manager. Seam finishes will conform to the finishes available to the factory in which the production department is having the stock garments made. All the thread colors need to be correct. All trimmings must be like the stock goods ordered. Threads must be trimmed. Garments need to be well pressed and hung on the correct store hangers exactly as the stock garments will be shipped. The production sample is the model for all future garments of this style to be copied. It must be a perfect example of what the manufacturer intends to ship.

Many large retailers demand a duplicate sample of the production prototype prior to delivery. They use this sample as a comparison to the stock they later receive in their warehouse. The sample will be used for fit approval prior to shipment and then stock comparison after stock goods are received. The retailer can use any variation from this original sample as evidence that the garments it actually receives do not conform to original specifications.

SPEC SHEETS

Once the fit and over all appearance of the production sample is approved by the designer

PATTERN CARD

STYLE # DE30-7323-CJ	CUSTOMER:
SIZE RANGE: XS-S-M-L-XL	STYLE # **DE30-7323-CJ**
DESCRIPTION: COLORBLOCKED SMOCK MAXI-DRESS	SIZE RANGE: XS-XL
	RATIO: SEE ORDER

STYLE # DE30-7323-CJ

SIZE RANGE: XS-S-M-L-XL

DESCRIPTION: COLORBLOCKED SMOCK MAXI-DRESS

P.O. #17527	BC #250324	REG #2467029

UNITS: SEE ORDER

DELIVERY DUE DATE: SEE ORDER

CHINA PRODUCTION: 876

SIZE RANGE: XS-XL	
RATIO: SEE ORDER	
PROD. PATTERNMAKER: **PAT NOMURA**	
RELEASE DATE: 11-26-08	DESIGNER: JULIE

PATTERN PIECES

	SELF	
1	TOP BODY	
	CONTRAST 1	
1	FRT RUFFLE	
1	BK RUFFLE	
	CONTRAST 2	
2	2ND RUFFLE	
	CONTRAST 3	
2	3RD RUFFLE	
	CONTRAST 4	
2	4TH RUFFLE	
	S/O	
1. Self straight cut 1 1/4" X 65" for 3/8" spaghetti.		

TIE MUST BE BE IN BOW FOR BULK SHIPPING

HANGER LOOPS 4 1/2" ON FOLD AT SIDE SEAM

TIE KNOT & INSERT BEADS 3/8" spaghetti straps 10" fin. BOW TIE 20" FINISH, CTR & TACK W/KNOT @ END. SET STRAPS FRT & BK 2 1/2" IN FROM SIDE SEAM FOR SZ MED

TIES MUST BE IN BOW FOR BULK SHIPPING

Top body s/o 11 rows smocking & 1/2" apart fin. 12" after steam FOR SZ MED.

SET 1/4" ELASTIC TO EMPIRE SEAM EMPIRE SEAM FINISH 12" FOR SZ MED.

Flat merrow top each ruffle edge & hem. shirring even set in each panel

ALL PANEL SHIRRING IS 1 1/2 TO 1 RATIO

TRIMS

QTY	ITEM	STYLE	COL	SIZE	PLAC
1	ELASTIC	1/4"		1/4"	EMPIRE SEAM
2	ELASTIN	CLEAR	CLEAR	1/4"	SS UND/ARM
8	BEADS				

LABEL: **PLACE LABEL @ CENTER BACK**

NECK BY S.N.T.S.

CUTTING INSTRUCTION

RELAX FABRIC BEFORE CUTTING

1-ST FIT	
2-D FIT	
3-D FIT	

PRESSING INSTRUCTION

PRESS GARMENT W/ LIGHT STEAM ONLY. MAKE SURE THAT

NECK AND ARMHOLES ARE PRESSED EVEN & NOT STRETCHED.

FIG. 11.4a. EXAMPLE OF COMPLETED PATTERN CARD.

PATTERN CARD

		CUSTOMER:	
		STYLE #	

STYLE #

SIZE RANGE: XS-S-M-L-XL-XXL

DESCRIPTION:

P.O. #	BC #	REG #

UNITS: SEE ORDER

DELIVERY DUE DATE:

PRODUCTION:

PATTERN PIECES

A	SELF

STYLE #

SIZE RANGE: XS-XXL

RATIO:

PROD. PATTERNMAKER:

RELEASE DATE:	**DESIGNER:**

TRIMS

QTY	ITEM	STYLE	COL	SIZE	PLAC

LABEL:	PLACE LABEL @ CENTER BACK
	NECK BY S.N.T.S.

CUTTING INSTRUCTION

RELAX FABRIC BEFORE CUTTING

1-ST FIT

2-D FIT

3-D FIT

PRESSING INSTRUCTION
PRESS GARMENT W/ LIGHT STEAM ONLY. MAKE SURE THAT
NECK AND ARMHOLES ARE PRESSED EVEN & NOT STRETCHED.

FIG. 11.4b. EXAMPLE OF BLANK PATTERN CARD.

a specification sheet is filled out. The information of the spec sheet stays with the sample for clarification in the next stages of production. These sheets may vary from computer-generated forms done by production engineers to handwritten sheets filled out by production pattern assistants. In many smaller companies, the production patternmaker or an assistant in that department will fill out as much information as demanded by the production manager.

Most spec sheets have information in such detail that any question a worker might have along the production cycle can be answered by checking the details on the spec sheet. A technical flat sketch of the front and back of the garment is also shown on the spec sheet. If there is some decorative detail on the garment, a blow-up sketch of that area of the garment may also be shown on the spec sheet. All trimmings and findings, like thread color and content, are listed, so that all factory or contracting parties know what is expected. Some companies actually sew a completed spec sheet to the production sample to ensure that the two are never separated. When the spec sheet is lengthy or very involved it is called a **design spec package**, or a *tech pack*. It is rarely the responsibility of the designer to complete spec sheets. Most production departments want the actual spec sheets to be filled out, whether by hand or computer, by a specialist. This is very exacting work with careful measurements and data. (See Figures 11.5a and 11.5b.)

The purpose of a spec sheet is to clarify everything about a style that is necessary to know during the production cycle. Measurements for the finished garment are listed so that when the garments are reproduced they can be checked to see that they are done correctly. For example, the amount of cut elastic that is needed for a pull-on pant waist is listed on the spec sheet with all the other sizes' cut measurements and finish measurements. The spacing for each button is measured and reflected. Every detail pertaining to the garment is put down in black and white as a ready reference.

Some companies list the fabric company and all the fabric information including content, weight, and special factors that might include the stretch or shrinkage expected.

If the garment has special treatments, like jeans that need stonewashing, specific instructions will detail how that finish should be created.

Swatches will either accompany the sheet or be attached so that the garment, and the preferred swatch colors, will follow the production cycle so that they can be compared at every stage of production. Buttons or trim may be attached to the spec sheet in order to make sure the correct notions are used for the garment. Nothing is left to chance.

A special section of the spec sheet is usually reserved for measurements. Finished measurements are given for necks, waists, cuffs, and any other section of the garment that is considered crucial to the correct fit. Measurements are given for each graded size. Each garment that is sewn must conform to the tolerance level set on the spec sheet. If the finished waist measurement for a size 10 girls' skirt is 24 inches, and the tolerance is ½ inch, skirts that measure 25 inches will be set aside and either fixed or held as **seconds**. By measuring garments at random, contractors or garment inspectors can ascertain if most of the garments are sewn within the tolerance allowed by both the manufacturer's standards and the retailer's agreement.

Some spec sheets include a step-by-step explanation of the construction process. When this operations sequence is required, a specialist will carefully list the sewing steps to complete the garment. Each step of garment construction is broken down into separate sewing operations. This analysis shows the most efficient method of construction, and it assures the level of quality that the manufacturer and the retailer, demand from the factory. For example, sleeves on a girl's dress can be set with the side seams open. The next operation closes the seam from the cuff of the sleeve all the way down the side seam of the garment. This method is much more efficient than completing the sleeve and then setting the sleeve into a closed armhole. Closing the seam in that manner is faster, but the result

SPEC SHEET

STYLE # DE30-7323-CJ

SIZE RANGE: S - M - L - XL

DESCRIPTION: COLORBLOCK SMOCKED MAXI DRESS

P.O. # 17527	BC # 250324	REG # 246726

UNITS: SEE ORDER

DELIVERY DUE DATE: SEE ORDER

COUNTRY OF ORIGIN: 876	RELEASE DATE: 11-26-08

TOPS							
POINT OF MEASUREMENT	TOL (+)	TOL (−)	S	M	L	XL	
BODY LENGTH (CENTER BACK)	TOL 1/2	1/2	29 1/2	30	30 1/2	31	
CHEST WIDTH 1″ BELOW A.H	TOL 1/2	1/2	10 3/4	11 1/2	12 1/2	13 1/2	
BOTTOM SWEEP OPENING	TOL 1/2	1/2	56 3/4	57 1/2	58 1/2	59 1/2	
SHOULDER STRAP	TOL 1/2	1/2	9 1/2	10	10 1/2	10 1/2	
FRONT STRAP PLMNT FROM SIDE SEAM	TOL 1/4	1/4	2 1/4	2 1/2	2 7/8	2 7/8	
BACK STRAP PLMNT FROM SIDE SEAM	TOL 1/4	1/4	2 1/4	2 1/2	2 7/8	2 7/8	
TOP BODY-EDGE TO SEAM	TOL 1/4	1/4	5 1/2	5 1/2	5 1/2	5 1/2	
1ST RUFFLE-EDGE TO SEAM	TOL 1/4	1/4	6 3/4	6 7/8	7	7 1/8	
2ND RUFFLE-EDGE TO SEAM	TOL 1/4	1/4	6 1/4	6 3/8	6 1/2	6 5/8	
3RD RUFFLE-EDGE TO SEAM	TOL 1/4	1/4	6 1/4	6 3/8	6 1/2	6 5/8	
4TH RUFFLE-EDGE TO SEAM	TOL 1/4	1/4	6 3/4	6 7/8	7	7 1/8	

SEWING INSTRUCTION

★ **STITCHES:** 10-12 STITCHES PER INCH

★ **SEAMS:** 1/4″ 4-THREAD OVERLOCK JOIN SEAM

★ **THREAD:** USE 100% SPUN POLYESTER TEX 27 TO MATCH
USE THREAD TO MATCH FOR OUTSIDE STITCHING.

FIT COMMENT: 12-22-08

APPRD. LOOKS GREAT - ADD LABEL

1/4″ ELASTIC 1 1/2 ON FOLD @ SIDE SEAMS

TIE KNOT & INSERT BEADS 3/8″ spaghetti straps 10″ fin. BOW TIE 20″ FINISH, CTR & TACK W/KNOT @ END. SET STRAPS FRT & BK 2 1/2″ IN FROM SIDE SEAM FOR SZ MED

Top body s/o 11 rows smocking & 1/2″ apart fin. 12″ after steam FOR SZ MED.

SET 1/4″ ELASTIC TO EMPIRE SEAM EMPIRE SEAM FINISH 12″ FOR SZ MED.

Flat merrow top each ruffle edge & hem. shirring even set in each panel

CUTTING INSTRUCTION

RELAX FABRIC BEFORE CUTTING

PRESSING INSTRUCTION

PRESS GARMENT W/ LIGHT STEAM ONLY. MAKE SURE THAT
NECK & ARMHOLES ARE PRESSED EVEN & NOT STRETCHED.

FIG. 11.5a. EXAMPLE OF COMPLETED SPEC SHEET.

SPEC SHEET

STYLE #			
SIZE RANGE:	S - M - L - XL		
DESCRIPTION:			
P.O. #	BC #	REG #	
UNITS:			
DELIVERY DUE DATE:			

COUNTRY OF ORIGIN:		RELEASE DATE:				

TOPS							
POINT OF MEASUREMENT	TOL (+)	TOL (−)	S	M	L	XL	
BODY LENGTH (CENTER BACK)	TOL 1/2	1/2					
CHEST WIDTH 1″ BELOW A.H	TOL 1/2	1/2					
BOTTOM SWEEP OPENING	TOL 1/2	1/2					
SHOULDER STRAP	TOL 1/2	1/2					
FRONT STRAP PLMNT FROM SIDE SEAM	TOL 1/4	1/4					
BACK STRAP PLMNT FROM SIDE SEAM	TOL 1/4	1/4					
TOP BODY-EDGE TO SEAM	TOL 1/4	1/4					
1ST RUFFLE-EDGE TO SEAM	TOL 1/4	1/4					
2ND RUFFLE-EDGE TO SEAM	TOL 1/4	1/4					
3RD RUFFLE-EDGE TO SEAM	TOL 1/4	1/4					
4TH RUFFLE-EDGE TO SEAM	TOL 1/4	1/4					

SEWING INSTRUCTION

★ STITCHES:

★ SEAMS:

★ THREAD:

CUTTING INSTRUCTION

PRESSING INSTRUCTION

FIG. 11.5b. EXAMPLE OF BLANK SPEC SHEET.

can be less than desirable if the seam is not clipped under the arm. If the garment is going to a mass merchant, and the seams are finished with a serger on ¼ inch, the first method should be compatible with the price of the garment, perhaps $19.99, and the value expected at that retail price. However, that method will not be acceptable for a specialty store's organza Easter dress that retails for $175.00.

Filling out spec sheets is a slow and boring job made more tedious by the required attention to detail. It is vital to the eventual outcome of the production garments. The more information that can be contained in clear, concise terms, the better chance the garments have of appearing as they are meant to look. With American apparel being manufactured in all corners of the world, by people speaking various languages, it is imperative that the sketches presented are technically exact, and that the wording is clear so that a simple translation from English is understandable.

TESTING OF FABRIC AND GARMENTS

During the pre-production process, a series of tests are performed on both the fabric before it is sewn up and on the sample garments that are fully constructed. The testing is done to make sure the garments that are produced will conform to the required standards. Many manufacturing companies maintain a testing site that is equipped with a washing machine and clothes dryer. Garments and fabric squares can be routinely tested and measured to avoid quality problems during the production cycle. (See Figure 11.6.)

The fabric is tested for shrinkage upon receipt from the fabric mills. Normally a square of fabric is cut one yard by one yard and washed as the fabric company suggests it should be. If the shrinkage is within the tolerance, the production samples will be cut and sewn.

Finished samples are tested again to make sure the various components are compatible with each other when laundered together. Several problems can occur when garments are composed of different fabrics, linings, or trims.

FIG. 11.6. MOST CLOTHING MANUFACTURERS HAVE ON-SITE TESTING AREAS TO MAKE SURE THE FABRIC AND GARMENTS LAUNDER EASILY WITHOUT TOO MUCH SHRINKAGE.

The three biggest issues are shrinkage, **crocking**, and skewing. Even if individual fabrics shrink within their tolerance measurement, they may not shrink to the same percentage as another fabric that is sewn together in the same garment. This can cause one of the fabrics to bunch up unevenly, or the garment can skew, which is to hang off grain. An example of this problem would be a junior knit top with contrasting woven collars, cuffs, and placket. The woven trim could have fused interlining. The woven trim might test fine as a fabric before it is sewn into a garment, but it could shrink differently than the knit and pucker the seams where it is attached. Alternatively, the interlining could shrink causing the trim collars, cuff, and placket to pucker.

Crocking happens when the color of a fabric actually rubs off. The fabric may not have been finished properly during its production cycle, and the color is not set. The dye may actually rub against other garments or fabrics in the same garment causing stains to appear. The easiest way to test for crocking is to take a swatch of the fabric and rub it against a white sheet of paper. If color is smeared onto the white, crocking may be a production problem.

When garments are constructed of several different fabrics sewn together, the fabrics have to be able to be laundered together without the dominant colored fabric changing the color of the contrasting goods. An example of this would be a blue print dress with white collars and cuffs. The dress must be tested to make sure that the blue does not bleed onto the white trim. Denim is notorious for bleeding. Bright red dye on printed cotton goods can also present problems when combined with white contrast goods.

Designers are supposed to take shrinkage and bleeding into consideration when designing garments, but in the haste to be creative and get the line out on time mistakes can occur. It is in the testing stage that those problems can be identified and solved.

GRADING PRODUCTION PATTERNS

After the garment has passed inspection for fit, appearance, and mandatory testing, the garment, spec sheet, and production pattern are passed off to the next expert in the pre-production cycle. This expert will do the grading of the production patterns. The purpose of grading a pattern is to create an entire set of patterns to fit each size in the range as purchased. The production pattern that is made in the sample size is the model for the grader to use to cut both smaller and larger versions. There is a base standard of **grade rules** that are followed to make the sample pattern pieces increase or decrease at specific points in order for the grade up, and the grade down to fit each additional size correctly.

Grading can be done manually. It is usually done with a grading machine, or by using a computer program. Pattern pieces are graded in length and width as the sizes change. Part of the increase in length is assigned to the bodice and another proportionate part is assigned to the below waist portion of a pattern. Conversely, the grade increases or decreases in circumference must be distributed to both front and back of the pattern pieces. Girls' clothing will sometimes have minuscule amounts of grading in circumference but a significant grade from hemline to hemline in order to account for growing bodies.

Designers have little or no influence on how patterns are graded. It is a matter of mathematical computations, and the grading measurements are not up for discussion. Some garments are designed to accommodate several sizes and need no grading except in length. A poncho for a girl or a junior might not need to be widened if it is a full cut garment. In this case, the designer and production patternmaker could strongly suggest that only a partial grade be applied. By increasing the width of the pattern, it is possible that the poncho could become bulky and out of proportion.

After the sample pattern is graded to a full pattern set that includes all the sizes in the size range that was sold, the entire set will be used for a marker. For example, a junior top pattern may have been sold in sizes small, medium, and large. The grader would have a pattern set that includes all those sizes hung together on one pattern hook or all sizes complete in the computer.

Making Markers

A marker is made by simply arranging all the pattern pieces of all the sizes necessary to cut a garment in one continuous layout. The pattern pieces are laid out within the width of the fabric that will be cut in such a manner as to utilize the fabric according to its grainline. Markers unrolled look like long rolls of paper that have been marked with the outline of the pattern pieces as a guide that will be followed to cut out all the sizes of the new style. The small sizes are made to fit in among the larger sizes in order to conserve fabric.

When a purchase order for garments is written, the retailer orders each style with a specific breakdown of sizes within each dozen sold. For example, in a 7–14 range the sizes are usually two size 7s, two size 8s, three size 10s, three size 12s, and two size 14s. This totals one dozen pieces. The marker would have to outline of two patterns of size 8, three patterns of size 10, and so on down the size range. Junior tops are usually cut size small, medium, large, and sometimes extra large. If the store is purchasing

Critics have claimed it's something else. Forever 21 said it was working to settle what's left of a couple dozen copyright- and trademark-infringement lawsuits, and the company was embroiled earlier in the decade in a legal battle with employees of Forever 21 subcontractors who claimed they worked six days a week, sometimes 12 hours a day, for far less than the minimum wage. The matter was settled out of court and the company, which admitted no wrongdoing, agreed to take steps to ensure that its garments were not made in sweatshops.

Sales, meanwhile, continued to climb. The company has forecasted revenue of $1.8 billion this year, up from $1.3 billion in 2007. And for 2009? The projection is $2.5 billion.

Along with European competitors H&M and Zara, Forever 21 created the inexpensive fast-fashion concept, spurring other apparel sellers to pick up the pace.

"They run lean and mean," said Debra Stevenson, president of Skyline Studios, a consulting firm in Los Angeles. "They have a lot of young people working for them, and they do understand their culture."

Chief Executive Don Chang has been working to understand shoppers since 1984, when he opened the first store in Highland Park. Business was slow, which helped him shape a strategy.

"The customer's always looking for the price," he said. If a purse didn't open, Chang asked questions. What's wrong? The fit? The fabric? "What kind of clothes do you want? I'll bring it for you."

Ilse Metchek, executive director of the California Fashion Assn., remembers her first visit to one of the early stores, a "hole in the wall" jammed with merchandise. "They had no talent for display, none," said Metchek, who called a couple of manufacturers and suggested they come have a look. "They said, 'My God, he's selling at retail for less than we could have made it at wholesale.'"

And Forever 21's styles were "right on," Metchek said. Jin Chang, a former hairdresser who is now chief merchandise officer, had an eye for fashion that the company was willing to bet on.

While their business was growing, the Changs, who are in their 50s, were making a mark in other ways. With a partner, they built the four-story Oxford Palace Hotel in Los Angeles' Koreatown and co-developed the San Pedro Wholesale Mart in downtown's Fashion District. It was the city's first commercial condominium project and built when most people "didn't believe in downtown," said Kent Smith, executive director of the L.A. Fashion District Business Improvement District.

Anyone who has looked at the bottom of a Forever 21 shopping bag has a hint about another important aspect of the Changs' life. Each bag is inscribed with "John 3:16"—the New Testament passage that says, "For God so loved the world, that he gave his only begotten son, that whosoever believeth in him shall not perish, but have everlasting life."

The inscription is "evidence of their faith and their commitment to God," Senior Vice President Larry Myer said.

The Changs have given millions of dollars to the Ttokamsa Mission Church in Los Angeles, where they attend the 5:30 a.m. prayer meetings Monday through Saturday when they're in town, Pastor Ken Choe said. "They are prayer warriors."

The church is part of the Christian Reformed Church of North America and directs more than 70% of its budget for overseas missions. Jin Chang has visited China, the Ukraine, and the Philippines to serve meals to missionaries and local pastors, Choe said.

Don Chang teaches at the church and, Choe said, has a "zeal for the Lord" that the preacher sometimes envies. "It's very rare," Choe said. "That's why I believe God has poured his blessing on him."

The church has helped build schools in China, Afghanistan, Cambodia, Vietnam and the Philippines, and Chang gave $3.4 million to build an auditorium at Faith Academy in Manila, a school for children of missionaries.

The Changs' business is looking toward Asia as well. Forever 21 plans to open its first store in Seoul this year and hopes to develop more than five malls in South Korea and elsewhere in Asia. The first store in China opened this month near Shanghai and more are expected in that country over the next year. Forever 21 will debut in Thailand this year and will open in Japan over the next two years.

Once the company has its "global infrastructure" in place, Senior Vice President Lee said, it may go public. But not now, Chang said. "If a company wants to grow, I think private is much better," he said.

If the retailer files an initial public stock offering, there should be no shortage of interest, said Frederick Schmitt, a principal at Sage Group investment bank in Los Angeles. Financial institutions and private equity firms have hovered in recent years, "waiting for them to go public, or trying to buy them," he said.

"It's sizable, it's growing, it's seen as a good operator and they're understood to be very profitable, so that makes it an attractive acquisition target," Schmitt said. Shoppers, and investors, are fickle, of course, and trends constantly change. But although "everybody's saying the economy's bad," Chang said, "we're doing better. We are strong."

Source: *Los Angeles Times,* Monday, June 23, 2008. Home Edition; Business, Part C, pg. 1, Business Desk. Reproduced with permission of the copyright owner. Further reproduction or distribution is prohibited without permission.

Chapter 12

Cycle of Production

The line is selling. Orders are being written. The designer has done a great job giving the sellers exciting product to wow the buyers. The sales department has orders in hand, and they continue to obtain more. The orders are credit checked and approved. The pre-production style preparation is continuing to turn out production patterns and samples as quickly as is physically possible. Finally, the selection of new styles ordered by retail customers will go into production. When the garments are finished, they will be shipped to retailers' racks for shoppers to purchase.

STAGES IN THE CYCLE OF PRODUCTION

Producing first quality garments is not an easy undertaking. The production manager has to get the garments cut, bundled, sewn, finished, inspected, and shipped in a narrow window of time. Sales departments hate to say no to buyers, and they seem to take orders with delivery dates that are just short of the production department's estimated **turn time** or **turnaround time**. The turn time is the span of time it takes to do all the pre-production work on the sample and patterns, complete all the production stages, and deliver the garments to the retailer's distribution center. If there are any truisms in the garment industry one is, "whatever can go wrong will go wrong" if the time constraints are forced. The normal steps of production can be done in house, where the manufacturer actually cuts and sews their own goods. Alternatively, the manufacturer may contract out for some of the procedures. The basic steps to cut and sew garments are the same no matter where the goods are placed.

The production process is made difficult due to several coinciding situations. First, orders taken by salespersons are often written with unrealistic dates because the buyer wants to be the first one to receive merchandise. This causes a rush to production, which may accidentally promote errors with patterns, fitting, or fabric ordering. Second, many orders for retailers are taken in a short span of time, over days or weeks, rather than spread evenly throughout the year. This causes a backlog of garments that

FIG. 12.1a, b. (a) Top. THIS PHOTO SHOWS A RECEIVING CLERK COUNTING THE ROLLS OF FABRIC BEING DELIVERED TO A CUTTING ROOM. (b) Bottom. THIS IS A PARTIAL INVENTORY OF STOCK PIECE GOODS AT A MANUFACTURING COMPANY IN LOS ANGELES.

need to go through the pre-production phase all at once. This leads to overwork in pre-production jobs and may accidentally promote sloppy detail work. Finally, the fabric and trimmings companies are involved in the same time crunch as the manufacturers are, with orders for goods that may also have unrealistic shipping dates. This can cause delays in cutting or finishing goods. Late fabric means the labor window for actual sewing time is shortened. This can lead to quality issues.

It is the scheduling of different phases of garment cutting and construction, and the

handling of all the problems that are inherent in product management that makes the manufacturing of apparel so difficult. The production department has to keep track of what each style needs at each stage of its production cycle. The delivery dates dictate the urgency of sometimes pushing styles ahead of other styles, while keeping all the different commitments on time. A production department could have any number of different styles in production for a season all at once. For example, a girls' top manufacturer could have 40 styles in work for a September 30 cancellation date. Some of those styles will be at screen printers, or at cutters, or at embroidery contractors, or being sewn. Keeping tabs of what is where and when it will be finished is not easily done.

Generally, the first step starts with the receipt of the stock fabric. The production department assigns a schedule for the order of cutting goods. To determine which garment gets cut first depends upon the delivery date of the materials. Production managers always complain that they can't cut air. Late fabric delivery throws production schedules off from the outset. The outside treatments necessary for the style are also taken into consideration. If a garment needs the pockets to be embroidered, and that work is stitched by an outside contractor, the cutting of the garment may be moved up in the schedule in order to make time for the decoration to be applied. If a garment has a great deal of needlework and takes longer in the machines than normal, a production manager may want it to be cut ahead of simpler garments. The production department makes the cut list and instructs the cutters to cut in the order the cuts are assigned.

Cutting the Garments

The stock rolls of fabric are inspected on site. If perfect, the fabric is spread in long plies, or layers, on a cutting table. This can be done manually by rolling the goods out and making layers upon layers of fabric. The process can also be completed by a robot that is preset with a specific measurement. The length of the fabric that is spread is dependent upon the length of the marker. The number of plies, laid on top of each other is determined by how many garments need to be cut. **Laying up** the goods is a common term for this process. The fabric is spread face to face, which means rolling the fabric to the end of the marker and then rolling it back continuously. The exception of this would be if the fabric plies were to be spread as a face-up marker. This means that the fabric roll must be cut across the goods at the end of each ply, for the length of the marker, rather than just folded end over end. The simple action of spreading the goods can be made more difficult if the fabric is slinky or stretchy. Stretchy knits are spread and left to settle, or shrink, back to their natural state before cutting. Extra slippery fabric is sometimes **nailed** to prevent it from moving when cut. Slinky fabrics may need paper spread between layers to fortify the weight of the fabric in order to make a sharp decisive edge. Very sharp, thin nails are used as pegs to hold the fabric in place when necessary.

Once the fabric is spread to the desired amount, the marker is placed on top of the goods. The cutter may use handheld electric knives called rotary cutters that look like a carpenter's saw. (See Figure 12.2.) Computerized cutting with a program uses plot markers to help the machine cut correctly. However the garments are cut, it is a time consuming chore. It must be done carefully in order to ensure that the garments start with proper seam allowances and notches. Sloppy cutting can cause unlimited production problems, possibly making it impossible for garments to fit correctly or meet **tolerances** on the spec sheets.

All the notching of garment pieces is done on the cutting table. Notching garments is a time-consuming process. After the knives cut around the pattern pieces a notching blade is used on woven fabrics to cut in the notch.

All punch holes are done by another special machine on the cutting tables prior to bundling. When fabric is layered ply upon ply, the height of the stack of plies can be cumbersome. The angle in which the punch hole is made could move by fractions of an inch from the top ply to the bottom. This is why punch holes must be marked narrower than the size of the finished pocket. Wide punch holes that show make the garments un-shippable as first quality. When the style is fully cut out, notched, and punched it is referred to as **the cut**.

The fabric that is left over from the cut, usually scraps and odd shapes or material, is called **fallout**. Fallout is recycled or discarded as trash. Some recycling firms make deals with manufacturers to pick up their fallout and utilize it to compress it into other products like carpet padding.

Bundling the Garments

Once the cutter is through cutting the goods, they are bundled. The plies of each part of the garment are tied with strips of cloth to hold the group of pieces together. For example, one bundle would contain only size 10 right bodice fronts in blue. Another bundle will contain the size 10 left sleeves in blue. Those bundles would be grouped together. If the fabric has more than one dye lot, the number of bundles per size per pattern piece will be split into additional bundles so that the dye lots are kept in distinctly different tie-ups. This means the garment's pieces are gathered together by size, color, dye lot, and a

FIG. 12.2. THE CUTTER MAY USE HANDHELD ELECTRIC KNIVES CALLED ROTARY CUTTERS THAT LOOK LIKE A CARPENTER'S SAW.

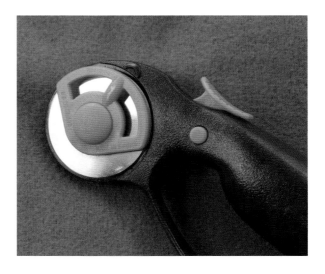

predetermined number of units. For example, if a cut has 1,200 pieces of a junior top in two colors, the production manager may want bundles of two dozen per size per color. The bundles retain the marker paper on the top of the first ply. This identifies the style number with the size of the bundle. Bundle amounts vary according to the weight of the bundle and the mass of the garment. Bundles are generally kept to a manageable size so that people can move them around. One small fabric square cut from the fallout from each cut is bundled showing the entire lay up to use, if necessary, to show the quantity cut for inventory purposes.

If outside work or special treatments need to be applied to separate sections, or to parts of a garment, those parts are separated, sent for the treatments, and later joined back into the appropriate bundles. An example of this would be yokes on a junior shirt that get embroidery work. The embroidery process would be applied to the yokes prior to assembling the shirt. Pockets on a jean could be separated from the bundle, decorated with beads, embroidery, or screen printing, and rejoined to the bundle in order for the jean to be sewn.

In order to keep track of what each bundle contains, the marker is marked or stamped clearly with the style number and size of each piece. Lost bundles containing one part of a garment can waste the entire garment. For example, a lost bundle of size 10 sleeves would make the entire garment unfinished if additional fabric were not available to recut those missing sleeves. Bundles are consolidated and carefully managed in order to avoid this potential disaster.

Large muslin-covered pushcarts or trolleys transport the bundles to the next destination, which could be as close as next door in the factory, or to a truck for transport to another facility or even another country. American manufacturer's cuts can be transported to Mexico for assembly, or cut in Mexico. When American manufacturers use more distant sewing factories—for instance those factories in China—the goods are cut there.

Managing the Placement of Cuts for Assembly

Manufacturers that own sewing facilities and do their own garment assembly control the workflow in those factories. These companies adjust to the volume of their own business cycles by regulating the number of operators employed, or by taking in sewing work from other companies, as their management deems necessary to keep their purchase order commitments, and their machines from being idle.

The manufacturers that contract out for the construction of their garments must make careful decisions about which factories they hire to handle their cuts. Looking for factories in which to place goods is called sourcing. There are several things that need to be taken into account when sourcing. (See Figure 12.3.) The Chinese government has invested millions of dollars to have state of the art facilities.

Some of the issues that must be examined before sourcing are social issues. Does the factory pay their help sufficiently? Is the country where the factory is located a stable environment or prone to social upheaval and war? The political and economic arenas must be conducive to business. Can this same work be performed profitably in the United States to keep jobs available domestically? Retailers have been embarrassed by news accounts showing their product being sewn in sweatshops or made by underage workers, and they want to be assured by their vendors that any garments coming into their stores are made in legal shops that pay appropriate wages. Production managers doing sourcing have to investigate each factory carefully in order to avoid problems. Once these questions are answered, the production department examines the more garment specific issues of production.

Labor cost is one of the first limitations on placing goods in factories. The garments in work have been sold with specific labor prices on them, and that price must be agreeable to the factory in order for all concerned to make a profit. The factory's past experience needs to be considered. If the contractor performed well

FIG. 12.3. SOME OF THE FACTORIES IN CHINA ARE STATE-OF-THE-ART FACILITIES THAT CAN ASSEMBLE HUGE QUANTITIES OF GARMENTS.

on previous cuts, that is a good indication of success with future business. The contract shop specialty is another consideration. A contractor that specializes in quick turn T-shirts will not succeed sewing prom dresses. The assortment and availability of equipment must also match the needs for production. An order for Wal-Mart of 24,000 pieces cannot be put into a factory of 50 machines. If a top has lots of marrow edging, the factory must have adequate machinery of that type to sew the goods in the time allotment. The time factor has to be investigated in every area of handling the goods. This examination must encompass both the size of the factory and its location. Long distance contractor sewing arrangements can add extra days to the turn time after completion for travel time for the shipment to arrive and pass through customs. After careful scrutiny, the production department matches the cuts to the production capability, and the garment assembly process begins.

APPAREL INDUSTRY LABOR ISSUES

Factories come in all phases of sophistication. Some have conveyor belts moving bundles along, and others seem to come right out of Charles Dickens's London. The term sweatshop is still appropriate in too many locations, but great strides are being made with modernizing the apparel industry.

Designers who work in the apparel industry must be aware of the social implications of working for companies that exploit factory workers. Many retailers are taking a more active role in the supervision of the production of the merchandise that ultimately ends up in their stores. Designers need to be aware of their company's sourcing standards. For many years, the efforts to get American consumers to buy apparel made in the United States failed because of the lure of lower prices for competing imported apparel. Now 90 percent of the apparel sold in the United States is sewn offshore. The current efforts made to entice consumers to buy apparel that is sewn in factories that do not use children, prisoners, or poorly paid and exploited workers, is suffering from the same lack of consumer interest. Consumers around the world consider price first when purchasing apparel marketed by ready-to-wear retailers, and they only worry about the social issues when pressed to do so. Current health issues with imported toys, plastics, and medicines have created additional consumer awareness, and wariness.

Designers working in the girls' and junior markets are more susceptible to having their styles made in low paying factories because of the competitive pricing of the apparel in those categories. Since a designer is simply an employee and not in the position to be a deter-mining agent of where goods are sewn, the only real option in regards to standing up for social responsibility, is to work for manufacturers that make every effort to source their goods in facto-ries that treat their workers fairly.

FACTORY CONSTRUCTION SYSTEMS

The spec sheets spell out exactly how the gar-ments must look upon completion. Some spec sheets even give the order of each step in the construction process of a garment. Spec sheets do not instruct factory supervisors in the man-agement of the employee's labor operations to achieve the most efficient method of working on a cut. There are several ways the completion of garments may be approached.

The obvious way that (which is almost never used in girls' and junior clothing) is for one sewing operator to sew up the entire garment individually. This is a practice left to very expen-sive couture clothing, or perhaps to a boutique seamstress sewing one-of-a-kind pieces of ap-parel. This method is never used in mass-mar-ket apparel.

A more logical approach is what is known as the **progressive bundle system**. This is done in a basic assembly line method. In this system, the bundles are opened by an operator, and that worker will do one or two operations, close the bundle and it is moved on to the next operator who performs a couple of additional proce-dures. The bundles are generally a dozen to two dozen pieces per bundle and are easily pushed to the next operator. The bundle is passed down until completion. Although this method is very straightforward, snafus can cause breaks in the flow. If one operation is much more difficult than the others are, adjustments have to be made to even out the pace of the sewing steps. It is best if the bundles move consistently from one operator to the next. In this simple progres-sive system, operators can be expert and fast in one operation, and they are not held back be-cause they are attempting procedures that are outside their realm of expertise. Additionally, in this system workers are paid according to how

many operations they successfully manage in a day's work. It is a **piecework payment** system.

In another method, called **team or modu-lar manufacturing**, the operations are actually done by a team, with each person in the team doing whatever is necessary to complete the work. This system utilizes team reward incen-tives, but each member of the team must be ca-pable of doing every sewing operation on every type of machine in order to complete a garment. The competitive nature of this method can stir faster production, but group responsibility over individual accountability can also affect quality. One worker benefit is that operators change up their operations so that there is less repetitive motion to stress joints in hands. For instance, for the morning Worker A sews sleeves on. In the afternoon this same worker might be doing the buttonholes on a placket.

Both systems have assets and drawbacks. The choice of the type of system that is used is up to the owner of the factory not the manufac-turer. The manufacturer needs only to demand the garments be sewn on time and show good workmanship.

CONTROLLING THE QUALITY OF GARMENTS

Prior to starting the actual construction on a new cut, factories are instructed to submit samples for approval. These contractor samples are carefully examined to see if they match the construction of the production sample that was supposed to be copied. The contractor dupli-cates must be inspected, measured, and then approved prior to the cut goes into full produc-tion. Some companies refer to these samples as **sew-bys** because the rest of the cut is supposed to be sewn by copying the original sample.

Contractor samples must be approved before the stock sewing begins. Who approves the sam-ples varies within different companies. In large companies, there may be a construction engineer who is in charge of this procedure. In small com-panies, the production patternmaker or even the designer may be asked to check each contractor sample. Sometimes designers will be asked an

each garment to offer all those essentials plus offer consumers good value, great fit, and styling that is unusual, wonderful, chic, whimsical, adorable, edgy, appropriate, and all-around terrific. Is there a woman who doesn't remember a favorite dress or outfit she wore on her first day at school when she was a little girl? Is there a woman who doesn't remember the one dress that made her feel like a princess? Is there a woman who doesn't remember what she wore when she was first kissed as a teenager? Wouldn't it be fantastic to be the designer who helped create the special memories for the girls, tweens, and teens who were wearing the design sketches that morphed into checkouts and turned into someone's favorite clothes?

Designer's Diary

Dear Diary,

Months ago, I was in a store, and I saw our company's styles hanging so low on a display rack at Macy's that I rearranged them to the top and put some other styles on the bottom. Yesterday I was back in Macy's and guess what? Our new shipment, my new designs, were displayed on the mannequins in the aisle near the escalator. I got chills. There was even a little girl in line with her mother *buying* my little kilt skirt set. OMG! Pinch me because I can't believe it. It is so cool to see my sketches become a child's wardrobe.

On Monday, I start the catalogue project for summer and do velvet holiday dresses for an ad. It never stops, but finally I get to see the result. Before I was just designing for a doll, but now I can visualize my clothes on real little girls. Carmen gave notice Friday. I am so sad to see her go. She got offered a great job for one of our competitors and I can't figure out why our boss didn't just match the money. Good patternmakers are essential. Listen to me. I thought she was a real pain in the butt and inflexible until I realized how much her input mattered. In the meantime, I got a sizeable raise.

. . . 10 Years Later

Dear Diary,

I can't believe I found this journal in an old trunk. I moved just after the last entry, and I must have left the trunk in storage at Mom's before getting my own house. I laughed when I read about Carmen losing her job. She is now my production partner. We stayed in touch for the several years we worked at different manufacturers, and that worked well, because we learned different lessons from very different companies. My label for juniors is called Just Because and Just Ducky is for the girls' line. Our clothes are eco-clean and made entirely in the United States. American Apparel showed the garment industry that fair trade clothes could be made here for a profit, and we copied their example. Carmen and I started the company in an old loft. Now we are moving to a bigger place on Los Angeles Street. Keep an eye out for our latest designs!

cancellation purchase orders can be cancelled when the garments are shipped beyond the date written on the contract or if the quality of the apparel is not up to the standards of the retailer. A cancellation is notification that the order is no longer in effect.

the cut as soon as a style is through the cutting and bundling process it will be referred to as the cut. Each cut has a number so it can be traced through production.

electronic data interchange system (EDI) electronic transfer of information from one point to another by way of computers. For example, transmission of purchase orders from retailer to manufacturer, allowing more rapid response to consumer demands. (Calasibetta, Tortora, Abling 2002, p. 136).

extension when a buyer allows the purchase order cancellation date to be extended to a later date without cancelling the garments.

fallout the fabric remaining in the spaces between pattern pieces after a garment style is cut. Such fabric pieces may be used in recycled textiles. (Calasibetta, Tortora, Abling 2002, p. 153).

hanging when garments are on hangers on racks or rails they are hanging. Hanging goods means it is hanging in house without a purchase order but ready to ship out.

laying up goods the process of rolling out fabric, ply over ply, for the cutting process.

markdown a financial discount taken by retailers when the purchase order is going to be shipped late or in any way different from the original approved sample.

nailed when goods slide around on the cutting table cutters may use large pins called nails to hold the goods in place during cutting to preserve the shape of the pattern pieces.

piecework payment when sewing contractors pay their line sewers by the completed sewn piece instead of by the hour. If it is fairly calculated, which makes sure the process can be done quickly enough to make minimum wage in an hour, it can be used as an incentive for speed. If the system is unfair, the sewing cannot be performed fast enough to make minimum wage and the worker is cheated.

progressive bundle system or **bundle system** in the garment trade, a method of garment production using an unorganized flow of work from one employee to another. Garment pieces are tied together into a bundle. The operator takes the bundle, performs one or more operations, bundles the finished work, and passes the work to the next employee. In the **development bundle system** items move in units or bundles in a more highly organized manner from one operator to another (Calasibetta, Tortora, Abling 2002, p. 47).

sew-by a sample garment sewn and submitted to the apparel manufacturer for approval by a contractor. Sewn production goods are compared to the sample to check quality. Also called a counter sample (Calasibetta, Tortora, Abling 2002, p. 401).

speed rail system the racking system in a warehouse that allows hanging garments to be inventoried and shipped along narrow pipes, called rails, easily. Trucks have rails to hold hanging goods and the fitting from the truck racking system fits to the speed rail allowing the loading of garments to be done efficiently.

team or modular manufacturing apparel production system in which employees are organized into teams of seven to nine operators who are all able to carry out production tasks. The team is responsible for the construction of a complete garment. As a result, production is more flexible than in the mass-production system. (Calasibetta, Tortora, Abling 2002, p. 329).

tolerances a range of acceptable variations from the dimensional measurements called for in the size specifications. Tolerance is stated as a + or − in inches or metric dimensions. (Calasibetta, Tortora, Abling 2002, p. 455).

turn time or **turnaround time** from the moment an apparel company gets an order until the time they can ship it to the retailer is turnaround time. Apparel sales personnel will tell a buyer that their turn time is 6 weeks, or 4 weeks, and so forth. The reality is that the turn time varies from style to style and depends on the quantity. Turn time usually presupposes that the factory has open production time and that the fabric is on hand to cut.

Activities

1. Go to a shopping mall and find a girls' department. Slowly look through the inventory, and see if you can find five different quality control problems. Look for hanging threads, missing buttons, poor pressing, tears, or loose threads on seam finishes, and so forth. Make a list and bring it to class to discuss what you perceive as problem areas for production.
2. Go to a shopping mall and find a junior department. Slowly look through the inventory, and see how many different countries are represented in the neck labels. Download a map from the Internet or make a copy from the library and put Xs on all the places the clothing was sewn. Compare the lists in the classroom.
3. Be the production staff for a day. Take five garments (from magazine photos or from the Internet), and pretend that they were sold and the pre-production stages are complete. Do a listing of all the different stages each garment would have to go through to be completed. Rank the most difficult to the easiest to produce and present your findings in class.
4. Sketch three ways each sewn sample for the miniline could be used for next season. The next line is just around the corner.

Weekly Planner

The objective for Chapter 12 is to get an overview of the stages of the production phase to the end process in the girls' apparel industry.
1. Read Chapter 12.
2. Do activities for Chapter 12.
3. Review the Designer's Dictionary
4. If possible arrange for live models to show the garments for the class. If live models are not available, put the clothing on classroom mannequins for display and classroom critique.

Congratulations. You have completed your first girls' mini-line!

Box 12.1

House of Tween Style

Build-a-Bear meets 'Project Runway'—with a dash of,

'I made it myself!'

By Booth Moore, *Times* Fashion Critic

If there was any more evidence needed of the mainstreaming of fashion, it's this: Kids used to go to Build-a-Bear Workshop or Color Me Mine to get their creative juices flowing. Now, they can design a piece of clothing, decorate it with graphics, rhinestones and charms and take it home, all in less than an hour.

Opening today in Beverly Hills, Fashionology is an interactive fashion design experience aimed at girls 8 to 14. The Build-a-Bear Workshop-meets-*Project Runway* destination was created by Elizabeth Wiatt and Jamie Tisch, who are fashion plates themselves, as regular guests at stylish soirees on both coasts and friends of designer Tory Burch.

Fashionology takes the teenage urge to customize sneakers and jeans to a new level, letting girls use touch screen kiosks to select a basic garment (hoodie, tank or capri pants for example) and a fashion "mood" such as Rock, Malibu, Peace or Juku. They can then choose accompanying graphics and embellishments by clicking "Sew It!," "Bling It!" or "Pin It!" icons.

Since there's no sewing involved, the experience is more akin to decorating cupcakes than baking them. But even a jaded fashion critic has to admit it was pretty fun adding rhinestones to the neckline of a hoodie and a sunset graphic to the back with the touch of a screen,

even if the piece was several sizes too small. We put Fashionology to the test with the target demographic, inviting a few tween girls to try it out. The experience met with a string of enthusiastic "awesomes!"

"I usually never go shopping, but this way I can make it how I want it," said Lena Vogler, 11, who chose a white hoodie with owl and peace sign graphics and an owl-shaped charm that clipped onto the waistband.

After a few minutes at the kiosk, Lena and her pal Jacqueline Moeller, 10, headed to the U-Bar where "fashionologists" printed out their patterns, used heat presses to add graphics and assembled a tray of embellishments to take to the "Make It!" table.

Settling in to decorate her black rocker-themed hoodie, Jacqueline said she was used to customizing her clothes with magic markers, so this was a step up. "Making it yourself and getting to walk out with it is really awesome."

Once the girls were finished, they put their hoodies on and got ready to model them under the spotlights on the Fashionology stage. Their photo was beamed onto the store's 70-inch TV screen for all to see and e-mailed to them so they could share it with friends. The experience costs $20 to $90, depending on how minimalist (or maximalist) you go. I managed to jack up the price of my hoodie to $88 pretty quickly, although the running total on the screen made it easy to subtract design elements and lower the price. The only complaint came from the moms who wished they could design too. (Adult sizes are on the way.)

The lively interior was designed by Roman Alonso at Commune Design in L.A., and the colorful imagery and empowering text ("Dream It! Make It! Wear It!") on the walls is a nod to 1960s L.A. activist Sister Corita Kent.

"We didn't want to talk down to the girls. We wanted them to feel creative and empowered," said Tisch, who met Wiatt 15 years ago when the two were dating the men they would marry (Wiatt is married to Jim Wiatt, the head of the William Morris Agency, and Tisch is in the process of getting a divorce from producer Steve Tisch).

"It's about the positives of fashion, not beauty or body image," said Wiatt, who has girls ages 6 and 8. "It's not about how girls look in the clothes. It's about creating the clothes."

Tisch said the inspiration for Fashionology came from her three tween children. The same goes for Wiatt, a former literary agent and magazine editor who left the workplace to be a full-time mom and work on environmental causes.

"Jamie and I were both teaching our kids to sew, and we had the bloody fingers to show for it. We got together and decided it would be great if there was a place we could go to teach them to sew." That lightbulb moment happened 18 months ago, and the two called an "emergency meeting" at Starbucks in Brentwood.

They started cruising sewing and notion stores for research, originally planning to open a business called Sew My Style, where girls would learn how to use sewing machines. When that proved to be too complicated for the under 15 set, they simplified the idea. Big Buddha Baba, a company of Los Angeles software designers who have worked with Disney Imagineering and on kids museum exhibits, helped them create a design experience that would use computers instead of needles and thread.

Wiatt and Tisch bankrolled the enterprise, and in a few weeks, they plan to open an online version of the store. A boys version of the experience could also be in the future, with different graphics and garments.

"We want to do things thoughtfully," Tisch said. "But we have a business plan to go nationwide very quickly." Expect to see a second store by early next year.

Something tells me there are going to be even more kids dreaming of becoming fashion designers when they grow up.

Fashionology, 338 N. Canon Drive, Beverly Hills, (310) 550-7997, fashionology.com.

Source: *Los Angeles Times,* Sunday, June 15, 2008. Home Edition; Image, Part P, pg. 6, Features Desk. Reproduced with permission of the copyright owner. Further reproduction or distribution is prohibited without permission.

Designer's Library

Batterberry, Michael, and Ariane Batterberry. *Fashion The Mirror of History.* New York: Crown Publishers, 1977.

Burns, Leslie Davis, and Nancy O. Bryant. *The Business of Fashion: Designing, Manufacturing, and Marketing.* 3rd ed. New York: Fairchild Books, 2007.

Calisabetta, Charlotte Mankey and Phyllis Tortora. *Fairchild Dictionary of Fashion.* 3rd ed. New York: Fairchild Books, 2003.

Chang, Andrea, and David Yi. "Retail—Macy's May be Poised to Sell Itself." *Los Angeles Times,* July 19, 2007.

Contini, Mila. *Fashion from Ancient Egypt to the Present Day.* New York: Crescent Books, 1965.

Earnest, Leslie. "New Chief Dives in at Pacific Sunwear," *Los Angeles Times,* July 7, 2007.

Ewing, Elizabeth. *History of Children's Costume.* New York: Charles Scribner's Sons, 1977.

Farrell-Beck, Jane, and Jean Parsons. *20th-Century Dress in the United States.* New York: Fairchild Books, 2007.

Gerome, John. "In a Corner Nashville, Western Swings the Thing," *Los Angeles Times,* July 30, 2007. http://articles.latimes.com/2007/jul/30/entertainment/et-timejumper30 (Accessed November 1, 2008).

Grossberg, Josh. "Casting Couch: Zeta-Jones Tunes Up for Cleopatra." *E! Online,* October 24, 2008. www.eonline.com/uberblog/b65501_Casting_Couch__Zeta_Jones_ Tunes_Up_for__lt_i_gt_Cleopatra_lt__i_ gt_.html (Accessed November 1, 2008).

Kim, Victoria. "PacSun is Slimming Down," *Los Angeles Times,* January 5, 2008.

Kwan, Amanda. "Gossip Girls Set Fashion Trends." *Associated Press,* August 26, 2008. www.azcentral.com/style/fashion/articles/2008/08/26/20080826gossipgirl.html (Accessed November 1, 2008).

Magsaysay, Melissa. "Hogwarts Chic." *Los Angeles Times,* September 9, 2007.

Magsaysay, Melissa. "Hooked on Look." *Los Angeles Times,* July 28, 2007.

Sills, Leslie. *From Rags to Riches: A History of Girls' Clothing in America.* New York: Holiday House, 2005.

SUGGESTED READING

Abling, Bina. *Fashion Sketchbook,* 4th ed. New York: Fairchild Publications, Inc., 2004.

Allen, Jeanne. *Showing Your Colors: A Designer's Guide to Coordinating Your Wardrobe.* San Francisco: Chronicle Books, 1986. (This book is a perfect way to see how colors go together in a garment. It is visual explanation with few words.)

Alvarado, Jane D. *Computer Aided Fashion Design Using Gerber Technology.* New York: Fairchild Books, 2007.

Amaden-Crawford, Connie. *A Guide to Fashion Sewing.* 4th ed. New York: Fairchild Books, 2006.

Armstrong, Jemi, Lorrie Ivas, and Wynn Armstrong. *From Pencil to Pen Tool: Understanding & Creating the Digital Fashion Image.* New York: Fairchild Publications, Inc., 2006.

Aspelund, Karl. *The Design Process.* New York: Fairchild Books, 2006.

Brannon, Evelyn L. *Fashion Forecasting Research, Analysis, and Presentation.* 2nd ed. New York: Fairchild Publications, Inc., 2005.

Carolyn L. Moore, Kathy K. Mullet, Margaret B. Prevatt Young. *Concepts of Pattern Grading: Techniques for Manual and Computer Grading.* 2nd ed. New York: Fairchild Books, 2008.

Joseph-Armstrong, Helen. *Patternmaking for Fashion Design.* Upper Saddle River, New Jersey: Prentice Hall, 2000.

Keiser, Sandra J., and Myrna B. H. Garner. *Beyond Design.* New York: Fairchild Books, 2008.

Malossi, Giannino, ed. *The Style Engine.* New York: Monacelli Press, 1998.

Myers-McDevitt, Paula J. *Complete Guide to Size Specification and Technical Design.* New York: Fairchild Publications, Inc., 2004.

Nugent, Laura. *Computerized Patternmaking for Apparel Production.* New York: Fairchild Books, 2009.

Peacock, John. *Fashion Since 1900: The Complete Sourcebook.* London: Thames & Hudson, 2007.

Peacock, John. *Fashion Sourcebooks. The 1970s.* London, Thames and Hudson, Ltd., 1997. (This book is one of a series 1920s, 1930s, 1950s, and so on. These are little booklets of illustrations of the different time periods. This series is helpful for researching style lines and important designers.)

Sharp, Julia, and Virginia Hencken Elsasser. *Introduction to AccuMark, Pattern Design, & Product Data Management.* New York: Fairchild Books, 2007.

Credits

CHAPTER 1

1.1   Author's Photo
1.2   Library of Congress
1.3   *Arthur's Home Magazine,* 1879
1.4   David McNew/Getty Images
1.5   Postcards from author's collection
1.6a   Courtesy of Fairchild Publications, Inc.
1.6b   Victoria Snowber/Getty Images
1.6c   © Masterfile
1.7   Antique Paper Dolls The Edwardian Era, Dover Publications © 1975
1.8   Courtesy of Fairchild Publications, Inc.
1.9   Courtesy of Fairchild Publications, Inc.
1.10   Veer
1.11   Veer
1.12a   Author's Photo
1.12b   Author's Photo
1.13a   Author's Photo
1.13b   Author's Photo
1.14   Veer
1.15   Robert Llewellyn/Corbis

CHAPTER 2

2.1a   Courtesy of Randi Beer
2.1b   Courtesy of J.C. Penney
2.2   Erik Snyder/Getty Images
2.3   Veer
2.4   Veer
2.5a   Courtesy of Randi Beer
2.5b   Courtesy of J.C. Penney

4.3b   Author's Photo
4.4   Author's Photo
4.5   Courtesy of Fairchild Publications, Inc.
4.6   Courtesy of Randi Beer
4.7   Courtesy of Randi Beer
4.8   Courtesy of Randi Beer

CHAPTER 5
5.1   Author's Photo
5.2   Courtesy of Randi Beer
5.3a   Veer
5.3b   Veer
5.3c   Veer
5.4   Courtesy of Randi Beer
5.5a   Courtesy of Fairchild Publications, Inc.
5.5b   Courtesy of Fairchild Publications, Inc.
5.5c   DMH Images/Getty Images
5.6   Author's Photo
5.7a   Author's Photo
5.7b   Author's Photo
5.8a   Author's Photo
5.8b   Author's Photo
5.1OA/B   Author's Photo
5.11A/B/C   Author's Photo
5.12   Author's Photo

CHAPTER 6
6.1   Jon Feingersh/Getty Images
6.2   Courtesy of Randi Beer
6.3a   Courtesy of Randi Beer
6.3b   Courtesy of Randi Beer
6.4   Author's Photo
6.5   Author's Photo
6.6   Courtesy of Fairchild Publications, Inc.

CHAPTER 7
7.1   Anaïs Martane/Corbis
7.2a   John Birdsall/Alamy
7.2b   William Taufic/Corbis
7.3   Veer
7.4   Courtesy of Randi Beer
7.6   Courtesy of Fairchild Publications, Inc.
7.7   William Gottlieb/Corbis
7.8   Author's Photo
7.9a   Author's Photo
7.9b   Author's Photo

CHAPTER 12
12.1a   Eightfish/Getty Images
12.1b   Author's Photo
12.2   Ted Foxx/Alamy
12.3   Stringer Shanghai/Reuters/Corbis
12.4   Author's Photo
12.5   Gail Mooney/Corbis

Index